HUNTING CONCRETE LIONS

A MEMOIR

Michael Cannan

MANANN
PUBLISHING
LONDON   NEW YORK   LOS ANGELES

Published by Manann Publishing 2017

Copyright © 2017

First edition.

ISBN: 978-0-692-89482-8 (Paperback)
978-0-692-89483-5 (ebook)

Whichever way you throw me, I will stand.

PROLOGUE

When I regained consciousness, I found myself lying flat on my back with a sizeable fluorescent light staring down at me from the ceiling.

Bloody painful that. The old eyelids would not stop blinking away against the glare.

Vaguely aware that I had been choosing my battles unwisely, I gave up the struggle and let my eyelids close.

Best to let the fog clear. Get my head around the current situation.

First things first: I made a mental note to do something about those bastard overhead lights – the minute I was better armed and back on the front foot.

A few seconds had passed when fear jumped inside me and my eyes snapped open again. Bloody hell. The fluorescents. The antiseptic-smelling air, and that dreadful machine bleeping behind me. Something was definitely not on the level here.

With a glance in all directions, I tried to sit up but found my left wrist, then my right one, then both ankles strapped down by four-point restraints, and to a gurney, no less.

Good God. What have I gone and done this time?

Alerted by a murmur of voices and something moving nearby, I tilted my head and saw more gurneys and people in white lab coats passing by out in the hallway.

Time for my best shot at a medical evaluation.

Location?…unknown. Circumstances?…unclear. Mental state?…a touch of terror on that front…

Conclusion?

Still alive, apparently. The rest of my status looked dodgy.

Figuring one of those blokes in the white coats might have an answer to this bollocks, I called out.

"What's the craic here, mate?"

Silence.

Straining my neck further forward, I saw that my track pants had been pulled down around my knees. My designer t-shirt was up around my chest, leaving exposed my pasty underbelly and thighs. A bedpan of some sort was tucked under my Calvin Klein underwear.

Out of the jumble of voices and passing forms, a black lady with a greying afro appeared overhead and stared down at me. The fluorescent lights formed a halo around her whole head.

"Michael, do you know who I am?"

I stared up, racking my brain for an answer.

"Do you remember anything about yesterday?"

In the chaos of what passed for a grown man's mind, I scrambled again, trying to piece together the previous few days, but nothing came to me.

"No…I…I don't remember anything."

"Nothing at all?" the lady said with a slow shake of her head.

I shook my head in return.

"Where am I?" I thought to ask.

"Santa Monica," she said. "UCLA Medical Centre."

So, still in America, north of the Mexican border and in a reasonably respectable neighbourhood. Thank God for that.

I fought momentarily with the restraints and fell back against the bed.

"Would it be too much to ask to get me out of these bloody things?"

"Are you hungry?" she said in response.

"I'm ravenous."

Another nurse soon appeared holding a wooden tray. The tray had three small bowls scattered on top of it.

That nurse left and the old black gal soon had a spoonful of quivering green Jell-O coming my way. I strained forward to meet the food. All I needed was for her to mimic an aeroplane.

A few shots of that Jell-O and I was done. The other nurse returned.

"Michael, I can release one arm and a leg from the restraints, as long as you show no signs of aggression."

That old Indian bloke, Chief Joseph, came to mind. *From where the sun stands now, I will fight no more forever.* That was my new motto.

"No fighting," I assured the nurse. "I'm done."

She released my left arm and right leg, and I allowed them to dangle freely over the bed. That small allowance of freedom felt like quite a luxury.

"Can somebody tell me what's going on?"

"We're just trying to find you a bed in another hospital," the nurse who had emancipated me said. "We've checked but there aren't any available."

I stared blankly.

"We have to follow certain procedures under the circumstances."

"And what circumstances would those be?"

The anxiety in my voice had elevated with the question, along with the thickness of my Manx accent.

"You're on an involuntary psychiatric hold," she told me. "You've been very sick, so we're legally required to hold you. It's for your own safety."

"I really need to go home."

"Go home where, Michael?"

"The Isle of Man."

"You must be kidding. No airline will take you in this condition."

The look on my face said, "You've got to be takin' the piss", but she wasn't. Both nurses went out, leaving me in my restraints.

3

My soul searching commenced. The self-recriminations and self-loathing. The desperate attempts to explain away my fall from grace. Only a few weeks earlier, I had been relaxing in a sprawling hacienda, a kept man in what was one of the wealthiest communities in California, or the world, for that matter, with a couple of acres under my arse that the well-heeled locals were cocky enough to call a ranch. The type of place where the rich go to pickle and only the gardeners can understand the street names.

The last thing I recalled, I was nicely stoned on OxyContin, a cold lager in one hand, my bare feet propped up while watching the first game of the baseball playoffs on Natasja's home theatre system. Natasja was out there flipping filet mignons for two at the poolside bar. Her lovely face was smiling up at me from the cover of a glossy fashion magazine on the coffee table.

Easy to gloat back then. A big 'fuck you' to every teacher, employer and drunken bastard who had ever questioned my ability to succeed.

So how the hell did I get from there to here? As it turned out, the joke was on me. Only I could have ballsed up so much good fortune.

Before Natasja had bailed me out, I was holed up in Auckland, New Zealand, in a small basement apartment tucked away at the back of an old building, a fence for a view and a battered yellow Mitsubishi parked on the downslope out the front. The slope was spot on for jumpstarting the dead battery in the mornings. It also worked wonders with draining water out through the rusted floorboards whenever it pissed down with rain.

On the flip side of that downer, I found myself driving a white Corvette convertible and with the Fortune 500 types of the world as my neighbours. If you wanted to find me, start up around San Clemente way and motor down the coast. You couldn't beat the journey. Carlsbad, Encinitas, Solana Beach and Del Mar. Turn left at La Jolla and amble up from the sea through rolling hills and citrus groves.

Catch me at the gate. I'd be installing concrete lions on the posts. Christmas cards were on the agenda – Natasja wearing a Santa's hat, me a monogrammed smoking jacket with a brandy snifter in hand. Top it all off with the Pacific Ocean for a backdrop.

I had it made.

And then...

I felt a knife dig into me, remembering how I'd cocked it all up.

Several hours passed very slowly on that gurney. Then they rolled me out into a long fluorescent-lit hallway. At the end I was lifted into an ambulance. The lights and shadows of the city played on my face as we drove. I had two Deadhead types silently keeping an eye on me.

We pulled into the driveway of a small home, enclosed by a fifteen-foot fence. Barbed wire on top added a fitting touch. When the van stopped, I was wheeled out and assisted to my feet. Two nurses escorted me inside.

Locks and bolts slammed shut as each steel door closed behind me.

Within the otherwise quiet home, someone shrieked. Christ. I had spent most of my adult life fearing just this. Consigned to a nuthouse. And here I was, finally arrived.

In horror, my thoughts hurtled back to my youth on the Isle of Man. Mum with her Bible and the old man with all that heroic Viking shit he had lumbered me with as a boy. Spears and rabbits in the woods, only I was the rabbit now, gored, my hind legs pumping wildly with the last jolt of nervous impulses emanating from my brain.

A nurse was talking to me.

"Michael, electro-convulsive therapy will be used if you show any signs of abnormal behaviour."

This definitely got my attention.

Led to the communal area, I was further horrified to find coloured building blocks and an abacus waiting there to entertain me. A handful of the nut cases were watching TV – the final game of the World Series. That one hurt. In the space of a few weeks, I had gone from Natasja flipping mignon for me to *One Flew over the Cuckoo's Nest*.

By the time I was escorted into my room, the drawstring from my track pants had been removed. So had the shoelaces from my trainers. No taking chances that I might hang myself.

The room was equally suicide proof, the bed, sink and toilet all moulded to the floor. There were no sharp edges on the furniture, no exposed wall sockets, no wires anywhere.

The room had a solitary window with wire mesh in it, in case you thought to break it, and steel bars, in case you were sane enough to try to escape. The sun was setting outside. A distant mountain range was lit up with an orange glow. I could have been on Mars.

I lay down on the bed in my designer sports gear. I had never felt so scared and alone. I didn't know where I was. Nobody knew where I was. I wasn't sure any of them still cared.

When a nurse passed, I remembered my manners and called out in my best BBC voice:

"Do excuse me, sorry to trouble you, but would it be possible to get something to help me sleep this evening?"

"No," she said.

My foot and leg began to twitch like that speared rabbit.

"Okay, no problem," I said.

She left.

"For fuck's sake," I mumbled to myself. "How do they expect me to get through the night?"

CHAPTER ONE

I come from a small fishing village on the Isle of Man – population a few thousand. Our two-story home was off a narrow winding lane, in a neighbourhood full of narrow winding lanes, where every house had a low stacked stone wall bordering the street and a fine view of the surrounding hillsides and forest from nearly every window.

The place had the pleasant feel of the Irish countryside. The land was green around us. The sea was nearby and our old home was a right cosy place to be in a storm.

Directly in front of our house rose an ancient Viking burial ground, a stone's throw from our driveway. The burial ground was a hillock that had become overgrown with ferns, casting mysterious shadows over the many forgotten graves.

As a lad, I would go up there to be alone with my thoughts. With the seagulls circling high overhead, my mind was stirred to dreams of swords and shields and Viking warriors. I'd be imagining I was on the hunt for buried treasure or some such when the old man's voice would break the stillness, bellowing out from our front door:

"Vikings never give up!"

One Sunday morning my father said, "I saw you up amongst the Viking graves. Follow me."

At a few inches shy of six feet and stocky, my old man was hardly impressive in stature, but he more than made up for his lack of dimensions with an oversized personality. Quick-witted and charming.

We walked down the lane to where a steep path passed between two homes and from there further up into the forested hills. Soon the world had grown dark and mysterious about us. All smelled earthy from the rotting vegetation. The pine trees creaked and groaned in the breeze. A cold, damp mist was rolling over the mountain.

"Manannan's Shroud," Dad said, referring to the mist. "Manannan throws it over the island to shroud us from our enemies in times of trouble."

"So who was Manannan?" I asked.

"Manannan was the Isle of Man's first ruler, the Irish god of the sea, ruler of the Otherworld and keeper of the magic tools. The Isle of Man was his throne. Manannan means 'Him from the Isle of Man'."

All that sounded like magic and I listened in a state of wonder.

"What else, Dad?"

"Manannan's wife was the beautiful goddess Fand, the Pearl of Beauty. Like your mum. That's why I married her."

Intrigued, I stared up at him as we walked.

"So what happened to Manannan?"

"He turned himself into the Triskellion. The three legs of man. You can see it on the Manx flag. *Quocunque jeceris stabit*."

"What does that mean?"

"*Quocunque jeceris stabit*?"

"Yeah."

"That's Latin for 'Whichever way you throw me, I will stand'."

I was staring up with a blank look now.

"Never mind, son. Just remember *quocunque jeceris stabit*."

We came to a glen and my father pointed to a rock. "Sit yourself down."

I did and listened as he started in with a lecture.

"There's an old quote that says, 'Give me a child for seven years and I'll give you the man'."

I nodded along.

He snapped a lengthy branch from a tree and went about smoothing it into a makeshift spear with his Swiss Army knife.

"You're eight years old and should know the history of where you came from."

I gave him another nod.

He scavenged about and found a piece of flint on the ground.

"Perfect for an arrowhead."

Throwing the flint into the air, he seized it on the way down, grabbed another piece of flint off the ground and used the second one to fashion the first into a point with serrated edges. Flakes of flint went flying all over the show.

"This is how your Viking forefathers would have done it," he told me, admiring the spearhead.

While I worked on the image of a Viking warrior with a Swiss Army knife, my old man used his to split the tip of his makeshift spear, and having done that, set the arrowhead into the mouth of the cut. He then secured the spear and arrowhead together with coarse twine he'd brought along in his pocket.

All the while, he rambled on about the Isle of Man being a Viking stronghold. Because it was strategically located between England, Ireland, Scotland and Wales, the Vikings had used it as a staging area for their raids around the Irish Sea. His tale was embroidered with depictions of brave warriors, silver and gold and glamorous birds. When it came to food and women, he went on inordinately about how Viking warriors had gorged themselves.

"You're a Viking, son, and Vikings stop at nothing to get what they want."

I could never tell if the old man was spinning a yarn or not. He often said the truth was no fun but at least things were starting to sound intriguing again.

"What did they look like, Dad?"

"They were the biggest and the best, tall and muscular with long hair."

"But how come you've got no hair, Dad?"

"It's growing back any day soon."

This last comment was said with a hand on his bald head.

"So is that why we live next to a Viking burial ground?" I asked.

He nodded and pointed at the pinnacle of the burial mound below us.

"That's where the great Viking leader King Magnus is buried. The most fearless warrior of them all, and we're his direct descendants."

We were looking north with the plains and the sea and the coast of Galloway far off in the distance.

"We're some of the only pure Manxmen left. A direct blood-line back to the greatest seafaring warriors of all time. They travelled as far as North America, you know. Africa and all over Europe. Conquering everything that came in their way. And always taking the best women."

Having concluded on that note, about our ancestors running off with helpless damsels, my father contemplated the Irish Sea in silence. He had been preoccupied for a long moment when a rabbit suddenly jumped up onto a moss-covered log. Alerted to its presence, the old man crouched in the stillness of the forest and signalled for me to be quiet. He drew back his spear and launched it with such ferocity that he slipped on the pine needles and fell on his arse. The spear lodged itself into some undergrowth.

"Dang it all," he said, gathering himself. "Go and grab the spear."

As I did, an image of the rabbit rolling off the log appeared in my head, gripping its sides with laughter.

With a disgruntled laugh, my father grasped the spear and started in about the Vikings again. The biggest and strongest and best. And first into battle.

"That's how you pick your friends, Mikey. Ask yourself, 'Would I go to war with this person?' "

I nodded to confirm my ongoing interest, no longer convinced that the old man's tales contained any truth but enamoured with this Viking business, especially if it meant running off with naked birds and all that.

"I'm a Viking," I whispered to myself. I liked the sound of that for sure.

The church bells rang out from the centre of town, to which my father responded as if he had just heard a call to arms.

"Let's go," he said and jogged off with the spear in hand. "Hurry up! Shoulders back! Chest out! Stomach in! Drive with the arms, son! Drive with the arms!"

Back at the house, my older sister, Sal, was sitting at the dining room table, neatly pressed. She had blonde, curly hair that was almost white and sparkling blue eyes and cheeks that were blushed with life.

I went upstairs and struggled to clip the bow-tie to my white shirt. I hated Sundays and church. With black trousers and black shoes on, I cast one last look at the pictures of top-less women pinned to my bedroom wall. I had snipped them from the national newspaper and arranged them between my favourite players from the Liverpool Football Club.

"Back soon," I said to them and headed downstairs.

Shoulders back, chest out, stomach in. Drive with your arms.

The scent of my mum's perfume filled the house. A strong, oriental scent, warm and spicy. It made my head ache.

Five minutes down the road, we all passed through the large oak doors of our church. In the foyer, we were confronted with an enormous painting of Jesus facing off with the Devil. The Devil was done up as a red beast with cloven hooves, ram's horns and a pitchfork. Jesus was bearded and wearing a white cloak. It appeared they had met in the desert.

"Good will always overcome evil," my mum reassured me as we passed. "Jesus always defeats the Devil."

For that he had been nailed to a cross and given a barbed wire crown for his head.

Baffled I was, to say the least. That image always scared the crap out of me.

When the church organist struck a deep chord, I felt it in my chest. My breath stopped. Along with other families, we wound up the wooden stairs and past the purple velvet curtain and gold rope that concealed the organ. I kept my eyes averted, fearing whatever beast might be lurking in there.

The townspeople filled the pews, the men in dark suits, the women in black and white. Everyone had their hands clasped in front and heads bowed. The vicar called out from the pulpit for us to open our books. The first hymn started.

"Onward, Christian soldiers, marching as to war, with the cross of Jesus going on before…"

The singing echoed up amongst the stained glass windows and high ceilings. I looked over and saw my father lip syncing the words through a grin. Something was not right.

The hymn ended and the vicar launched into his usual fire and brimstone, peppered with Christian humility and Viking myth. An eye for an eye, a tooth for a tooth and turn the other cheek. Fire and sulphur and the gnashing of teeth. From the Isle of Man you could see all six kingdoms: England, Ireland, Scotland and Wales, Man and the kingdom of heaven. Burning bushes and the saviour of the world.

Know the truth and it shall set ye free. On and on…

The vicar raised his arms, inviting everyone up for Holy Communion. A white wafer and a sip of wine. The pearly gates were straight ahead.

I clipped my sister's ankles going forward and got a warning from my old man.

"Leave your sister alone."

"I haven't done anything," I said, trying not to laugh.

My sister somehow converted her stumble into a graceful glide forward, and we both knelt before the altar. I cupped my hands and projected my arms to the front, doing my best to hold back the laughter. Sal sniggered. My body broke into a shake. The more I fought it, the worse it became. I swallowed hard and held back the tears.

"Michael!" my mother whispered sharply.

"It's her," I said and pointed at my sister.

With another look between us, Sal and I finally broke out into laughter.

"In the name of the Father, the Son, and the Holy Ghost."

The vicar placed the body of Christ in my hands. I swallowed the white wafer and chased it with what turned out to be grape juice.

Gutted I was. What a huge disappointment.

Every Sunday the vicar finished off with the same old line: "And he will come again."

A real cliffhanger it was, leaving me to wait, though for the life of me I could not figure out who the hell was coming. Jesus or God? Whoever he was, I expected him to bust through the church roof in mid-service, the congregation saved with their arms outstretched, stripped to the ankles, ready for rapture.

Once everyone had received communion and the gilded collection plates had been passed around, the bells chimed and the congregation filed out of the church. Everyone lingered in conversation outside. I squirmed and was relieved when some of the families finally drifted off towards their favourite pub. The road was lined with them, a pub or two opposite every church. Chapel Lane Independent Methodist Church faced the Viking Hotel and Bar. St Paul's Church of England. The Roman Catholic Church. Trinity United Reform Church; they were all surrounded, every house of the Lord offering hope and salvation, the pubs offering relief of another kind from damnation.

I considered it to be just one more bit of Viking business.

When I asked the old man if we could visit a pub, he brushed me off.

"They refer to the Isle of Man as 70,000 alcoholics clinging to a rock, so the answer's no."

Back at the house, I quickly peeled off my clothes and threw them in the corner of my room. The centre-forward shirt for the Liverpool Football Club went on. Shin pads fastened with socks and tape, the boots double laced. I pretty much lived in my football kit.

I heard the old man rummaging around in the upstairs landing sports cupboard. It was stuffed with balls and rackets of every sort: football, tennis, golf, cricket, along with badminton, squash, and even some scuba diving gear. Our life revolved around sports. Mum had taught physical education at Merchant Taylors School, and Dad had played for and coached the Island Football team.

Following a knock on the door of my room the old man came in. I half expected to see him with wetsuit and harpoon.

He took one look at the *Playboy*-like foldouts plastered all over the wall behind me and burst out laughing, hands to his knees. "What the hell's that lot?"

"What?" I said innocently.

He pointed. "What football team's that?"

"Tits Wobbles United," I said.

"How on earth did you get that stuff past the front door?"

"Finnegan's dad brings them home from the building site," I offered as an excuse.

I had clipped them from page 3 of *The Sun*. It was considered a good working-class newspaper. If it was good enough for them, it was good enough for me.

"You'd better take them down before your mum gets a look."

I heard her call from the stairs, and Dad answered.

"Jude, come and have a look at Mikey's new football team."

"Dad, nooooooo!" I whispered.

"I don't like the sound of this," she said, coming up the stairs.

Giving my collection a disapproving look, she jabbed the old man in the ribs with her elbow. "He gets it from you. And don't wear those boots in the house," she added in my direction.

I heard a clatter of studs on the front path and opened the bedroom window.

"FINNEGAN!"

He was decked out in the same Liverpool football kit as me and sprinted along chucking bits of ferns like they were spears.

"Mikeeeeeyy, Mikey, Mike, Michaellll," he shouted in a variety of pitches.

Finnegan and I had become friends after he ditched the local Catholic school and joined the Protestant school with me. A brave and skilful Irishman on the football pitch, with sparkling eyes and a dimpled face, but not so bright at academics, the poor dyslexic bastard. Sit him down with a pencil and paper and the boy was stumped. Smart as a bag of rocks he was. He was trying to explain the two-minute run from his house to mine, and in his excitement the words came out all wrong.

"I that there," he said, pointing backwards, "Then I, ahh…"

To exorcise his frustration, he started humming the Rocky theme and jabbing his fists in the air.

I'd have gone to war with him.

"Meet me round the back," I shouted and scrambled out my bedroom window onto the roof, the studs of my shoes slipping on the tiles as I pulled myself across the window ledge to the garage roof. My jump over the oil tank landed me near my sister and her friends making daisy chains on the grass.

"The crowds are on their feet," I said for the girls and did a skidding stop on my knees. I looked to my adoring audience and found them shaking their heads.

Dad jogged across the pitch.

"How many goals did you score at football this weekend?"

"Twenty, at least," I replied.

"And what do you want to be when you grow up?"

"A professional football player, just like you."

"Semi-pro – when I lived in Australia," he corrected me.

The old man began showing off his football skills.

"We've got a big game next Saturday, lads, and I need you both in top form."

He stood in goal while we took shots. Then my sister's prettiest friend left and I couldn't be arsed playing. What was the point of performing without her watching?

After the workout, the old man coached us on the finer points of the game. His advice was always the same:

"You've got two ears and one mouth. Use them in that ratio."

Yeah, yeah. I was still fantasizing over my sister's friend.

Getting ready for bed that night, my mum and dad kneeled on either side of me.

"Gentle Jesus, meek and mild, look upon this little child..."

Meek and mild? More confusion. Clearly, Jesus was no Viking.

CHAPTER TWO

Three years passed. Another Sunday came, but our family did not attend church that day. As a family we hadn't attended church for the past two years. I had not bothered to ask why. I wasn't one to fuck with good fortune.

I was sitting on the sofa watching the *Tarzan* matinee with Sal.

My parents were still seated at the dining table, following our usual Sunday roast dinner.

"Kids, can you come back to the dining room please," my mother called out.

It was her teacher's voice. Something was wrong.

"It's the middle of *Tarzan*," I called out from the living room.

"Please, can you both come through?"

The teacher's voice again. I began to worry.

"I haven't done anything wrong!" I yelled back.

"Come on," Sal said and was off. There was nothing to do but follow.

Sal took a seat opposite my father, who was at the head of the table. I sat facing my mum. The remains of the roast chicken and potatoes, vegetables and Yorkshire pudding were still sitting on the long table. My mother and father sat rigidly, staring at each other. Feeling the tension in the room, I dug into the left-over spuds, nervously shoving one after another into my mouth.

"We have something to tell you," my mother said. "You both know where the Viking Hotel is, don't you?"

Ya fucking kidding me. How could I possibly not? The Viking was also known as Heartbreak Hotel. It housed newly separated couples and random one night bookings from the local pubs.

My mother placed the palms of her hands on the table.

"Your dad's going to the Viking for a while. He needs to be closer to work."

My eyes flooded with tears. My heart choked with fear and sadness. I swallowed hard. Please God, no. This is not happening.

A voice in my head reminded me. Good Vikings show no emotion.

A second voice begged to differ. The Viking Hotel's half a mile down the road. How the hell is that closer to work?

"Men don't cry," my father told me with furrowed brow.

Right, Dad. Shoulders back. Chest out. Stomach in. Drive with the arms. Drive with the arms.

"Why?" my sister said. "Why? Why's he going?"

She went on frantically demanding answers until she too was crying.

"Your dad has a work project and he needs to move to be closer to work."

"It's only for the duration of the project," he offered in a lighter tone. "Just for a couple of months. You guys can visit anytime."

His voice cracked.

"Noooo," my sister cried out and bolted from the room. Her chair went flying in the process. Her door slammed.

I remained seated, trying to process what I'd been told, trying to understand how this sudden right turn fitted into my old man's version of Viking lore.

Neither of my parents had displayed any unhappiness before now. There were never any great rows between them or major disagreements in front of us kids.

Sure, the old man could be an arsehole at times, and on one occasion, late at night, I'd heard my parents arguing behind closed doors, but my father had a respectable job as the assistant manager at the Isle of Man Bank. He always paid the bills and had coached us lads at football ever since I was four. He was my hero of sorts, and my mum, too. Besides being a housewife, she coached tennis, netball and swimming. A kinder and gentler and more giving soul you could not find.

In fact, all my friends and the local kids loved my parents. We had a perfect home. We took annual holidays – Australia, Singapore and all over Europe – and Sal and I were both grade A students.

It was the perfect bloody family, right? So what had happened? The world around me was suddenly reverting back to Viking-like savagery.

A short while later, my father went out of the door with his suitcase. All of us gathered to wave him goodbye.

"You're the man of the house now," he told me, his head held low out on the front porch. "You've got to look after the girls."

I nodded. "I'll look after them."

Shoulders back. Chest out. Stomach in. Stiff upper lip.

My father climbed into his maroon Sierra, reversed quickly up the steep drive and backed into the cul-de-sac. The Viking burial ground formed the backdrop as he pulled away. I watched until he had disappeared out of sight.

That night I lay awake in the dark, still deeply pained and baffled by the whole situation. Time crawled along. My mind was a blur of questions, anger and grief. What the bloody hell will the townspeople say? The prospect of this business going public filled me with dread. I had never been confronted with something like this before. The old man had taught me from day one: Look good at all times, lad. Always look the part.

Very late that night, a story began to emerge that fitted the confusion. My dad had been promoted and was moving into a luxury apartment. Big pay rise. A new car. Soon, the family would be traveling the world.

I walked through the school gates the following morning to find the news had preceded me. It was a small town. News travelled fast.

"Mike, Mike," Finnegan said. "What's this that ya dad's leavin'? It's not true, is it? He's the footy coach. No way."

Divorce was rare in our town. My friend's parents were all still married. I laid on the bullshit. "Nah, he's moving into a huge luxury apartment, just to be closer to work. He's the main man now. A massive pay rise. We were getting a new top of the line Sierra 4x4 to go with the deal. And a holiday to Disneyland."

A toxic feeling of guilt and shame washed over me the minute those words came out of my mouth. Before that moment, denying to my mother that I had stolen the biscuits from her pantry rated as the biggest lie I had ever told. Now I had told one of monumental proportions, and with a potential outreach of 850 students. Worse still, I had made Finnegan my unwitting accomplice.

With confession on my lips, I let it pass and instead concocted a preemptive defence in my head...lest anyone should ever question my bullshit.

"Yeah," Finnegan said, interrupting my private movie. "But Tracy Smith's spreading this crap around school that he's having an affair. Reckons her parents said so."

I was ready to smash the bitch's face in, but that's not how things were done in our town. You hit a woman, the local lads came by to pay you a visit, not the police.

I scoured the schoolyard until I found my sister.

"Sal, Tracy Smith's spreading rumours about Dad. Sort it out, will ya?"

She bolted off across the schoolyard and returned a few moments later. "That's put an end to that."

Tracy Smith stormed across the yard, red in the face from my sister's slating. When I saw Tracy later in the day, her face was still red.

But what if her story was true? There were groups of kids chatting around the grounds and staring my way. Were they gossiping about my dad's departure? Was their laughter aimed at me? I felt naked and wanted the ground to open up and swallow me whole.

The rest of the day, I moped around school alone, vacillating between shame and rage. Was there something wrong with me? Had I done or said something to drive my dad away? Every look my way and I was ready to iron somebody out.

When a lad began mouthing off to me, "Where's your dad gone?" I squared him up with two good rights to his face. The arrogant prick. He was taller than me and quickly lamped me back on the nose. I was pissing with blood as a crowd formed.

Bloody livid now, I went after him with a flurry of punches. One right hook landed on his cheekbone with a nice crunch.

He went to his knees. I went and stood over him, ready to kill.

Just then the sports coach brushed through the crowd and yelled, "CANNAN!!! Get in my office!"

The cane across the arse. That was the usual punishment for fighting at school but this time I got away with only a reprimand.

"Watch yourself lad or next time you won't sit down for a week."

At home, Mum just shook her head. "Your dad'll be proud."

With that she handed me some ice from the fridge to pack on my nose.

A day or so later, Mum dropped Sal and me off at the Viking Hotel. My eyes darted around the shopping precinct beneath the hotel, glancing worriedly at the windows and cars. I asked Mum to drop us close to the hotel entrance and hurried inside with the feeling I was visiting an incarcerated felon. On the way up to the reception desk, we walked past the model of a Viking longboat, hung from the wall. The man behind the front desk was smoking a cigarette.

"Here to see my dad," Sal said.

"Who's your dad?"

"Peter Cannan."

"You're Pete's kids, are ya? 218."

He waved us across the worn carpet and past the saloon doors to the public bar. The doors swung back and forth. Smoke and laughter spilled into the foyer. The whole place smelled of stale beer.

At the top of the stairs, we stopped and looked out of the windows. The local precinct and hotel parking were below us. St Paul's Church was across the way facing the market square. The harbour and fishing boats were visible beyond the church. Fishing and smuggling were no longer mainstays of the economy, but the rank stench of herring and mackerel still suffused the narrow main street adjacent to the marketplace.

Sal and I started down the long corridor. As we turned down another long corridor towards Room 218, I heard the old man's familiar voice. An open door quickly shut. A woman with thick, dark hair sauntered down the corridor our way, her hips swaying. She flicked her hair like in one of those shampoo commercials.

"What's Miss World doing here?" I said to my sister.

"Bitch, bitch!" my sister said and broke into tears.

Hearing the ruckus, my dad opened his door and came out into the hallway.

"I hate you!" my sister screamed at him.

"Sal, she's just dropping round some groceries. We work together, you know."

"Yeah, she's just dropping round some groceries, Sal," I said.

Sal pushed my father away. "I hate you," she yelled again and ran down the corridor, crying.

My father made eyes at Miss World and she headed down the corridor the other way. He then went after Sal and I followed them, sucking on my asthma inhaler.

"Just wait here, kids," the old man said outside. "I'll call your mum."

Mum arrived and pointed at my nose. "I suppose you've seen this."

The old man smiled and nodded approvingly. My mum didn't.

"Get in the car," she told us and remained behind to talk to Dad.

"What happened?" she asked when she got back into the car.

"That bitch Davina was there," Sal screamed in the front seat.

Mum's face straightened. Her lips pursed. Tears were still streaming down Sal's cheeks. Nothing was said as we drove away.

Back at school, I continued on with my bullshit about my dad being the top banana and moving back home soon. One day an older kid ran past me, taunting me.

"Ha, ha, your dad's shagging the secretary."

I threw out my arm, intending just to disrupt his flight a bit but ended up lamping him with a good right in the nose. He dropped, clutching his face, the nose bleeding.

"Oh shit!" I said reflexively with a hand held out, feeling all remorseful. Then I remembered about being a Viking and decided, to hell with him. Finnegan was there and walked away with me.

"I hear of anyone else mouthing off and he'll get the same," I told him.

At the end of the day, I went to wait for my mum in the staff parking lot. She had returned to teaching Religious Education and sport at our school and was there to give me a lift home every day.

"How's everything going?" she asked as I climbed into the car.

I threw my bag on the floor of the car and slumped down with a squint in her direction. The other kids had been calling her a Bible basher. Did she not know how embarrassed I was by it all?

"Why?" I asked disdainfully.

"I just wondered if you're getting on okay, or if there's anything I can do to help."

I ignored her all the way home and settled in front of the TV as soon as we had walked in the door. My mum took a seat next to me.

"Can we just carry on the conversation, please, Mike?"

"What conversation?" I got up and left the room.

She followed. "Well, I've been getting reports from the other teachers."

"What reports?"

"Can you just stand still, please, so I can talk to you?"

I walked up the stairs. She gripped the banister and watched me from the ground level.

"Just stay where I can see you, please?"

She came up a couple of stairs. I hid around the corner, unable to look at her.

"I'm fine here. Tell me what you want to say."

"Some of the other teachers have mentioned that you've been a bit disruptive."

"What do you mean, disruptive?"

"Calling out and shouting in class. Always joking. I mean, it's okay on the occasion but not when it affects the rest of the class."

"Who told you that, Miss Bloody Keating? She's an effing nightmare."

Fucking bitch, I mumbled under my breath.

"It doesn't matter who told me. Look, they're going to move you down one from the top sets."

I went in and slammed the bedroom door. The pain of another public humiliation came with me. I had finished my junior school education in the top three of the year for academic achievement – only behind two highly studious, bespectacled young redhead girls – which had automatically placed me in the A set classes in Secondary School. Now I was lined up in the public stocks.

For a cure, I began envisioning a colossal supper. Eat like a Viking. Slice upon slice of chunky toasted white bread, smeared in salty butter. Food equalled sedation. Sedation equalled peace at night.

The months dragged on with the old man and his new bird still down at the hotel. Mum put on a brave face through it all, showing no emotion. My sister kept chucking fits. I was the man of the house and all that, but I had ceased caring about the whole mess. It was the Viking way. You raped and pillaged and moved on. No one hung around to cry over the victims.

One windswept day, on a sports field in Douglas, the main town of our island, the local officials held the yearly junior football trials. This was a major event on the Isle of Man. The trials provided an opportunity for lads like me to be scouted by the pro teams in England. Players came from all over the island to participate. If selected, you had a chance to play in tournaments in the north of England.

I pulled on the number 9 shirt. Centre forward, the same position as Dad. Having made the team the previous year, he had to be proud.

I sprinted onto the field with a gathering of family and friends shouting at the referee and players from the sidelines, a mixture of encouragement, profanities and advice.

"Fuck's the matter with ya, ref?"

"Break his fuck'n' legs."

"Get in hard."

The match had not yet started.

The air was so cold that day, the ball left seam stitches imprinted on my flesh each time I headed the ball during pre-match warm-ups. Once, when the ball hit the back of the net, I turned to seek Dad's approval but he was busy entertaining some other parents with one of his many tales. The anecdote was animated by an abundance of hand gestures. The last I saw, he and the other parents were doubled over in laughter.

The referee's whistle signalled for the game to kick off. Dad paced back and forth along the sideline, barking encouragement. Each time I made a strong challenge or played with skill, he offered me a subdued clap of his hands. When the other parents praised me, he offered them a sarcastic nod. Yeah, he got lucky.

If I lost a challenge, my father turned away in disgust. What an outrage. My every failure was a direct challenge to his masculinity.

"Christ, Michael, stand upright in the challenge! What's the matter with you, for chrissake, Michael? Go in hard, get aggressive!"

"Fuckin' detest that fuckin' prick," I muttered back under my breath.

What business did he have barking orders at me from over on the sidelines? The arsehole had run off with another woman.

I turned towards him and saw the same intense stare back that had paralysed me since I was a little kid. *The bastard hates me. I'm making him look bad.*

Certain that everyone watching the game knew of his affair, I felt like an idiot. Yeah, that's right. I'm the only fool who doesn't know.

The more my father barked directions, the more I detested him. The day would come when I was bigger and stronger than him. Then I would iron him out, all right.

Ignoring him, I continued taking my anger out on every opponent, leaving behind heavy casualties. By the time my dad came over with his advice at the end of the day, I was ready to tell him to fuck off.

The selections went on for a couple of weeks. At the end, I was left sitting in the locker room with three other lads. The chosen players had already jogged out. The coach dropped his clipboard.

"Better luck next year, lads. Thanks for coming."

The tension in the car ride home made my gut ache. I could feel Dad's disappointment and anger. I wished he were dead.

My mother opened the front door as we pulled up to the house.

"The boy needs more hardening up and less mollycoddling," my father told her and delivered me up.

As I started in through the front door, my sister rushed out to my father's arms. Beaming, he held her head against his shoulder.

"That's my girl. That's my girl."

I looked back once, in growing envy and anger towards the whole world. What did I have to do to earn that sort of affection?

"How many goals did you get?" Mum called after me. "Did you make the team?"

Ah, fuck off, I wanted to tell her. Fuck everyone, including the Vikings. Fucking bollocks to everything. I went up to my room and hid. First academic relegation. Now athletic rejection. My public humiliation was complete.

As a consolation, the old man secured me a membership at the local golf course with his connections in the bank. I started rubbing shoulders with well-respected businessmen and wealthy retirees. Rolling hills and pine forests. Snaefell Mountain served as a backdrop. The first time I strolled out onto the fairways and manicured greens, I felt like the dog's bollocks. When the old man arranged for Finnegan to join the club, I forgave him a bit.

Finnegan and I played as often as we could: before school, lunchtime and after school. We hung out in the clubhouse in the evenings.

With the old man's encouragement, we started taking bets on every angle: longest drive, nearest the pin, best score on each hole, fewest putts, and the least amount of clothes. The gambling continued into the clubhouse: slot machines, darts and snooker. Whatever we had.

Next thing you knew, we were guzzling down a few half lagers with our recreational activities and everything became fair game for a sup. Four holes of golf after school and we had a few beers. A lunchtime sandwich at the club and we chucked down a beer. Evenings, weekends, rain or shine, everything came down to "Fuck it, I'll have another". I never gave it much thought up to that point and never gave it much thought from that point forward. My brain was hardwired to want more.

As time passed, lager turned to whiskey, cigarettes to cigars. At the country club, this all seemed cultured and stylish. Sporting gentlemanly attire. Living the leisurely lifestyle. What was next? I could hardly wait to become a teenager.

With the passage of time, Dad moved into a different room at the Viking, then to a small apartment. I turned up one day and found Miss World leaving. I turned my bike around but heard the old man calling my name. Red-faced, I went back.

"Why did you leave?" he asked.

How could the fucking idiot be so blind? He still did not understand.

A year or so later, the old man bought the family home from my mother, forcing us to move into a smaller house alongside the main coast road. Mum had returned to teaching full-time to afford the bills. She never showed any anguish at the move, just went about decorating the dilapidated house with our old furniture and renovating it into a warm, welcoming home.

Dad moved into our old family house and had it furnished up with a nice clinical touch. In place of the fluffy old family sofa, he bought something as stiff as a board. A couple of pictures on the walls and new beige carpet and he thought it was a showroom.

Other than for a couple of beds, the rest of the place was empty.

I dreaded our regular Wednesday night visits, especially his lectures. Driven to the point of anger and frustration by him, he would then berate me for showing emotion. That was not the Viking way. Show your weakness and people will jump all over you. There was no place in his world for tender feelings.

When it came time to leave, he always invited me to stay.

"This is your castle. You'll always be safe here. I bought you a new bed. You can pick your own bedroom furniture. It will be an adventure."

An adventure? It was more like a psychological endurance test. I loved him but preferred not to be in the same room.

Having eyed a basket full of silver coins on the side cabinet, I decided it was my just compensation for putting up with all his bullshit. During his work hours the next day, I broke into the house and began a series of robberies. Whatever change I could grab, I nicked. I had a slot machine habit to feed over at the local snooker hall.

PJ's was located next to a poor council estate and had a reputation for trouble. It was a melting pot for dropouts – a mixture of dissident Catholic and Protestant kids, rabble from the special units at school and abandoned teenagers from the local children's home – all gambling, drinking, smoking and fighting, and all while trying to play snooker.

Having ditched my friends from the top sets at school, I fell in with this bunch at PJ's. Mum was my letter of introduction. She taught many of these troubled kids at school and had a real affection for them, and they adored her in return. As Mrs Cannan's son, I was warmly welcomed into the tribe. I'd take the piss out of them, and they'd take the piss out of me, all in good nature.

It felt good to be accepted anywhere in the world, but Mum hated the idea of me being seen near the place.

"Keep away from that dive PJ's place, I've heard reports that you've been down there," my mum would call out after me as I tried to sneak out of the house.

With no male figure to rein me in, I was full of chin and belligerent behaviour. Eager to be with my friends, I was always sneaking out of the house at night.

The cold, dark evening was heavy with the scent of coal fires. You could see the smoke billowing from the chimneys of the tall town houses lining the road. I stopped to spark up a king-size Regal cigarette, straining the end for a nicotine rush. The nicotine and a gust of wind at my bollocks nearly gave me a hard on.

PJ's opened at six o'clock and I was usually first to arrive. Finnegan met me there most nights but I often saw this lad there at PJ's – the last name, Howcroft. He was in the lower sets at school, where they learned to lay bricks and plaster walls. He was one year older than me – had big ears, tight abs, jaundiced-looking skin and a stunner for a sister. Her name was Caitlynn. At sixteen, she had been crowned the carnival queen and paraded through the park and town on the back of an old milk float, smiling and waving like royalty. She appeared on the front page of the local paper, looking like a young Audrey Hepburn. I had to have her.

A big block of apartments separated my house from Howcroft's place, so one night I waited across the road for him to leave home, then headed for his front door as soon as he had disappeared, checking the gelled hair as I strode up, shoulders back, chest out, stomach in. My heart was pounding.

I rang the bell and waited. A figure appeared on the other side of the frosted glass door. It was Caitlynn with a bath towel wrapped around her torso. From what I could tell, the towel was hardly covering her crotch.

"Who is it, Caitlynn?" a deep voice called out in the background.

"I dunno, babe," she called back.

I almost ran. The door opened before I could get away. I was standing face to face with Caitlynn, half-naked, still wet, the towel struggling to keep her tits caged. Her wet black hair hung down to her shoulders. The Audrey Hepburn eyes searched me. I tried to stay focused on them and not the towel.

"Who are you?" she said as if perturbed.

"Michael. Is Howcroft there?"

"No, you've just missed him. He'll be heading down the prom."

"Okay, thanks."

She shut the door in my face.

Oh, I get it, playing the old hard to get game. I saw right through her. She wanted me but couldn't let the boyfriend know. Three years older was no big deal to me.

Slowly, slowly catch a monkey, I said to myself as I headed off down the prom. The fantasies played out in my head. One day, with the boyfriend gone, I'd be invited in for a cup of tea. Nod along while she did all the talking, like Sal and my Mum had taught me. Monkey see, monkey do. Then I'd be on her.

CHAPTER THREE

As the months flew by, Mum became inured to my increasingly antisocial behaviour. The more she told me what to do, the more I did the opposite, until she stopped interfering altogether. No more lectures on my late night carousing and the smell of alcohol and cigarette smoke in clothing. Instead, the accumulation of religious icons around the house grew in direct proportion to my deteriorating behaviour. Her concern was now being expressed in the form of religious literature and artwork. Mum was a lay reader at church, so she had all the works right there at her fingertips.

Jesus Heals The Sick in paperback purposely placed on the kitchen table or bedside cabinet. Jesus and the prophets in watercolour staring on as I took a shit. For the life of me I could not escape their bloody presence.

A year or so later, my mother informed me that it was time for my confirmation. Apparently I was ready to renounce the Devil and turn to Christ. Filled with an aversion to anything religious, I protested.

"Why, Mum? Why do I have to be confirmed?"

Mum explained about her own religious upbringing – she had lost her mother at an early age and God and religion had helped ease her grief – so she had made a commitment to raise her own children with the same Christian values.

"And I had an experience, and, well, it changed my life."

"What experience?"

"I'll tell you when you're older and able to understand."

I in turn pleaded, sulked and refused confirmation until she relented.

"Well, I'd been praying in a room with the vicar and I asked Jesus fully into my life. Then I felt a very strong wind from the centre of the room cover my body. I could hear it. The holy spirit. I knew it."

"And there was no windows open?"

"Nothing, every window and door was shut."

"Then what happened?"

"I was in a state of bliss. I just felt such love for everyone, especially your dad and you kids. I felt born again. Dad asked who came first in my life, God or him, and I told him that it was God. That's when our relationship began to fall down. Dad felt like I'd committed adultery."

She began to well up.

"No more. I promised your dad I would never talk badly about him or share what happened."

"So you have to ask Jesus fully into your life and the wind will come?" I said.

"Yes, he hears everything. You really have to mean it, though. Really ask him into your life."

She reassured me with a hug.

"You see? The family will all be reunited in heaven when we die – that's provided you've asked Jesus into your life."

Hearing all that, I got ready for church. I had to have Jesus. I had to go to heaven and be saved.

I adopted an ongoing mantra wherever I went.

"Please, Jesus, come into my life, come into my life, I accept you."

Then I waited patiently for the wind.

Clearly I was not sincere enough, so I got down on my knees, clutching my chest and pleading, real Shakespearean like, but still nothing.

At the end of each day, I would kneel at the end of my bed and begin the prayer.

"Gentle Jesus meek and mild, look upon this little child…"

I prayed to be perfect in every thought and action. I prayed to say the perfect words. If I didn't have anything nice to say, I would say nothing at all. I continued to pray for every person I knew. An hour or so a night, but still the wind did not come.

I felt frustrated and helpless. Unable to remember everyone's name, I would describe their appearance and where they lived, hoping the prayer would find them.

As time progressed, I prayed for each person in my school and town. Then on the Isle of Man, England, Ireland, Scotland, and Wales. People on the TV. Random animals that had been hurt. Lepers. Starving children in Africa. I pulled out a world map and spoke the name of each country and prayed for every person within that country. I prayed until I cried, but still no wind.

I must be going to hell, I thought. I could not remove the image of fire and brimstone and the red horned beast from my mind.

I explained to Mum that the wind hadn't come.

"You have to really mean it," she said. "Ask from your heart. He sees and hears everything."

So there I was, down on bended knee, clutching my chest and clenching my fist.

"Please, Jesus, please hear me."

Any more words felt insincere. I just hoped the strained look on my face communicated my conviction.

For confirmation, the bishop lined me up at the altar, poured aromatic oil over my head, placed his hands on me and hammered out a few set prayers. Rendered me damn perfect they did. I remember a plaque on the wall at the vicarage reading:

Watch your thoughts, for they become words. Watch your words, for they become actions. Watch your actions, for they become habits. Watch your habits, for they become character. Watch your character, for it becomes your destiny.

The old man had Miss World and the old girl had Jesus, so as soon as they were done anointing me with the cross, I headed off down to the snooker hall to smoke a cigarette and officially renounce any future spot in the clergy.

The place was empty and dark when I walked in, nobody playing. A cigarette lighter lit up in the darkness amongst the seats in the back, briefly revealing a young man. I heard rustling sounds and knew he was up to something.

"Ow, ow," he said and waved his hand like he'd burned his fingers.

I placed a couple of coins in the gambler and kept half an eye on things in the back. The young man appeared to be rolling something and slicking a tongue along the edge. A few moments later, a figure came into view.

"How's it goin', Mikey?"

"All right, McQuinn. What's happenin', yissur?"

Yissur being Manx slang for mate.

"Bit a this an' that. Are ya comin' outside?"

Declan McQuinn had been a ringleader and troublemaker at the Catholic school. The schoolkids nicknamed him Diabhal, Irish for Devil. I was attending the Protestant school directly across the road and knew that Protestants were right and Catholics wrong and that was that. Rocks and insults were frequently exchanged between the two schools. Now it appeared that McQuinn and I had gravitated towards a common solution.

We walked outside and around the corner until we were out of view of the road. McQuinn lit a long, rough-looking, cone-shaped cigarette. He sucked in and held his breath.

"Ever had a blast on this tackle, Mikey?" he said on the out breath.

"What's that then?"

"Squidgy black. Gold seal, like. Don't say fuck all."

"Drugs?" I said.

"Hash. Good ones, though. No crap."

He carried on smoking and shaking his head.

"Helluva buzz. Get a blast a that in ya."

He passed me the joint. I took a pull and blew out.

"Hold it in, don't waste it," McQuinn said.

Remembering Jesus, I offered up my version of a prayer. I'm not a bad lad, really. It's just a bit of pot.

"Have another," McQuinn said.

I took a good drag and coughed. The two of us passed it back and forth and were soon having a good laugh. Fucking relief, I thought. A sedated bliss and otherworldliness had fallen upon me. Everything I had been looking for in church, and all it took was a long draw.

"Any more?" I said.

"You can buy some."

"I'll have to get some cash."

I wandered home, half giddy and suddenly ravenous. I threw a couple of slices of bread in the toaster and chased it down with some processed cheese and a few milk chocolate biscuits.

My mother's handbag was staring at me from a seat at the kitchen table. I lifted the flap back and walked away, straining my ears for any sound of Mum in the lounge next door. When nothing came of it, I walked back over and delicately twisted open the gold purse clasps. When all was still quiet, I opened up the purse and pinched a £1 note.

The toaster popped, scaring the shit out of me. I put everything back as it was and stumbled upstairs with cheese on toast, a pack of sour cream Pringles and the rest of the biscuits stuffed under my arm. I knew God could hear my thoughts: God, Jesus, listen, it's just a loan. I'll pay it back, honestly, I will.

In the darkened bedroom, I opened one of my sister's fashion magazines and had a half-arsed wank into an old sock. Afterwards, I fell naked to my knees and bowed my head, wanting Jesus to come into my life, wanting to be pure, wanting to feel all awakened and chosen, the way my mum had felt.

"I accept you," I said but nothing happened.

"Jesus, I accept you into my life...come into my life, Jesus."

Still nothing.

"Fucking cunt."

I winced in anticipation of the lightning bolt, but nothing happened so I sparked a cigarette and opened the bedroom window.

Fucking doomed I am. Fucking sinner. Fuck it all.

I robbed my mum's purse of another £5 and called McQuinn. Drugs were easier. Plus, a few tokes and you'd forget all about the fire and brimstone.

Along with failing grades, I lost interest in everything involving a team. Who cared? My family was disbanded. I was an outcast. I no longer had any sense of pride.

Testosterone kicked in over the next few years. By the time I was 15, I was nearly six foot tall. My voice had deepened enough so that if I thickened the accent a bit and looked stern, I could get served alcohol at a pub.

I had a new hobby and the Viking Hotel was my weekend gateway. I got a strange, anxious touch of nostalgia each time I entered in the front and went upstairs to the saloon style doors. I'd like to see Miss World parading down the corridor now.

The interior of the pub hadn't changed. Smoke filled the room. Irish folk songs bellowed from the speakers. The slot machines spit out the occasional winner. The same people were sitting in the same seats. Only their weight changed and the size and coloration of their noses.

Old Howcroft was always civilized. Never had a drink until I arrived. I called him wingnut, in honour of his impressive ears. He called me big nose, in honour of the ugly lump smack bang in the middle of my face.

There had been many fights in which it had been broken.

Howcroft also called me Fod, short for Cannan fodder. I was still trying every possible angle to get in his sister's knickers, and never failed to let him know it. One word about that and the veins in his neck bulged like a couple of piano wires, both fists clenched.

"If I hear one more fucking word about my sister…"

"Easy, old boy, you wanna chaser with that pint?"

"Ahh, don't mind if I do."

With the old man gone, I could practically do whatever I wanted without fear of reprisal. Drinking, smoking, and knocking about with the dregs of society. Lower companions gave me an elevated sense of self-worth.

It was the life. I had finished the GCSE exams. An A in design. My father wanted me to get a trade. I was fancying a degree and all that. On the beach. The easy life. No more responsibility for me. I had dreams of a summer job, save a few quid and head off in some direction, any direction. I had no fixed plan. A couple of grand would do the trick.

"Morocco," I told Howcroft. "We just head south and keep going. The best drugs in the world. Cheap, too."

"Now you're talking, Fod."

"Birds, two a penny."

"Loads of them, yissur."

"Rapin' and pillagin' on the front lines. Real Vikings we'll be. Great craic, Wingy."

As the drinks flowed, I found it necessary to shorten wing-nut to wingy.

"Another?" he said.

I nodded at the glass. "Rude not to."

He returned from the bar with another round of drinks and the newspaper under his armpit.

"Here Fod, check this out. Article in the paper here about this bloke being paid to travel the world and fuck all these rich women."

"Imagine that, Wingy. A bird with loads of money. Big ol' palace with a pool and jacuzzi. Concrete lions on the gateposts an' all that."

We drank and ran our mouths off about shagging rich American birds and living in the US of A, land of opportunity.

On the way home we had to hold each other up. Stumbling and swaying down the road we went.

Howcroft noticed the figure in the dark arches beneath the church before me.

"Gidawook."

He was an old bum around town. I once asked Dad why they called him Gidawook.

"Because at school he couldn't say 'Give me a look at your homework', so he would just say 'Gidawook'."

Gidawook had all these involuntary twitches of limbs and torso and fingers. The kids taunted and teased him. I had seen him walking aimlessly around town at all hours of day and night. Everyone knew him.

At seeing us, Gidawook adjusted his heavy brown trench coat and yanked his pants high up his belly. Howcroft and I began muttering "Gidawook" under our breath. He looked over at us, his eyelids fluttering. His lips puckered and smacked.

"Fuhuhhuuck ooffff," he mumbled.

God, I felt for the poor fucker.

Howcroft became alert all of a sudden.

"Must have let him out of the nuthouse. Reckon he was the last person on the Isle of Man to get electric shock treatment."

My head cleared too.

"Imagine us ending up in a bloody nuthouse."

My absolute worst nightmare.

I met Howcroft at his house the next day. When the tide was in, you could jump from the pier next door into the sea. The pier was a quarter of a mile long and once had a miniature train running to and from a café at the end. Steep headlands stretched down the coastline, dotted with rocky coves.

Howcroft and I climbed around the fenced entrance and went for a 20-foot belly flop into the inky, ice-cold water. We had started fleshy pink and came out looking pale blue. The seagulls circled overhead, having a good look at our folly.

Howcroft's girlfriend was watching from the rocks beneath the pier with her best friend, Sandra. Sandra was twenty-one and quite pretty, provided she didn't laugh and show her teeth.

"Meet us at the apartment," the wingnut's bird shouted after she had watched us jump several times.

"We'll get changed and meet you over there!" Howcroft shouted.

We heard bottles rattling in their shopping bags as the two women walked away. With them gone, the two of us went back to dunking each other in the freezing water.

"Why don't you bang Sandra, Fod? Get it out of the way."

"I'm saving myself for number one," I said with a nod at his sister's bedroom window.

"Yeah, in your dreams. Anyway, her fella's back from the army now."

We changed at Howcroft's and bolted up to the fourth-floor apartment across the road. The girls were already pouring drinks in the kitchen when we came in. Howcroft quickly pulled his bird into the spare bedroom. Not long after the door had closed, the bedsprings started squeaking. I sat with Sandra watching TV. She began tapping me on my arm.

"Is that foreplay?" I said.

"If you want," she said and ran a hand up the inside of my thigh.

She unbuttoned my shirt next and ran her nails down my chest. I grabbed at her tits. She had her lips at my face and neck, breathing real heavy and dramatic. At one point, she backed off, her eyes rolling about in her head. Then she came in for another kiss. Her breath stunk. My cock was hard. She fumbled with my belt, unbuttoned the fly and ran the palm of her hand down my cock. It was all over in six seconds, if that long.

"Don't worry, we can try again," she said.

Don't bloody worry? My best Marks and Spencer's undies were a mess. I left punching the wall on my way down the stairs, humiliated. I had a fantasy of being the world's greatest fuck. I'd planned to fuck her for two hours straight. What if she told her friends, for fuck's sake?

A few days later, I walked across the road armed with four cans of the auld wife beater and two bottles of Lambrini. It had been buy one, get one free at the Co-op. Sandra opened the door.

"Oh, you gentleman. Two bottles for me?" She clutched them to her chest.

"Worth every penny you are."

After a few drinks, Sandra took my hand and pulled me into her bedroom. Our clothes went flying. She pointed at the bed. "On ya back."

Her tits knocked together as she straddled me. She thumbed my cock inside her snatch and held my wrists above my head. Her feet were wrapped around my shins. I clenched my teeth as she thrashed her hips back and forth. Minutes passed and I had yet to come. I shut my eyes and thought of Caitlynn. When I opened them, all I could see was the underside of Sandra's chin. I came before she did, but that did nothing to stop her. The crescendo built to a moan and stopped dead. Sandra fell off and rolled over.

My training for this exercise had been a catalogue of hard-core misogynistic porn videos. The twisted pile driver. The Indian headstand. The g-spot sniper.

I had not wrestled Sandra into any of those positions, but I was willing.

Did she want me to fist her arse?

Not really. Okay. Whatever. At least the burden of my virginity was now gone.

I looked up at the clock. "I'd better get going. School tomorrow."

While gathering up my underwear and socks, I saw Caitlynn's light was on through the window. The promised land, only I had sold out. I walked home with my soiled conscience and my cock stuck to my undies. I had visions of Caitlynn getting thumped by her big army man.

Amazing thing it is your conscience. A few weeks later, I was back over at Sandra's apartment for a session. People were standing around talking and dancing. I had set up shop on a kitchen counter with a can of Stella and my feet on the back of a chair. Without a knock, the front door burst open and Caitlynn walked through with a couple of girlfriends.

"Nightlife's shut," she said as she stumbled in with a bit of a laugh. "We heard the party was goin' on over here. Hi ya, Mikey love. Av you seen our Howcroft?"

She seemed to be staring at the wall directly behind my head. I noticed her makeup was not the most accurately arranged.

"Aye, I think he's in there with the missus." I pointed at the bedroom.

"You wanna drink, Cait?"

"Pour us a glazzawine, will ya love?"

She hung on the doorframe for a moment and swung out of the room. I poured the drinks and sat back, not believing my good fortune. Caitlynn soon came back through the door and walked straight towards me. I held up her glass. She ignored the glass and stood between my legs.

"Wot av we ere, then?" she said as she unbuttoned the top two buttons of my shirt. With her hands on my lapels, she pulled me towards her and we kissed. It turned into a full snog with tongues and saliva. I could not, for the fucking life of me, believe my luck.

She pulled away and pushed her tongue into her cheek. "Aye, aye," she said.

"Caitlynn," I said and pointed to the room where Howcroft was. "Say fuck all, yeah?"

She laughed and sat next to me on the counter. She talked and talked. I nodded along.

The next weekend we took acid together. I can't remember much about what happened. You don't remember much about acid. You're just left with all these vague, fantastical images and reveries, wondering, what the fuck. I don't even remember how we got on to taking acid. Mostly I remember some wild sex and the metallic taste left in my mouth.

Anyway, Caitlynn and I were now an item. Every day around noon at school, I'd hear her hammering away at the horn of her black Volkswagen Golf outside. The boys giving me shit over my bag of weed and three-quarter length pigskin leather jacket as I closed my locker and made an exit from the building. Caitlynn was out there circling the staff parking lot with one arm waving and a fag hanging from her lip.

We drove to Caitlynn's house with one thing on our minds. Howcroft had taken a work gig as a brickie for the local commissioners. Caitlynn's mum was busy in the kitchen.

"Hi, Eleanor," I said as we raced through the living room, Caitlynn laughing. By the time we hit the stairs, I was loosening my tie and grabbing at Caitlynn's skirt. The inside of her bedroom smelled of hairspray, ashtrays and floral perfume.

Panned out on the bed, I braced myself for action and Caitlynn started barking out instructions.

"A little more pressure...use the thick of your tongue... change direction...long strokes...now the tip...grab my arse and massage."

My head was stuck between her legs. By the time she finally came, my jaw was about to drop off.

"Your turn," she said and commenced to tie me to the bedposts, my socks on two corners, my belt and school tie on the others.

"Eleanor, Eleanor," I called out to her mum, just for the craic.

"Shut the fuck up," Caitlynn said and went to work on my cock.

All of a sudden, I heard the back gate bang open and looked at Caitlynn.

"Just the postman, luv," she said.

As she carried on, the back door slammed shut, then the living room door.

"Hey love, what's up?" I heard Eleanor say.

Caitlynn's enterprise halted abruptly.

"The fucking door had better be locked," I said.

She nodded and placed a finger to her lips. We heard Howcroft's voice.

"Boss told me to leave the building site, said I was an angry man. Should have put him on his arse."

"Aw, love. Sorry to hear it. Mikey's upstairs. Go and say hello."

I heard his metal toecaps bounding up the stairs, three to a stride. Caitlynn leapt behind the bed and crouched with her knickers in hand. I was struggling to get free of my bindings.

"It is locked, innit?" I said, nodding vigorously.

It wasn't and the door flew open. Howcroft's look of shock came with a high-pitched laugh, which I had never heard the likes of before.

"Fucking hell," he said. "That's all I fucking need. Cannan fodder tied to my sister's fucking bed."

He slammed the door shut.

"Fuck's sake, Mum. You didn't tell me he was bollock naked and tied to her fuckin' bed, for cryin' out loud."

We heard Howcroft go down step by step. We joined him a short while later. He was downstairs sitting with Eleanor.

"Come on, yissur, let's go for a beer after school," I said.

He gave me the finger.

"Better get you back to your classes," Caitlynn said.

I offered her mum a sheepish goodbye.

Later that day, I ran into Howcroft in front of the pub.

"Sally's fair game," he said, going in.

"Every dog has his day."

"I'll have my day, all right." He made a lewd gesture.

"Well, if anyone's gonna be shagging my sister, I'd rather it was you."

CHAPTER FOUR

At sixteen I began studying for my driving licence and passed on the third try. As a reward, Dad bought me a sunburst orange Ford Fiesta.

By now the old man and Miss World were shacked up at her country farmhouse a few miles outside of town. It was a charming place populated with one bereft lamb, believing it was a dog, a few ducks as gatekeepers and a motley collection of Shire horses. Never liked visiting the place. Bad feeling about the whole setup all around.

Dad and I spoke a couple of times a week by phone. That way there was no chance of him smelling the alcohol and nicotine on me.

On the phone, he always started out by enquiring as to my general health.

"How's it going?"

"Good. You?"

The pleasantries out of the way, a handful of dirty jokes usually followed. When he lowered his voice, I knew what was coming.

"What's the difference between a magician and a stripper?" he asked me one day.

Stumped, I admitted as much.

"One has a cunning stunt…"

Infectious laughter through the phone. I was pretty much doubled up too.

"Saw Caitlynn modelling in the newspaper the other day," he said once we straightened ourselves out. "What's she doing with you?"

He laughed again. I didn't.

Bloody rich coming from you, arsehole. What the fuck is Miss World doing with an old bastard like you? I wanted to spit through the phone.

He ended the conversation with the usual banter. His way of showing affection. Actually, I got the impression he was quite proud of me for shagging Caitlynn.

By that next summer, I had become tight with McQuinn, that Catholic bloke from the poor side of town. He lived in one of those real rundown housing estates and the two of us had become further acquainted from hanging around PJ's together.

On my seventeenth birthday, I drove over to his place, eager for drugs. By now McQuinn was renowned around town for being an addict. He mixed with junkies and convicts, most of whom had been to prison. I feared guilt by association, but the allure of getting wasted was worth just about any risk.

Parked up the adjacent side road, I waited until McQuinn clocked me from his bedroom window and waved for him to come outside. A minute later, the door to the house swung open and McQuinn bolted down the path.

His dad appeared in the opened door, filling the frame.

"Ya wee bastard. Get your arse back here now or don't come back at all!"

The old man was shaking his fist at him. McQuinn jumped into the passenger side.

"Drive, drive. He's goin' nuts."

McQuinn was fidgeting with a prescription container. The pills and a lighter were rattling in his hands. He popped a couple of tablets into his mouth.

"What you got there?" I asked.

"DF118s."

"What the hell are they?"

"Painkillers. Strong ones. Drive over to the beach."

The lighter and prescription container remained in his lap.

"Any weed?" I asked.

"Got a few bits and pieces."

Hearing the tin foil rustle put a smirk on my face.

I drove over to the north shore promenade and down a short slipway facing the beach. The day was cold and clear. Waves were crashing down the shore. With the windows up, the bright sunlight warmed the car interior.

"Got some sugar," McQuinn said.

"Sugar? What's that?"

"Don't say fuck all, Mike…brown."

"Brown?"

"Ya know. Smack…heroin."

He pulled out a folded piece of tin foil and a small envelope. "Don't breathe, and do that window up tight. And turn the music down. Fuck, turn it off. This is gold dust."

He formed a crease in the foil and used a corner of the envelope to remove a few grains of the light brown powder. His tongue was out as he placed the powder on the foil. His hands were trembling. He centred the powder again.

I was both apprehensive and intrigued. This was heroin. The dark side. As dark as it got.

"Fucking hell, Mike."

"What!?"

"It's not you, man, sorry. Just don't do anything."

I held my breath while he placed a tube of tin foil between his lips and lit a flame beneath the other foil. The powder turned to black as it boiled and vaporized into smoke. It smelled of strong black coffee, but sweet. McQuinn's foil tube chased the genie-like smoke trail. I was still holding my breath. My heart was racing. Time seemed to have stopped. Alchemy and black magic were at work.

"You'll be wrapped in cotton wool and the best-looking man in the world," McQuinn said as he slowly exhaled the smoke.

46

His gaze drifted off towards the deep blue ocean. My thoughts turned to all the posters hanging around town – a skull, with two needles instead of crossed bones – warning about heroin. My only knowledge of it came from a high school melodrama. Talented and athletic young man slowly self-destructs, his relationships, health and life turned to ruins from increasing addiction, until, last scene, he's lying there dead with a needle in his arm.

Fuck it, I thought. I'm only smoking. No needles. Just this once.

"Don't let any out," McQuinn warned as he lit the foil.

I inhaled and held it. Moments later, a bone-deep warmth spread throughout my body. The tension in my jaw fell away. In a dead state of euphoria, I wanted for nothing. My life suddenly seemed both manageable and secure. A profound sense of acceptance and control had come over me. A lobotomy had been performed on all my abstract thought processes.

It definitely did not fuck me up the way alcohol did. I did not feel driven to act insanely and say stupid shit.

"It's all been a lie," I said.

The deep, calm tone of my own voice surprised me.

"What?" McQuinn said.

I did not bother to answer. Both of us were staring out of the windows of the Fiesta. My eyes opened and shut to the waking dream. With a glance at my reflection in the rearview mirror, I saw Elvis staring back.

Pink Floyd's *Dark Side of the Moon* played over and over. I was comfortably numb on perpetual loop.

I woke up early the next day and everything was normal. No hangover. No sickness. No sadness. I was happy and mellow. A warm afterglow remained of yesterday's pleasant feelings. Heroin was a miracle drug, I thought. Made me the man I wanted to be. I was home.

Drugs in general were scarce on the Isle of Man. It was difficult to import with the tight border patrol and strict searches at the ports. Heroin was especially rare. Like any drug, it tripled in price the minute it arrived.

McQuinn knew the only dealer. He lived in a small village several miles from our town. We spent long hours in my car, on a small lane across the road from his house, waiting for the donkey to arrive. The tension was palpable. Waiting. Anticipating. Waiting. Anticipating. We chugged cheap lager and bickered over trivial crap.

McQuinn was a bloody nightmare, desperate not to miss his fix. Admittedly, so was I.

If the boat came in from England, the game was on. If not, we headed back home to more days of intolerable waiting.

Usually when it came time for the magic, we'd drive to some secluded beach, recline in the car and get Bowie crooning on the stereo.

"Never a frown with golden brown…"

By the time school resumed, heroin had become an ingrained psychological need, if not yet a physical addiction. Everything else became secondary. I would wish away entire days, waiting for the man and longing for the drug. My mind nodded off in lectures. If I had some, I would smoke a small amount before school and a bit in the school toilets between periods.

"Just tired," I'd say if the teacher roused me from my desk.

One day at noontime, I decided to take the five-minute walk into town for lunch. This required permission from a parent or guardian but I didn't bother.

Back at school, I heard a voice call from across the yard:

"Michael, did you have permission to go down town?"

It was Mum.

"No," I called back.

"It's Monday night detention for you."

She was exercising the only form of control she had over me now, desperately trying to claw back some sense of structure and normality into our family life. Failing a guidebook on that one, she had chosen to lay down the law at school. It was a bit overcooked, in my estimation, but what was done was done.

Monday night came and I surrendered to my fate. I had never been in detention before but quickly realized this was for life's most abject losers.

Mum entered the class to speak to the teacher in charge. I was sitting with several of the kids from the 'special unit'. That term needed no further explanation.

When Mum and I exchanged glances, I saw the anguish in her face. She had failed as a wife. Now she was failing as a mother.

Though troubled by that knowledge, I could not stop smoking heroin. The more I did, the more I needed it. The more I did it, the more paranoid I became. Soon every car seemed to be following me. Every plane looked dodgy. The sight of every cop led to the heroin and gear being stashed in the car door panels.

Soon, everything worthwhile had passed from my life, Caitlynn included.

The last I saw of her, she was dancing at the Nightclub in her Lycra kit.

"Come and dance, come on," she said, extending her hand. "I've something to tell you."

McQuinn came in right then, his eyes shifting around the room. "Got some," he said.

"Serious? You got her?"

"I'll be leavin' in about twenty minutes. Got anywhere to go?"

I left Caitlynn dancing there alone. We ended up at old Gordon's place, a couple of miles out of town because his parents were away.

The following morning, I arrived home and was confronted by Mum. The pupils of my eyes were like piss holes in the snow. To avoid arousing suspicion of drug use, I averted my gaze and darted up the stairs as she spoke to me.

"I got up in the night to pour a drink of water, and I saw someone in the garden with a white jacket. The security light came on, so I called the police. When they came, they found

Caitlynn in the hedge. She said she'd lost you in the nightclub and was throwing stones at your bedroom window, trying to wake you."

"I wasn't here," I said stupidly through my half-closed bedroom door.

"I can see that now. Anyway, she was so upset she couldn't apologize enough. You know, she really cares about you. The police asked if I wanted to press charges but of course I didn't. Look," my mum added and showed me a big bouquet of flowers through the door. "She dropped these around this morning to say sorry. She's such a sweet girl."

Caitlynn was but I had no choice in ending my relationship with her. I was in another one now, one that I could not control.

The next day, I began to experience flu-like symptoms. It had been thirty-six hours since my last hit of heroin. Damn cold, I thought. My legs were itchy and restless. A small amount of heroin quickly put an end to all the symptoms.

Vaguely aware of the danger, I made a decision. Never cross that invisible line of physical addiction. From here on out, I would only touch heroin on special occasions.

That turned out to be my preliminary A-level Economics exam. A smoke of the goods in the toilet and I was ready to restructure the world economy. My pen flowed across the page. I was in and out of consciousness for two hours.

The teacher later announced to the class that he had marked his lowest ever score as a teacher. Three per cent. He handed me the paper and later suggested I look for a job. Mum used her influence as a teacher and persuaded him to let me stay.

I scraped through my secondary education buzzed on smack. The results of my exams were not exactly degree worthy. I was looking at the career of a sparky.

Having resigned myself to no more school, Mum kept leaving the university enrolment forms lying all over the house. I ignored them until she finally filled them out for me. I signed the bottom and off they went.

Later that summer, I received an offer to study for a Higher National Diploma in Electronic Design at the University of Derby. Mum had lived in Derbyshire and relentlessly encouraged me to go.

Leave the island. Get away from the small world mentality.

The Derby offer was lower than a bachelor's degree but enough to keep Mum off my back, so I agreed. First off, though, I was taking a year out. I had planned a long vacation to foreign shores with Howcroft and Gordon. After all those long drinking binges down at the Viking Hotel, Morocco was still on the agenda.

I spent the first part of that summer shredding documents in the stationery department of the bank where my father worked, an obligatory marijuana joint at every lunchtime break, when I would romanticize about the upcoming Moroccan adventure. Cheap drugs, fine wine and luxurious women, it was the ultimate Viking adventure. I would travel the world for a year, reinvent myself and return triumphantly to the Isle of Man.

My vacation with Howcroft and Gordon got off to a hell of a start. We took a boat to Liverpool, a train to London, another train to Portsmouth and a boat from there to Santander, on the northern coast of Spain. All three of us had backpacks and bedrolls. Howcroft had brought along an additional suitcase and oversized ghetto blaster.

We landed at 2 a.m. and walked six miles to the nearest campsite. By the time we arrived in the early hours of dawn, a rainstorm was whipping around us. With the tent set up, we lay back in our sleeping bags, exhausted. Within a few minutes, the tent had started to leak. A pole dropped and one end collapsed on our heads.

"It appears we mistimed the seasons," I said with the saturated nylon both glued to my face and flapping madly.

"I ain't fixin' it," Howcroft said.

"Me neither."

I heard a bottle being opened beneath the flattened tent.

"That's the ticket, Howcroft," I said. "Pass it around and keep your eyes focused on that cheap heroin in Morocco."

We took the train down to Madrid the following day, then over to Lisbon and ended that leg on a picture postcard peninsula, deckchairs pulled up, three cold beers in hand and admiring the view. I knew Morocco was the final destination, but this beach was the bollocks.

All was well for a few minutes until Howcroft attempted to remove his beer bottle cap with his teeth and lost two of them in the process. He was done, blood dripping from his lips.

We went our separate ways the next day. Gordon and I headed south with our thumbs out. Howcroft headed home. He was a liability on tour, a menace to himself. I later learned that he walked the entire length of Portugal back to Santander, where he caught a boat and a train back to the Isle of Man.

Our first ride was with a man driving a white pickup, soused on port. As with everyone else who picked us up down the coast to Algarve, we drank with him. Eventually, we found ourselves sitting in a bar in Lagos. Looking for any opportunity, I noticed an advert to crew for a small yacht posted on a bulletin board. I asked the barman and learned we'd missed the guy by a day. Out of luck there, we headed further down the coast towards Spain. That led us to a desolate campsite a few miles down from a local casino. I devised a plan and worked out all the details. We'd visit the casino, find ourselves a couple of wealthy birds and kick our feet up for the winter.

We strutted out of the tent that evening in black trousers, white shirts, black leather waistcoats and Italian loafers, the perfect gear for a three-mile hike down a dusty road. I split a note with the cashier at the casino and we hit the pokeys. The wealthy birds turned out to be non-existent, but I was soon broke anyway, blowing all my money on gambling and booze.

Down to a stash of cheap booze back at the campground, I had to reverse charges on a call to my father three days later. We had been stopped short of Morocco, but at least we were equipped with some impressive stories.

Back home at the airport, my father was there to greet me as I disembarked from the plane. Looking more despondent and frayed than I was, he stared into my eyes.

"Drunk and skint, eh? Got your priorities straight. The typical Manxman on holiday."

Christ, that was all I fucking needed.

"No, I've still got money," I said.

"What the hell happened?"

"We missed a luxury job crewing a yacht around the Mediterranean. We basically had to come back, but we'll be heading back for the next cruise season."

He squinted at me.

"You've still got money left?"

"Yeah," I said, still lying.

I had expected the old man to rip the back outta me. Don't recall there being too many stories of Viking warriors limping home with their tails between their legs, but I guess he had enough problems of his own and let it pass.

An old friend of ours who lived down the road had become a club DJ, so a small band of lads my age started hanging out there taking drugs and buzzin' with the music. A group of guys in their twenties were the kingpins of that scene. The ringleader drove a black Mercedes and had a load of money. The best-looking women surrounded them. I wanted in on the action.

When this new nightclub opened up in the centre of Douglas, I was all in for my latest initiation rite. Ecstasy. The boys chucked me a tablet and one more time I said, "fuck it". I didn't want the older lads to think I was a pussy.

Quickly, my whole life revolved around the nightclub culture: house music, designer drugs and a DJ massaging everyone's brains into a trance. The prominent bass drum beat made it feel like a tribal gathering. People of all ages and backgrounds flocked there, but Ecstasy was the common denominator. As the weeks progressed, I grew more and more hooked on the exhilarating release of serotonin. It was a one-hour rush of ecstatic bliss, followed by a couple of hours on a mellow plateau before you crashed back down to an anxiety-ridden state of exhaustion.

Naturally, I mostly remembered the ecstatic bliss and tried every imaginable combination of drugs to replicate that initial experience. Acid, Ecstasy, speed, ketamine, amyl nitrate, nitrous oxide, cocaine and various veterinary medications, but I could never get enough, and once started, I was unable to stop. I wasn't suffering so much a physical addiction as a psychological need to replicate the profound state of bliss and loss of inhibition. Who didn't want to feel completely present and connected to the universe, filled with a sense of bonding with all other human beings? "I fucking love you" was the dance floor anthem. Males ground their naked chests to that delusional beat. I had found emotional rapture and readily dismissed the accompanying panic attacks.

All was right with my world until one day I flicked on the TV and came across this documentary about drug use. They had a squirrel monkey suffering from brain damage after only four days of being dosed with Ecstasy. I'd been using it for months at that point. Load of bollocks, I thought. That could never happen to me.

That night I joined the lads for an evening on the bong. One hit and I went cold. My hands started to tremble. My flesh tingled like pins and needles. The TV and chatter in the room turned to a muffled drone. A heart-stopping sense of fear accelerated my heart rate right off the charts.

Tunnel vision set in. As everything raced away from me, I got up and sprinted for the door. Well before reaching it, I was slowed by a sudden sense of vertigo. Then I felt a sharp pain in my chest.

Fuck me, I thought. A heart attack, and I'm only seventeen years old.

Convinced I was dying, I jumped into my car and drove straight to the hospital. My sweaty hands were trembling at the wheel. My heart was still hammering away.

When I finally reached the hospital, I circled the emergency wing again and again, afraid the bastards inside would catch on and commit me to Ballamona, the local nut house. Prepared to die before suffering that indignity, I drove around the countryside for another hour until the attack finally subsided. Back in the safety of my own bedroom, I lay there fighting waves of adrenaline.

That was it for me. Drugs were out. Yet the panic attacks persisted. Over the coming days and weeks, I remained welded to the armchair in our house, gripping the armrests with my eyes fixed on the TV screen. Must be getting older, I thought. Part of becoming an adult. Or perhaps I had some sort of undiagnosed disorder. The panic attacks went on, disrupting my every waking hour. The anxiety caused fear and the fear led to me avoiding everything else.

December was a rough one. Locked inside the house, my thoughts became increasingly dark and paranoid. I thought the people on TV were whispering messages to me. Demons watched from the shadows. All was impending doom. Holding back tears was my only form of control. I obsessed over death, terrified of ending up in hell.

Where there was good, there was evil. If Mum was good and pure, then I must be pure evil. The Devil himself.

Being that fucked up in my head, I was utterly convinced that she had propagated the anti-Christ.

When she continued to question my well-being, I used the only defence I had – hostility. Finally, I broke down in tears one day.

"Mum, I'm really not feeling that good."

She looked on, both helpless and afraid.

"You've been in this room for months now. You'll have to go to Ballamona if this carries on."

Was she fucking reading my mind? More paranoia set in.

My friends, having become concerned about my absence, came knocking at the door. Mum made up a lame excuse why I couldn't leave the house. I for one did not want them knowing that a mission outside equalled a panic attack.

Late one night, I made it from the front steps out to the pavement and stood there for a minute. All was quiet except for my breathing and a heartbeat drumming in my ears.

Enough of that for one day.

The next day, I started up the road and was on wobbly legs in less than thirty paces. Heart racing, I turned back towards home in a state of paralysing fear. It seemed as if all the buildings and cars and passing people were laughing at me.

Back inside the safety of the house, I peeked out through the curtains. Was it all in my head? I had lost all ability to discern the answer to that question.

Each day I ventured a little further from the house until I had made it all the way around the block. Exhilarating. A sense of accomplishment was mine.

Slowly desensitized to open spaces and transportation, I took short car rides and walks up the nearby beach. I was regaining confidence, but my paranoia and delusions remained.

Seeing this, Mum pleaded with me until I finally agreed to see a doctor.

"Make sure you tell him everything," Mum shouted as I left the house.

I certainly would not be admitting to my new identity as the fallen angel, Satan himself.

At the front counter of the clinic, I was greeted by a bird who knew me.

"Hi, Michael, how are you?"

Oh fuck. Everyone's going to know now. I'll be the talk of the town. What am I doing in here?

While waiting, I picked up a leaflet on depression. Have you experienced any of the following for longer than two weeks: a change in eating habits resulting in unwanted weight loss or gain; a change in sleep patterns – too much sleep or not enough; feeling tired all the time; a loss of interest in people and/or activities that once brought you pleasure; becoming easily agitated or angered; feeling that nothing you do is good enough; thoughts of death or suicide, or attempting suicide;

ongoing physical symptoms that do not respond to treatment, such as headaches, digestive disorders and chronic pain.

Nothing in there about thinking I was the Devil or the heart racing.

This surgeon I knew, Dr Kensington, came by. "Michael, what are you doing? You look way too healthy to be in here."

That was a good sign. My name came over the intercom a few moments later.

"Michael Cannan for Dr Masterton."

I was drenched in Tchaikovsky on the way down the hall. Some sentimental bollocks from one of his classics. Thank God it was not *The Nutcracker*.

"Enter," a man's voice said at my knock. I went in and we shook hands. "Michael, please, take a seat. Now what can I do for you today?"

I slouched over with arms on my knees, talking to the floor. "I feel a bit off centre."

"Can you tell me a bit more?"

"Er, felt a bit low. And sometimes my heart starts racing. Not very often, though."

"Have you ever done drugs?"

"No, never."

I waited for the ejector switch, or for the men in the white coats. I was going straight to hell for lying.

"That's good," Masterton told me. "You know, sometimes people start down the road to drugs and never come back. It's a downward spiral. Like getting on a helter skelter."

He laughed at his own joke. I felt like I was already in a nuthouse. Did he really just use that fairground analogy?

"And how long's it been going on?" he asked me.

"Just started, really."

"Then come back in two weeks and we'll review your situation."

Two weeks later, I told him the same story, so he started me on the lowest dose of the mildest anti-depressant. When that failed to cure me, he gradually doubled the dose.

Still nothing. Taking a useless anti-depressant just left me feeling helpless and hopeless.

I continued telling the same story, of course omitting the truth. I was a drug addict. Not a word on that.

My thought was, if I can get off this island, where nobody knows me, and completely away from the paranoia and shame, I'd be willing to confess and get help. On the island, there were simply too many people to judge me. The word would spread. Michael Cannan is mental.

Somehow, I got accepted to the University of Derby. Deep fears still paralysed me. A few miles from home and I was gasping for air, but I had to get away.

When it came time to show up for the lads, I pasted a grin on my face and pretended to have my shit together. The lads looked surprised but welcomed me back with no questions asked. Just a few knowing looks exchanged as they passed the hash.

Not thinking, I had a blast on the pipe and was promptly hit with another panic attack.

Christ. I'm losing it.

More terrified of looking weak than I was of the drug, I took another hit and pretended to be feeling no pain.

Wired as hell I was.

Finnegan appeared from the bar with four cans of Stella Artois. I had not drunk for nine months. Halfway down that first can, I felt tremendous relief. Ready to settle in and all that. A job at the bank, nights at the pub, a house down the road. Acceptance of growing up. No wonder people drank. A few pints of lager and I had peace.

First things first, though. I was off to the University of Derby at nineteen with a healthy fear of public spaces and few interests. At least my drinking would not look so out of place in the college environment.

Following a boat ride, a train and a taxi across town, I arrived in Derby, England with Mum as my chaperone. Good thing. Derby was in stark contrast to our little island. I was bombarded with horns and bright lights, boisterous touts and jostling. All kinds of faces in the crowd. Different races. Graffiti scrawled on buildings.

Hectic as hell. Damn nerves shot right through.

A shopkeeper greeted us in the local monotone Midlands accent.

"Ay up, mi duck?"

What the fuck.

The close proximity of so many things induced the old claustrophobia. There seemed to be only one hope of escape from the sensory assault. Get rid of the old girl so I could drink in peace.

Mum and I arrived at a newly constructed Halls of Residence, six floors high, built around a courtyard and housing four hundred students. The courtyard was a fashion show of buffed-out guys and stunning women. In comparison, I had a wardrobe of ill-fitting clothes and worn-out shoes.

Up in my room, an old trunk containing my clothes lay on the floor.

"Oh great, it arrived," Mum said.

She wanted to open it and check the contents.

"I'll walk you back to the taxi," I said.

Mum hesitated as though torn between her need to shed the obligatory tear and deposit me safely in my room and the allure of her own freedom. I knew I wanted mine and found myself thinking, just go, woman.

I couldn't get her back to the train fast enough. The smell of lager was calling to me from across the road at The Queens Head. Liberation awaited, as soon as the old girl was on her way.

En route to the taxi rank, Mum went on and on about the town. It hadn't changed much. When she was younger, she used to cycle all around these parts. I sensed a real spring in her step now, as if realizing she was about to be free from the nightmare of me for the first time in twenty years.

"It's going to be winter soon. You at least need a jacket."

Jesus wept. Now we had to visit the nearest clothing store. I grabbed a jacket from the nearest hanger and tried it on.

"Changing room's over here," Mum said.

"It's fine. It fits."

I finally got her into a cab and waved as it pulled away. She was wiping at tears. A bit of joy and a bit of sadness in that, I reckoned. As soon as she was out of sight, I crossed directly over to the nearest pub.

The barman greeted me with that slow monotone Midlands drawl.

"Alrate youth, avya summat up wi'ya? Worra ya avin?"

"Two pints of the old wife beater, yissur."

Oblivion was straight ahead.

Among my many introductions to university life, I learned to enrol at the local doctor. That first visit, reeking of alcohol, I carefully selected a seat away from the direct lighting. Gidawook passed through my mind. Sweat kept beading up on my brow and cheeks. While thumbing through a car magazine, I rehearsed my speech.

The plan was to lay it all out. I was fucked. I couldn't go on with life any more, so give me anything, fucking anything that could possibly relieve me of the bullshit inside my head. I wasn't leaving the office without it.

When the moment finally arrived and I was seated before the doctor in his examination room, my well-rehearsed speech completely evaporated. I knew I needed some serious medication – Prozac or something to pull me out of the depression – but fear of being banished to the local nuthouse had frozen my tongue.

"Are there any issues you'd like to discuss with me?" he asked

"No," I replied, unable to spit out the words.

I left empty-handed.

The daily bus rides from the halls to university were hell. Packed with students. Intense paranoia. After a few days, my agoraphobia returned with a vengeance. I could not leave the dormitory without a drink and stopped attending classes altogether. Alone in my room, I imagined all the shit I would hear back home for dropping out.

I soon had a drinking partner in the dormitory, this slick-looking bloke, forever kitted out in designer clothes. He was dating a good-looking Dutch girl.

We were drinking heavy one night when he received a call saying she was dead.

He dropped to the floor and flipped around like a fish out of water. Scared as hell, I watched him muttering crap to himself. Then his eyes glazed over and he went stiff as a board. I slapped him on the face a couple of times. When that failed to rattle him, I called an ambulance. They carted him off to the local nuthouse.

I was well suspicious upon receiving a call informing me that it was now safe to visit him. I assumed it was a bit of treachery to get my arse locked up in the joint.

The place was a fittingly decrepit old infirmary. The long, dimly lit hallways were patrolled by drooling inmates in gowns. Bloody Gidawooks all over the show. They gaped at me. Their gowns gaped at me from the rear. I heard screams that were more animal than human.

I found my old mate sitting on the edge of his bed, looking completely vacant. It was as if they had hit him up with an elephant tranquilizer.

Begged me to get him out, he did.

I spoke to a nurse, who clued me in that there had been some sort of mental breakdown. They had to keep him in there medicated.

A mental breakdown? Jesus.

Undaunted by the association of mental breakdowns and designer clothes, I blew my entire student loan on a new wardrobe. Lifted the pride a touch. At least I looked like I had my shit together.

The next three months were spent mostly up in my room, self-medicating with Tennent's. Super T they called it. The chosen drink of the homeless. The word had become generic.

"What a load of Tennent's." It referred to anything of extremely poor quality.

As December rolled around, I received a note from the warden at the Halls of Residence asking me to come by his office to see him.

"Mr Cannan. Your kitchen was on fire and the fire engine had to be called out. The first two floors were covered with dry powder. Do you have anything to say for yourself?"

"I was trying to cook an egg, like."

He shook his head.

"It's not the first complaint we've had. You'll have to look elsewhere for a place to live next term."

I could not have cared less. I was leaving anyway.

Before I did, I decided to pay a visit to the head of my course at the university. Maybe I could turn all this to my advantage.

Primed by a large tumbler of whiskey, I arrived at the Department of Design and Technology and knocked on his door. A voice said "Enter" and I went in.

"I've a feeling there's been some sort of mix-up," I said, having explained my version of the first semester. "I'm actually on the wrong course."

He pulled out a ring binder and began flipping through the pages.

"No record of a Michael Cannan here. What course were you meant to be studying?"

"An HND in…er…something or other. What I'd like to do is get on to the bachelor's degree course. Product Design, Innovation and Marketing."

"It might be possible. What's your education background and what school have you come from?"

"Ramsey Grammar School, Isle of Man."

He came to life.

"Oh, the Isle of Man. Great motorbike races over there. Crazy those guys. Just bear with me."

He flipped to the back of his folder.

"Oh, I see your government pays ten times more per student than the local governments in the UK. Yes, I think the degree course would be a possibility."

I was gobsmacked. He continued.

"You'll have missed three months of core lectures. You'd have to start catching up over Christmas. It'd be a lot of work."

"Would it make more sense to start the following year?"

He smiled. "Yes, that would be sensible. We can make that happen." He paused with a finger to his lip. "Hmm, do you think you could recruit any more students from the Isle of Man, maybe put the word out? We could have you on commission."

Elated by this break, I was right on the ball and offered up my services.

"Of course I can help. I'll go round all the schools on the island and do a presentation for the University."

"Excellent, excellent. Keep in touch and we'll see you back here next year."

Relieved, I left his office on cloud nine. The presentation was never going to happen, but he had no way of knowing that. Best of all, I had bought myself a shitload of breathing room with the clan back home.

"No, no, not dropping out. Just developing myself profes- sionally an' all that."

I now had nine months to address the underlying mental problems behind my academic failures.

Back on the Isle of Man, I hit the first pub and set to work sorting that out.

My family and friends were extremely proud of my upgrade to study for a Bachelor of Science degree in Product Design, Innovation and Marketing. The premise of the course was to take poorly performing products, reinvent them and use fancy words and images to make them look worth an investment.

Bullshitting. It seemed perfect for me.

My entire life had been a practice run for that course of study, so I returned to that theme of my youth, becoming the biggest and baddest Viking. If I was going back to university, I wanted to look the part. Working from the outside in, I grew my hair long, beefed up with thirty pounds of muscle and looked into getting a new nose.

In the doctor's office, they called my name over the intercom and I headed down the hallway, drenched in another Tchaikovsky violin concerto.

When asked why I wanted the operation, I pinched the bridge of my nose and gave the doc a song and dance.

"Breathing difficulties. It's been broken a few times. Fighting. Judo. Rugby."

The doctor thumbed through my file and questioned me about the anti-depressant prescription.

"How's that going?"

"Nothing's changed, really. I've just finished university. Bit of trouble sleeping. Heart still races an' that. I'm all right, though."

Noting that it had been a long-term problem, he increased my dosage. After ten days of that, I awoke one morning feeling at peace. That night I abstained from drinking. I felt an inner confidence for the first time in years.

At my consultation with the ear, nose and throat specialist, I was asked what bothered me the most, the breathing or the appearance. I opted for a course of honesty.

"Probably the appearance."

I half expected him to throw me out. Instead he offered to do a septorhinoplasty.

"We'll correct them both at the same time."

When the old man visited me in the hospital, I still had the cast on. I was waiting for the inevitable questions. Cosmetic reasons, eh? That was the last thing I wanted him to think. What sort of Viking was that?

He examined my face and pinched his own nose.

"Wish I'd had mine done back in the day."

So vanity and Viking lore weren't mutually exclusive.

CHAPTER FIVE

I called Howcroft a few days after they took the cast off my nose. His girlfriend was living at the Viking Hotel. He invited me down for a drink. The minute the door opened, he began circling me and bobbing from side to side, having a good look at my nose.

"Phew, fucking hell. That looks different. And you can breathe okay?"

"It looks that good, I couldn't give a shit if I can breathe through it or not."

"Do you reckon they could do something with these?" he said, tapping the backs of his ears.

"I reckon. I tell ya this much, I feel like a new man."

His girlfriend, who had been watching us, barged into the conversation. "You'll never guess what. I thought I couldn't breathe. I thought I was going to die and I began to panic, so I drove to the hospital and they made me breathe into a paper bag and took some tests. Then they told me I was having a panic attack. They prescribed me these."

She held up a tube of pills.

"Let's have a look. Diazepam," I said, reading the label.

She nodded. "Mother's little helper. It was all in my head. I felt better after a few days and don't need them anymore. Do you want one?"

"Sure," I said and washed one down with a lager. I ate another, and one more for good measure.

Within no time, the requisite amount of stillness had fallen over me.

"Can I buy a few off you?" I asked in a low, even tone.

She sold me four. Knowing they were in my pocket was all the psychological advantage I needed over the devil in my head.

With the nose business out of the way, I embarked on stage two of my personality transformation: muscle building. I subscribed to *Musclemag International* and *Flex* magazines and joined the local gym. I consumed two chicken breasts, a protein shake and pasta every day. After six weeks of that, my physique had noticeably changed. The gym owner approached me.

"You do know, we don't allow the use of steroids or performance-enhancing drugs in the gym, don't you?"

I professed my honest innocence, but the man had aroused my curiosity. Might as well be hung for a sheep as for a lamb, I thought. Flicking through the pages of *Musclemag International*, I came across an article on a young professional bodybuilder. His body's symmetry was perfect. Yet it took five years of dedicated lifting, seven days a week. That was no bloody good. I only had seven months before the start of university.

I called an old friend of mine, Aidan, from school. I had seen him walking about with his shirt off the previous summer, and judging by his abs, he must have had some assistance. His brother had been a competitive bodybuilder.

Aidan was now studying archaeology at Manchester University. As good as a medical doctor in my eyes. I got his number from his mum.

In the course of my conversation with Aidan, I learned that he'd been tortured with his own panic attacks from Ecstasy use. I shared my story as a lead-in, but not for long.

"I'll cut to the chase, mate. Can you get any steroids?"

"Yeah," Aidan said. "I did a course last summer and made some incredible gains. My brother Logan was doing them when he won Mr Essex."

"So what would you recommend?"

"You have to be careful. There are side effects. Testicular atrophy, erectile dysfunction."

"Say that again. I caught testicles and erections and what sounded like problems."

"You know, shrink your bollocks and switch your nob off, and acne, all sorts of stuff."

"Fuck me. What happened to Logan?"

"Had a nervous breakdown. Said he was an emotional wreck by the end of it all. One day he stood in the mirror, about to use the syringe, and broke down. Couldn't take it any more. His girlfriend had left him. Said she'd had enough."

"Must have switched his nob off," I said, being lighthearted. "Definitely don't want any of that."

"You'll need a three-month cycle of injectable and oral forms of anabolic and androgenic compounds," Aidan said as if ignoring my concerns. "That'll give you massive muscular gains and alleviate any possibility of erectile dysfunction. You'll need a diuretic to reduce water retention and an anti-oestrogen to prevent the aromatization of testosterone to oestrogen, which causes gynaecomastia."

"What the fuck's gynaecomastia?"

"Bitch tits. Sloppy nipples."

"That would not be quite the look I was going for."

"Then once you've completed the course, you'll need Human Chorionic Gonadotropin…"

"What the fuck…"

"Purified urine from pregnant women. It jump-starts your natural production of testosterone."

"For crying out fucking loud. Is there one tablet that does it all?"

"No, but you could try Anadrol."

"What's that?

"They use it to bulk up bulls for show."

"Are you serious?"

I had visions of them parading me around with a fucking tag in my ear and a ring through my nose. Best in class. The farmers could bid for me at the local cattle show.

I came back to the conversation only to hear Aidan going on about his brother again.

"Yeah. Logan did that and put on fifteen pounds in a few days. There was yellow discoloration to his eyes and skin. He had pains in his liver, acne, high blood pressure and water retention. His nose kept bleeding and he had a permanent erection. Oh, and a big vein pulsing out the side of his head, but he said it was all worth it."

"Fuckin' lovely! So if his nob was working, why did his girl-friend leave?"

"An imbalance of hormones can affect you psychologically. It ranges from what they call roid rage to severe depression."

"So what was Ben Johnson taking when he won the Olympic Gold?"

"Winstrol. I took some of that. I've heard of people secret-ing milk from their nipples with it. I didn't, though. I took Dianobol. Arnie Schwarzenegger used to call Dianobol the Breakfast of Champions."

"All tablets? I don't want to be using needles," I said.

"Yeah, no needles."

"Course of that'll do nicely," I said.

"Okay, give me a few days," Aidan said. "Oh, you know you can lose your hair on this stuff, but only if you have a genetic predisposition."

My dad and Mum's dad had no hair.

"Nah, Dad's father had a good head of hair. Saw him in a photo. No problem there."

My tablets arrived through the post a week later. No phar-maceutical packaging. Bank coin bags containing white discs and pink hexagons.

I awoke after a couple of days feeling pumped. The constant erections required regular relief. Just a couple of tugs to ease the pain. No pornography required. A small amount of sugar before I worked out gave a vascular look to the muscle. The serious weights I had previously lifted became a light warm-up. Grunt and grimace through a workout, then stop to admire myself in the gym mirror.

Is that me? I thought with a bit of peacock posturing. I was on my way to being the biggest and the best Viking. No doubt about it. My arms soon looked like ham shanks.

The old man often cycled into town from Miss World's place and he rode right by the gym one day. One look through the glass front and he stopped dead. Came in while I was doing a bicep curl.

"Hey, Mikey," he said, nodding in approval. "What have you been doing?"

"Training hard, eating well," I said.

He looked at me askance.

"Well, whatever you're doing, it's working. My God."

He sat on the bench press machine. I sat on the machine opposite, placed the pin at the maximum load and ripped off a couple of presses like it was nothing.

"You been out for a bike ride?" I said with a casual look over.

"Yeah."

"See the missus?"

He shook his head. "Yeah, you know, never get involved with a woman with horses. They come before everything. That time when her Shire horse kicked me across the barn? She asked if the horse was okay. The doctor said I was lucky to survive."

"That's rough," I said.

"When you get a woman, make sure you get a good one. A kind one. Someone who wants to be with you for you. Looks fade," he said with his head down.

Yeah, you fuck. You had one of those and threw her away. She's called my mum.

I got a job as a postman that summer. Six days a week delivering Her Majesty's Royal Mail to the housing estates on the north of the island.

"It's a twelve-mile route, so nobody really wants to do it," the manager told me. "That's why we got you."

"What's the quickest lap time?" I asked him.

"I guess one lad got back by three o'clock. Stick to the roads and paths, though, or they'll complain."

I turned the route into my own Olympic event: across gardens, over trees, through hedges and back by two. On a light day, I got back by one-thirty. Just over a couple of hours start to finish. Steroids will do that. The mail was misplaced if I was behind on my times. Steroids will do that too.

One afternoon when I returned to the mail depot, the manager stopped me.

"Aside from three complaints, you've got a bit of a fan club down on Riverside Walk."

"Oh, that'll be old Deirdre, in number 26. Loves a laugh, old Deirdre. Always meets me on the drive, invites me in for a cuppa. Lovely old lady."

He handed me a shirt and trousers. "Much as they might be enjoying it, it might be an idea to lose the short shorts and cover your chest when you deliver the mail. Put a t-shirt on at the least. We're a government department, you know."

A side effect began to kick in. My hairline had begun to tingle and itch. One morning, I was lathering shampoo through my thick dark hair and noticed that strands covered the shower pan. A close inspection in the mirror revealed my hair thinning and receding at the temple points.

Christ! I'm losing bloody hair! The newfound female interest was nice but maybe not enough to offset the hair loss. When the problem continued, I picked up the phone.

"Aidan, the hair loss. What drugs do I need to reverse that?"

"That's irreversible. It stops when you stop taking the gear."

So stop I did. I felt like someone had removed the nozzle from an inflatable balloon. After all that shit, when the water retention finally vanished, I was left a couple of pounds heavier than when I started. The Dolce & Gabbana black spandex t-shirts had to go.

I found an advert about hair loss in a copy of *GQ* and gave them a call.

"Royal Leamington Hair Restoration Centre."

"Yes, I'd like to book a consultation. I want my hair back. I'll be in the United Kingdom in September."

Perfect.

My new accommodation in Derby was at The Ram Public House, but mainly I lived in the bar downstairs. The place greeted you with the bittersweet scent of greasy cooking, cigarette smoke and spilt ale.

No sooner had my bags touched the ground than I hailed a taxi for the train station. A man from the hair clinic was waiting for me at the other end.

"Mr Cannan, is it?" he said.

"That's right."

How the fuck did he know it was me? I had arranged to meet him at the station to avoid telling a cab driver "The Royal Leamington Hair Restoration Centre, please."

"So you want your hair back?" he asked me.

"That would be good. Took a few steroids and they didn't quite agree with me."

"We'll take care of you."

At the clinic, he introduced me to the doctor, who lifted the front of the Caesar cut I was now sporting.

"It's minimal hair loss. We wouldn't perform a hair transplant until it recedes a lot further."

His consultant showed me the alternatives. Out of a black briefcase came a two-ounce pump spray bottle and a blister packet of tablets. "The latest dual-action breakthrough in the treatment of male pattern baldness. Minoxidil, a topical solution and tablets originally designed for male prostate cancer that have shown to halt hair loss in most men. A new solution for devastated men on a global scale. Only eighty pounds a month."

I had hope. "And it'll grow back?"

"Possibly," he said.

"Good enough odds for me. How long do I take it for?"

"As long as you want to keep your hair. If it gets worse, you can do what I did."

He held up a photo, showing the top of a man's head with a circular bald crown. It resembled the same hair loss pattern of my old man.

"This was me before." He lowered his head to show a full head of hair. "And me now."

"Wow, that's impressive," I said. "How did you accomplish that?"

"I had a frechet scalp reduction."

"Er, what the fu...what's that?"

"A new technique where they place an expander under the skin, then remove the excess skin and bald area and suture together leaving no bald spot. It's still numb," he said, tapping his skull.

Fuck church and alcohol. Again, I was feeling hope.

"Mate, I'll let a cow lick my head if it helps," I said, recalling another option I had read about in the mags.

"I'm not sure if there's any truth to that solution."

Impressed with his ethics, I wrote a cheque from my second student loan account and bid them farewell.

"Remember, if you stop taking the medication, all the hair you've saved will fall out," he offered as a send-off.

"Okay, thanks," I said.

I reckon he skinned me with that racket.

Over the coming week, some minor problems developed: dry, itchy, flaky scalp, a decrease in overall muscle mass, generalized joint pain, low sex drive, low energy, increased oestrogen, increased weight, elevated blood pressure and heart rate, but it stopped the hair loss, which paved the way back to using steroids, which, after all, was the ultimate goal.

Somewhere between the protein powder supplements, creatine and everything else I was throwing at my body, I bought a book on steroids, did the research and found a steroid that "looked good" from the packaging. The external box, with its sporty brand and blue colour scheme, suggested top quality to me. The red stamp was an indication of safety. Further reading revealed that this drug was used for the treatment of osteoporosis in postmenopausal women and was successful in preventing muscle wastage in 30–40% of critically ill AIDS patients. Plus, it had less harmful effects on the scalp, skin and prostate. We had a winner.

Or so I thought.

After I had shoved a 22-gauge syringe with a 1.5 inch needle in the upper, outer cheek of my right arse, flooding me with artificial testosterone, my body sensed the excess amounts of hormone and shut down its own production of testosterone. My physical and psychological symptoms shifted accordingly. Now depression, high blood pressure, sexual dysfunction and inhibition of testicular function – or shrunken bollocks – became the status quo. I became sad, inconsolable and emotionally unstable. Nobody in the world wanted to be around me. And for all this, I was rewarded with a growing set of breasts.

Apparently, I was coming to see, you shouldn't fuck lightly with your body's chemistry. Add testosterone and it will counter with an increase in oestrogen. My nipples began to itch and swell. New breast tissue formed, in stark opposition to the original purpose of my taking the drugs. I was definitely getting in touch with my feminine side.

Staring into the mirror, I thought, this cannot be happening to me. It had stated clearly on the side effects/warning section of the package: men might experience breast enlargement, or words to that effect, but I had considered myself above all that. Thought I could beat the laws of nature.

I called Aidan about the breast enlargement.

"Mate, these tits are not quite what I had in mind."

"Tamoxifen. They use it to treat women with breast cancer. I'll send some down."

It suddenly dawned on me that I was trying to solve an emotional problem with a physical response. "Fuck this for a game of soldiers. I'm done," I said.

Remembering Aidan's words, another alarm went off in my head. "You're not suggesting that I could grow tits, then develop cancer in them, are you?"

Aidan laughed. "Just remember. When you stop, the body's natural production of testosterone can lie dormant for as long as you've been taking the drug. The body's not like a thermostat. After steroid use, your testosterone production won't immediately start up again."

"Keep going…"

"Yeah. You'll need a shot of a female fertility drug to jump-start your testosterone."

"Fuck that, mate. I do not need to be experimenting with gender roles."

Over a month had passed before my testosterone levels returned to anything resembling normal, but I did kick the habit. I completed the next two academic years with a D minus average and an A cup.

My room above the pub was just large enough to accommodate a single bed and a small cupboard. You had to crouch down in places to miss the low ceilings. The endless chatter and laughter of drunken students down in the pub was always drifting up to my room – the scent of stale beer, fish and chips and cigarette smoke thrown in with the mix – so if I ever needed to sleep during regular business hours, I was fucked. The scene down there usually carried on long after closing hours.

In a sign of changing fortunes, Martha, the owner of the pub, called me downstairs one afternoon and introduced me to a bloke named Archie.

"He'll be living with us now," she said.

I shook Archie's hand. He was a short redheaded lad with an impressive portfolio from his Product Design, Innovation and Marketing class. After one look I could see I had been wasting my education. I stared in disbelief at both the hand-rendered and computer-generated images of his work. This was along professional standards. Nobody in my course had produced anything even close to this level. As he flicked through some train interiors, I noticed a scribbled note from Richard Branson:

"This is the exact ambiance we are looking for."

This bastard with industry-standard skills and all the 3D computer-generated design software you could ever want was moving in with me.

"Do you think you could help me, mate? I've been falling a bit behind on my coursework."

He looked a bit bent out of shape.

"Just get yourself a proper computer, and I'll upload all my software onto your system."

Fucking unbelievable. I had just saved myself thousands of pounds' worth of expenditures, and made a new drinking mate in the bargain.

He waved me into his bedroom and pointed beneath his bed at a stash of eighties porn videos.

"All the porn you'll ever need."

I called my old man the next day, who agreed to give me the money for a new computer. Archie built the PC himself and installed the software. I had no clue how to use the tackle, but my fortunes were definitely looking up.

Archie got a load of shit about his red hair and he ripped the piss out of people in return. Always joking and ogling lecherously at the women in the bar downstairs. He had both a fascination for the filthiest sexual exploits you could ever imagine and a severe shortage of actual women.

My life grew even brighter when this bird named Chloe went to work behind the bar. My final year of school became a contest between my cock and my brain. Chloe's long, straight chocolate-coloured hair and fine figure were enough to fill the pub every night she worked. Add her wit and tart exchanges with the clientele, and she had won me over.

Every drunken soul who tried it on with her got a virtual pat on the head.

"Come round to mine and I'll bang ya," they'd say to impress their mates.

To which she'd reply, expression unchanged, "I really don't feel you'd be up to the job, young man."

The wisecracks never ended, and nobody could match her word for word.

I was smitten.

One night Chloe came in through the door, looking distressed. Turned out she had broken up with her old man. Wanted to be on her own now and all that, which always upped the stakes when it came to a bird.

The following Tuesday, I chased Chloe down at a local nightclub. She stood facing the bar as I placed my hand on the arch of her lower back going by. That got her attention. I ordered drinks with the blokes and acted as if nothing had happened.

Around midnight, I saw her preparing to leave and arranged to get in her way at the door.

"Mind if I walk you home?"

"It wouldn't be right. I've just split from Ryan. If we were seen walking together, it would be around the university in no time."

"Okay, just to the corner. I'm going that way."

"Maybe just to the corner."

We stopped beneath a streetlight at the corner. I checked down the road.

"The coast is clear," I said and kissed her.

She quickly pulled away. "This should never happen again," she said and walked off.

I watched her sashay down the road.

The next night she was working in the bar. I went down and ordered a pint of lager.

"Just for the record," I said to her with a smile. "What happened last night? That can never ever happen again."

"Ever," she said.

"Come upstairs and say goodbye before you finish," I said.

"No."

"I'll only come down and get you, then."

She looked away, but I knew I had her thinking. Six hours later, she was rolling around on my warped mattress in her black lace underwear.

"Did I come too quickly?" she said afterward.

I was thinking, will ya marry me?

The year went on with me fucking Chloe and buying Archie pints in exchange for a share of his homework. Naturally, Chloe was impressed with my course studies. I was entirely dependent on Archie for a passing grade.

For my dissertation assignment, I had to innovate and design a new product, then apply marketing theory to get the product to market. This assignment represented 40% of my overall grade. The previous year's grades and exams would comprise the rest of it, which meant I was fucked. I had a D minus going. The lecturers predicted a career trajectory that led to back alleys and rubbish dumps.

From an operation on a shoulder injury years earlier, where the post-op care had actually made my shoulder worse, not better, I began designing an orthopaedic rehabilitation unit that would improve this care. As always with me and my grand designs, I had visions of the sports world snapping up my piece of equipment. With my first million in sight, I went to bribe Archie for his help with a pint of lager. He told me to piss off.

"The 3D manuals are upstairs. They're all yours, buddy. Learn it yaself."

Well, fuck me. I had kept Chloe convinced that I was the best and brightest. Now I had to actually do something to back up that myth.

I pulled out the thick 3D computer-aided design software manuals and began reading through thousands of commands: solid models, surface modelling, assigning textures and lighting to produce a photo-realistic rendering. I was fucked. I might as well have been trying to learn a foreign language with my ears plugged.

I remained locked away for two weeks, drinking heavily, until I finally had something to brag about. I called Archie up to my room.

"Check that out, it's unbelievable. That's enough to pass right there. I'm done."

He tilted his head up and literally looked down his hooked nose at me. "It's a start, but that's all. Where do they place their feet, and what does it look like?"

"The footrest is an organic shape," I said, thinking out loud. "I'd need to learn three-dimensional surface modelling to produce that."

"Page 256," Archie said and walked off.

After another week I was able to model two footrests in three dimensions. Again, Archie came up to have a look.

"How do they stop their foot from slipping off the footrest?"

Another few days and I had added grips to the footrests. Archie looked it over.

"How do you know where to place the seat, and how far should it be off the ground? In other words, how does the user interact with the equipment?"

I was handed a book on ergonomics.

"Incorporate real-world dimensions into the design."

Drinking to oblivion each night and smoking heavily, it took me another few weeks before I was ready to call Archie again.

"Well, you're getting the block of marble to create the David. No block, no nothing," he said.

"This is better than anything anybody else will produce," I said, disheartened.

"What materials will the product be made from? Find the physical properties of the metals and materials and assign textures to the geometry. Page 678."

"For fuck's sake. Give me a break."

Archie reviewed the model again. That only led to more suggestions.

"Look at it from every angle and add a three-point lighting system and a surface for the product to sit on."

He grabbed a plastic ball and held it up to the light.

"Follow the light. Study how light acts and reacts in the real world, how the light creates specular highlights on the plastic surface. Study the light and how it reacts to different materials. It's all about light."

He placed the ball next to a wooden surface.

"Look how the wooden colour bleeds onto the surface of the ball. That's what you need to create photorealism in your scene."

Over the next few days, I added the materials and lights. I couldn't believe what I was seeing. It looked like a photo. I felt like the dog's bollocks.

"The light will make or break the scene," Archie said doubtfully, looking it over again. "Keep going. It's still not believable."

For fuck's sake.

Skulling lager after cheap whiskey, I spent day after day fucking around, trying to add depth and realism, changing the scale of the textures, creating proportion and balance. Every time I thought I was done, Archie would have a look and throw something else at me. Create a logo and colour scheme. It's all about attention to detail.

After months of my nose to the grindstone, I finally had a photorealistic, fully rendered image of the Torsion 40. I'd named it that because it allowed the user to perform 40 different exercises from multiple angles.

Archie reviewed the piece. "Okay, now leave it alone for a few days and come back to it before you continue."

"Continue!!" I shouted at him. "Are you kidding me! It looks fucking amazing!"

Archie was not fazed in the slightest. "Do you want to just pass or be the absolute best?"

"Okay, okay," I said.

Never satisfied, Archie eventually had me work up a 20-second animation clip to music. I'd never seen anything like it in my life, and I had produced it. When Chloe had a look, her eyes lit up.

"That is incredible," she said and threw her arms around me. "You are so smart, you can't ever leave me."

The dissertation got an A and helped me to graduate with honours. To the astonishment of all who knew me, I had a Bachelor of Science Degree.

One lecturer passed me in the corridor and commented, "You must be getting laid."

Chloe graduated with first-class honours and moved back home to Nottingham, twenty minutes away. Archie graduated at the top of the class and almost immediately started to receive offers.

One night towards the end of that year, he cornered me up in my room. I had no idea about what, but the look on his face was deadly serious. Like he had caught me stealing his porn or something. What came out of his mouth had me totally baffled for that moment.

"My old clients from the industry need someone to do three-dimensional computer-aided design for their aerospace and transportation projects. There's Bombardier, and Filberto Moretti, the former head designer at Pininfarina, who's worked with Lamborghini, Piaggio and Mercedes. He's now with Intertech and would be interested in talking. Plus Andrew Richards, who was head of design at one of the biggest industrial design agencies in the UK. He's now working as a consultant and wants to outsource his computer-aided design work. Plus, tons of local graphic design agencies and architects."

Archie was breathless. I still wasn't quite sure where he was going with this and told him so.

"They all want me to set up my own design agency. I think we should do it."

I gaped at him.

"We?"

CHAPTER SIX

During the previous four years I had been assaulted time and again with the age-old question: What are you going to do when you finish your studies? So far the question had been met with a "fuck knows" shrug. Now I had the lapel-straightening response of, "I'm the creative director of my own multi-disciplinary design consultancy".

People thought I was loaded and I let them believe it. At least I had the girl and the business. I was on my way to the modern-day trappings of Viking success.

When asked, Archie had told me, "I picked you for a partner because of the speed with which you picked up the CAD software. My only concern is the number of distractions you have passing through your bedroom. Now if you could direct a few of them to the office, that would be a bonus. I can pick up the castoffs."

Fair deal.

Archie and I moved out of the pub and into a rented house together. Across the road from the Ram pub, the university was converting an old five-storey rope mill into low-cost start-up studios for art, design and crafts. We secured two units on the fourth floor. An old business colleague of Archie's came in as a silent partner and leased the computer systems. Having a reputation, he wrote letters to the bank guaranteeing our salaries, which enabled us to receive loans of £10,000. The summer was spent decorating the studio with new floors, carpets, furniture and infrastructure. The exposed brick interior and spotlights finished it like an Ikea showroom.

As much as we were going about our venture all professional-like, the building was not exactly fit for the suited and booted business types. Ascending the stairs to our studio, you passed the likes of tie-dyed, pink-haired, heavily pierced glass blowers. Reggae music, bongo drums and the scent of hash and chemicals filled the corridors.

Shortly after we had opened our doors, I went in one night at dusk to find Archie with his eye glued to a telescope. It was pointed at a building across the way.

He frantically waved an arm at me without looking.

"Shhh, shh. Don't turn the lights on for fuck's sake. She's gonna get her tits out."

I looked out of the window at the Halls of Residence one hundred yards across the river. Four storeys high and about twenty-four windows in total. The lights were on and curtains open in each window, each with a different performance. It was Derbyshire Idol and we were the judges panel.

"She's been posing in the mirror for the last twenty minutes. We need a video camera. We can sell this shit." Archie grabbed his crotch with excitement. "I'm gonna go over there, knock on the door and give her one she'll never forget."

"I cannot wait to watch this," I said with sarcasm.

Every other word with Archie was about fucking some bird or how to go about fucking some bird.

As the night grew dark, he turned his attention to chatting online with random women.

"Log in," he suggested.

We sat facing each other across a desk with our laptops open. I entered the Hotmail grapevine chatrooms. This twenty-one-year-old Latina bird named Layla started talking real dirty to me. Gripped, I rolled deeper and deeper into the conversation.

Two hours later, I announced:

"Archie, she wants to meet me at the gates of Loughborough University wearing nothing but a raincoat."

"And?" he replies.

I grabbed my jacket.

"Heading to the store, back soon."

"Say hi to Layla for me."

A few strides down the hallway, it hit me. How the fuck did he know her name?

I turned around and burst back into the office. Archie was doubled over in laughter.

"You bastard. It was you the whole fuckin' time."

I never entirely trusted that son of a bitch again.

One day, soon after that episode, the dean of the university came around to visit the building, along with several heads of departments. As the investors in the building, they wanted to see how the inhabitants were utilizing the studios.

Coming into our studio, they all looked impressed.

"Well now, this is very different from the other studios," the dean said. "And what are these space age-looking machines?"

I gave him the rundown. They were the same tools that Pixar and Industrial Light and Magic used. Designed to handle all the polygons generated in 3D modelling. About £13,000 for the two. Archie followed up with a presentation from his portfolio. Names were thrown about: Bombardier, Intertech, Oracle, Jones Jeffries, RS Forth, Rees Partners. We were working with the biggest industrial design agencies in the country. The Continental lot as well.

Next thing you know, the dean wants to send around the press department. Do a cover story. Great promotion for the university. A couple of students showed up the next week to take snapshots. Archie and I stood together in our suits, gazing imperiously off into the distance. Our mugs were displayed on posters all around the university and beyond. The local news channel did a piece, along with the local press. The Isle of Man newspapers picked up the story. Local Boy Does Good.

It was an incredible amount of success, considering we had yet to land a project and hadn't a pot to piss in. Competition was high from foreign countries. The Chinese visual artists, in particular, were constantly lowering costs and raising the bar. Plus, our computers were constantly crashing from over demand. I was on edge the whole time.

Simply put, the long hours did not equal money.

Not to be deterred, I calculated my wealth from the sale of the company and decided the only thing missing from my newfound status as an international entrepreneur was a cocaine habit.

I called Aidan, my steroid dealer.

Up in Manchester, I was met by his salivating Pit Bull, snapping and straining at the end of a thick chain. Aidan came out in black trousers, white shirt and a black bow tie unknotted around his neck. The dog was called off and we headed into the kitchen. The curtains were drawn. The room smelled like a paint and body shop from all the chemicals in the drugs. Three black bin liners sat on the floor, filled with 250,000 Ecstasy tablets in each. Aidan pulled a book-size block of white powder out of the microwave.

"Here's what you're after. Peruvian Flake. The best cocaine in the United Kingdom."

"Fuck me, mate, I don't need that much. I just wanted a pick-me-up, ya know."

He shaved off enough powder into a coin bag to get me going. "There, give us a shout if you need more."

I arrived back in Derby to some spec jobs Archie had taken on for local companies. If they liked the work, we got a job. If not, we were fucked. A few paid jobs came in from Bombardier, Oracle and a small local architectural firm, but mostly my mum was supporting me. The hundred-hour weeks and a drive up to Manchester every several days helped to manage my coke habit.

We'd been fucking around lost for months when a call came in from a Mr Moretti. Archie set up a meeting at our studio. On Monday morning, he dressed in his best suit, shirt and tie. I was wearing a black suit and open neck maroon shirt.

Locked in the toilet, the seat down, a pound note jammed into my nose, I was whacking away at a coin bag of white powder with my debit card. I was ready for twelve rounds when I heard the buzzer go off in the studio.

"Archie, spray some deodorant down that corridor," I said, coming back. "It stinks of hash. Shut as many doors as you can. I'll bring him up the main staircase to avoid as many of the other residents as possible."

Mr Moretti was waiting for me in the foyer, impeccably dressed. I was trembling from the coke rush.

"I'm Michael, Mr Moretti. We spoke on the phone."

"Call me Filberto."

I calmly led him upstairs, contrary to the furious coke rush inside of me.

Archie met us at the door and gave Filberto the tour. He loved the place. At one point his eyes locked on the telescope Archie used for spying on birds in the Halls of Residence across the way.

"Oh, oh, you can see in the window," Filberto said, pulling away.

Archie went red in the face and fumbled with excuses. I hung my head. Christ, well, that's that. Over before it began.

Instead, Filberto went into a pitch about splitting up with his wife. He hadn't dated in years. Didn't know where to begin. Didn't even know what clothes to wear or what styles were in anymore.

"You should come out with us one night, Filberto," I said. "We'll show you the ropes."

"Yes, that would be good." He pulled a chair up to Archie's monitor. "Tell me about what's happening here and we'll see what we can do."

Filberto had a project to redesign the interior of the Globalstar train. It was a highly prestigious project, and he was down to the last two companies. The project would be awarded to either us or a French outfit. Archie dazzled him with theories of product and industrial design, rendered in 3D. I planned to get Filberto laid to seal the deal.

With my coke high coming to an end, I was considering how best to renew my fix when I noticed Archie's eyes widening. He did a pretend swipe beneath his nose. I touched mine and found blood. Shit.

"Do excuse me one moment."

In the bathroom, while cleaning up, I used the opportunity to take another whack at the powder. Getting caught would cost the project, but I needed the rush. There I was, as always, pushing the edge and flirting with disaster.

Archie was taking Filberto through his portfolio upon my return. The deal was set. Filberto wanted a quote based on thirty days, £250 per designer per day. That was £15,000 to start.

"We'll take it from there," Filberto said and left.

Archie and I did the obligatory formal handshakes.

"Lovely," I said. "I need a pint."

"In Barbados", I was thinking.

Once Filberto had confirmed the deal, Archie and I moved our beds into the studio. Driven to provide Chloe with every-thing she had ever wanted, I worked night and day. The image of her gazing proudly over my success drove me to ever greater efforts.

After days of sleeping in the office and not showering, the place smelled like a locker room. For me, a line of powder fixed that and any other annoyance. I spent a good portion of each day getting my nose to stop bleeding. Meanwhile, Archie grew ever more critical and suspicious of my habits.

Forty-five days later, we completed the project and pre-sented a series of visuals and an animation to Filberto. Later that week we received a call.

"We came in second," he said. "The Globalstar group believed the design already looked too British and awarded the contract to the French company."

I felt fucked, but the work we produced had won other transport projects for FS Italy, Virgin Trains, Stockholm Metro and Merseylink.

A year passed. My life was nonstop: long work weeks, week-ends partying in Manchester to overcompensate for the long work weeks, driving up to visit Chloe every ten days or so in Nottingham, driving back from Manchester and Nottingham with a stop at every other motorway service station to drink a can of Stella Artois and snort another line of coke.

One night I arrived back to Derby with the left side of my body going numb.

A fucking stroke, I thought and drove straight to the nearest bar for a pint of Stella. When that didn't fix things properly, I tried another, and another. A terrifying realization struck me. Alcohol had completely stopped working.

Still numb, I drove to the emergency room at Derbyshire Hallam Hospital and complained of chest pains and numbness. The nurse asked me to take off my shirt.

"Have you been using steroids?" she asked.

"Used to. Not for years now. I work out regular, though."

I wanted them to think I took care of myself.

She slipped a blood pressure monitor to my arm and began to inflate the cuff. "Any drugs?"

"No, none."

The doctor came in and had a look at the results. "Your blood pressure's up slightly, but there's nothing physically wrong with you, at least according to your ECG. We'll do some more tests, but I've a feeling this could be a mental issue."

"What about these chest pains?"

"Again, considering your test results, I suspect anxiety. The chest pains could be the result of improper breathing. The body freezes under stress. How's your stress level?"

"Long hours, over one hundred a week, every week."

"Perhaps you should consider a career change," he said and left.

I had been thinking the same thing. After eighteen months we had yet to break even. I had a bank loan out and owed my mum at least fifteen grand. The relationship between Archie and I was becoming strained. It was a pissing contest to see who could spend the most time at the studio and he was winning. He began distancing himself – dining separately with clients and taking private calls about contracts. After a few heavy days on coke, I left for a spot of rest and recuperation on the Isle of Man.

"Mate, it's not working," he said upon my return, "I'm going out on my own."

I sold my half of the company to Archie for about £2,000 and began looking for work in the area. Since every bit of my portfolio was a combination of work we had produced together, I was fucked. Archie always put on the finishing touches.

I landed a few interviews with companies in the East Midlands and scored a trial run with one company but was sweating so badly that first day, my entire shirt was stuck to my body. I did not return.

That led me to move in with Chloe and her sister in Nottingham. After a few weeks of that environment, things grew strained. Her sister was high maintenance. Both of them together was hell.

I questioned their oestrogen levels and sanity. Neither liked that. One night Chloe took exception to me spending her money on alcohol. I hadn't counted on the scrutiny and responded with fury.

"Do you not fucking know what I am going through? I've no job, no money, constant chest pains and I'm sharing a house with you and your damn sister."

After she had left for work the next morning, I packed my bags and drove up the motorway to my sister's house in Kendal.

That evening "Chloe" flashed up on the screen of my phone. I hit the reject button. The phone rang again. I hit reject, again and again and again. The phone went under my pillow. Silence was my most vicious weapon. I was well versed in emotional blackmail.

An hour passed. I checked the phone. Forty missed calls and ten text messages.

The text messages began: *Where are you? – What's happening? – I can't get through. – Are you ignoring the calls? – Please call me? – Please tell me you're OK? – Please, please Mike, don't do this. – I'm begging you, please call me.*

Sal's phone rang.

"Chloe," she said.

"You've not seen me," I said.

Chloe continued to try to contact me. I continued to communicate my hostility in cold, punishing silence. If I withheld my feelings, no one could hurt me. I felt all powerful – until she stopped calling.

I called the doctor that day and booked an appointment.

"I want to kill myself," I said when they asked how they could help me.

I told the doctor about the breakdown of my relationship and the loss of my business. Those seemed like legitimate enough reasons to get some drugs. The doctor prescribed the anti-depressant Seroxat. I was in business.

While in Kendal, I received a call from my mum to tell me that her friend Owen had asked if I was interested in a position doing computer-aided design for Manx Logistics.

The poor bastard, I thought. Owen was a director at the company and had been pestering my mum to be his missus all these years. Every Valentine's Day he showed up at our house in a new sports car, armed with flowers, a card and a marriage proposal. He really was in love with the old girl. Yet after fifteen years Mum was still having none of it. Now he was trying to use her son to win her over.

"Good ole Owen," Mum said.

I felt defeated, mostly. The previous year, I had been splashed across the paper as a success story. Now the big shot was limping home, poor and empty-handed. It was humiliating to be back in my cramped childhood bedroom, sleeping with my feet dangling off the end of my old single bed. I had Arnie the Terminator on a movie poster, helping me to make sense of my life.

On the plus side, after the debauchery of the previous few years, it was comforting to have the old girl's home cooking and affection on a regular basis.

The prospect of a steady income was reassuring too. I could pocket some cash and get back off the island soon. In the meantime, I'd find some relief with old friends.

First day back on the Isle of Man, I had gone directly for a walk along the harbour. The tide was high. The swing bridge turned, allowing yachts to pass through. The fishing boats were emptying their hulls from the day's catch. The deep chugging engine sounds and smell of diesel fuel reminded me I was home. The stench of seaweed at high tide made me think of Dad. I remembered him from days past, walking the harbour at high tide and having the craic with the fishermen. Ironically, I saw him again that day, walking on the far side of the harbour. We were estranged, apart from the odd phone call.

I slipped into the gloomy Schooner bar and went downstairs. McQuinn and Finnegan were standing in the back. McQuinn nodded and winked.

With barely a word, we left the bar and drove over to Finnegan's apartment. As we pulled up, Finnegan pointed two doors down.

"The dealer lives there. No shortage of brown, like in the old days."

"You know," I told Finnegan, going into his apartment. "I told myself over and over in Kendal, 'If you go back to the island, you'll go back to heroin. You'll become an addict.' The thought's been on permanent repeat in my head."

"I've been on it a while now," he said, creasing the foil and sticking the silver tube in his mouth. "It's got me. Spending £50 a night, sometimes more."

"I'll just stick to a smoke every now and then," I said. "I won't get hooked."

"So what's happened with Chloe?" he said.

"The whole thing's been a nightmare. Absolute hell it's been. I was as low as I've ever been in Kendal. Here, pass that over," I said, taking the foil and sparking the lighter.

The rush of chemicals to the brain was an instant relief. It was the embrace of an old friend. I lit a cigarette and strained on that to intensify the euphoria. In the company of lads who had known me from day one, I relaxed.

"Relationships, mate, don't know what all the fuss is about. Birds come and go, ya know? I feel stupid makin' such a big deal about it."

I was laughing on the outside, but things weren't feeling so great on the inside.

Before I could go to work for Manx Logistics, the company arranged for me to have a medical. On the day I was scheduled to go in, I smoked crack and heroin in an attempt to reduce my blood pressure and anxiety. My degree in product design was now being put to good use making a crack pipe out of an asthmatic inhaler. The doctor referred me to his wife, a hypno-therapist. He felt she could help me. I went and ran into half the island coming back out.

"Trying to get off the cigs," I told everyone, even those who hadn't asked.

I went to work at Manx Logistics and within a few weeks was hooked on heroin again. I functioned well on the gear. It made a shitty job seem fairly good craic, or at least to some degree tolerable.

As the months passed, my tolerance increased and my habit grew. Every penny I earned was spent on junk. To relieve the flu-like symptoms, I fell into a predictable routine of using each morning. When I was unable to score heroin, I upped the dose of anti-depressants and consumed large amounts of painkillers. It occurred to me that I had long ago crossed that line I had vowed never to cross: physical dependency. Courtesy of Owen, my various ailments and addictions were largely ignored.

Every morning I pulled into the staff car park, dropped down out of sight, opened the silver foil, flicked the lighter and gently eased the heroin smoke down my throat. At the sound of any nearby staff, I bolted upright, held my breath and nodded to whoever was going by.

Inside the building, there were always several people chat-ting away and drinking coffee in my department. I made my own cup, returned to my desk, turned on the computer and pulled up the same CAD drawing I had been staring at for the last two months. There were some green and red lines and some numbers with symbols next to them. If anyone passed by, I could switch from surfing the Internet to the technical drawing in a click of a button.

Nose to the grindstone. Being slack as hell did nothing for the old morale.

Promptly at 9:30 a.m., the door swung open and Owen waltzed into the office.

"Good morning, boyyyy," he said in his thick Welsh accent.

"Good morning, Mr Llewellyn, sir," I said. "How are we on this fine day?"

Marinda, his executive secretary, put her finger down her throat.

Owen stopped at the corner of my desk, his back to the rest of the staff.

"Oh, absolutely fantastic, boy. I tell you what. Life is so good. I could not ask for one thing more."

"Mum sends her regards," I said.

He went quiet, looked at the ground and shook his head gently. "Aye…Aye, helluva woman. So on Friday night, I go out in the new wheels. Have you seen the new Jaguar, by the way?"

I shook my head.

"I tell you what…"

Standing there at the corner of my desk, he gave me a blow-by-blow account of the entire weekend, down to each person and what they had said, followed by a schedule for the upcoming week.

"He said…she said…oh, you would not believe this…"

Every sentence came with a belly laugh and a slap on his thigh.

He drove me nuts, but I endured it for the sake of job security.

"So what have we got goin' on today, boy?" he said an hour and a half later.

I turned the monitor and gave him some bullshit about adding C++ code into the mainframe before running some Java scripts, then developing some Autolisp functions for AutoCAD. I told him I was consulting with the software vendors about implementing some Visual Basic.

"My word, boy. You'll be turning this company around."

"Always a team effort, Mr Llewellyn."

Marinda put her finger down her throat again.

"Come up to my room in a few minutes," Owen said before leaving. "I have some plans for you."

He left. I smiled for the rest of my office mates.

"You make me want to puke, Cannan," Marinda shouted as soon as Owen was out of earshot.

"Now, now, do wish me luck," I said, fixing my tie and swinging my blazer across my shoulders. "Full report on my return."

"Prostitutin' your own mother," Marinda said with a stare.

"Wounded," I said, bowing my head and touching my hand to the centre of my chest.

Before bounding up the stairs to the director's floor, I exited the building and did a quick fix on the foil in my car. I needed the damn gear to feel normal. I was trying to quit – daily – but to no avail.

"Come in, boyyyy," Owen shouted from behind the door when I knocked.

I entered the room but remained standing to show my respect.

"Please, take a seat," he said.

The long and short of it was, he wanted to send me to Rome for a week of training with our main software vendors. I was to go on from there to London, Jersey, Birmingham and Dublin to speak with our clients.

"There's gonna be plenty of opportunities. Aye, we'll start getting you out there."

I sat there with my dreams of Vikings and foreign conquests. At last I was being recognized for my talents. Plus, it was an opportunity to put some distance between me and the drugs. My physical and mental states had become untenable. I was tapping Mum up for cash towards the end of each month. I had lost track of how much I owed her since quitting uni. If I could get off the island and away from temptation, I could get off the drugs once and for all.

And then there was Chloe. I'd be in England. Maybe I would look her up again.

Owen leaned over the desk to get my attention. "I'm gonna give ye some advice, boy. Never let the staff see you drinking coffee. Take yourself into town for a break if you want a cup. Let me know and I'll come with you."

By fuck, this man knew his stuff. He was grooming me for the big league. CEO within the year, I thought.

"I'm with you on that, sir."

"We'll look at a salary increase. If you make your next invoice payable for…"

He placed a piece of paper on the desk, wrote a figure and circled it with his pencil.

"No complaints here, Mr Llewellyn."

Then he started in again with even more detail about the weekend. "He said…she said…then they…Then the cat had crapped all over the carpet…the car wouldn't start. Oh, we laughed, we laughed we did…"

Fuck me, three-quarters of an hour later and my eyelids were beginning to sag. Beads of sweat were dripping down the sides of my face. Nausea set in. I tugged at my collar to release the feeling of suffocation. The heroin had me. My chin was down at my chest.

"Boy, are you okay? You've gone sheet white. Put your head between your legs, boyy. Quick like. Get the blood to the head."

I slumped with my ears between my knees. Must not puke. Few deep breaths.

"That's it, boy, breathe. Are you okay?"

"Medical room, I think, Owen. Be best."

"Aye, get yourself down there, boy."

I hustled down the stairs and into the office.

"And?" Marinda said.

I gave her a wink. "Pay rise and a spot of Continental travel," I said on my way into the medical room. "I'll be in here. Do not disturb."

"Are you for real?"

I waved and closed the door. Off went the faux Italian loafers as I assumed the horizontal position. A cold compress went to my brow. I lay there taking deep breaths.

A pay rise and a trip to Rome. A shedload of opportunities. All I had to do was get back off the junk.

I left for Rome with a bag full of prescription painkillers to help me detox. I had Marinda book me a hotel near the only pub that I knew sold Guinness. The pills were all gone in the first few days, so I tried Guinness to keep me from going under. When that failed, I spent the night scouring strip joints for a bit of smack. There was nothing. Not even the back street hookers could come up with drugs. That led me to miss the last few days of work and the software company jumping me for not showing up.

Upon my return from Rome, I drove straight to Finnegan's house.

"Thank God you're here," I said when he opened the door. "Now please tell me you've got some gear."

He looked me up and down. "Fuck me, Michael. You look rough. Sort of green and grey like. I thought you'd be all clean by now."

"Not through choice, mate, I can tell ya."

I grabbed the foil off him.

"I tell you what, those Italians take their Catholicism very seriously 'cos I couldn't score heroin anywhere near the Vatican." I put the flame to the foil. "It'll have to be London for my next detox."

A flurry of business trips followed; London, Birmingham, Dublin and Jersey. My every wild and hopeful intention became tomorrow's agenda, but the change in location had no positive effect. The freedom of anonymity made it worse. I picked up the odd homeless person and chauffeured them around in search of drugs. They got money and I got high. I ended up in the worst housing estates, wasted on heroin and crack.

Over time, Owen became my first call in the morning.

"Not feelin' too bright this morning, Mr Llewellyn, sir. Best stay at home, see how I feel."

"Aye boy, just you get yourself well. Don't be burnin' yourself out."

The doctor increased my anti-depressants to a level where I could function, but the increased dose led to waves of adrenaline. That led to me retching in the company toilet on a regular basis. The adrenaline and heightened state led to severe agitation and a craving for alcohol and Valium to take the edge off. Heroin, alcohol and sedatives were now counterbalancing my use of anti-depressants. The doctor had prescribed a drug for depression that created the side effect of craving for a depressant, which in turn exacerbated my addictions. It was a nice, neat circle.

I walked around detached from my physical form and devoid of emotions. It was like the spirit had finally said "Fuck this" and vacated the human container, but the body somehow went on functioning.

The most visible symptoms of me inhabiting a corporeal body were sweating, shaking and chest pains. That led me back to the anti-depressants to reduce my anxiety. I developed a serious resentment about being a slave to the anti-depressants and attempted to quit. It became an endless cycle. The withdrawals would begin with dizziness, followed by electric-shock-like sensations through my head and body. My limbs would jerk involuntarily. I experienced flu-like symptoms. I felt nauseous and had diarrhoea. Eventually I would be reaching for a little blue pill and the whole thing would start all over again.

I concluded that the Isle of Man was the problem. I required a new job and a new location. It was time to get off the rock once and for all.

Chloe came to mind while I considered this. Suddenly that seemed like a great way to make a new start.

I knew I had it in me. I'd really pull it all together and get back in the game. I had a stack of skills and experience. One foot on the corporate ladder was all I needed. Land a high-powered job with a national design agency and I'd rise to the top. Chloe back on my arm and everything would be fine. The old man always said, "The further up the tree the monkey goes, the more people can see its arse."

I'd show everyone who had doubted me.

CHAPTER SEVEN

I spent the next couple of weeks fine-tuning my curriculum vitae and sent it to several recruitment agencies in England, along with samples of computer-aided design work. A request came back for an interview with Ridley and Partners, an international architecture and design firm based in London. The job description was to provide 3D visualization and animation services for the company's buildings and products.

I arrived in London early for my interview, and on a wet and dreary morning, I set off for the interview, sporting Hugo Boss and Versace. That was on the outside. On the inside I combined a warming blend of Pfizer, GlaxoSmithKline and Hoffmann-La Roche. My reflection certainly looked the business as I approached the five-storey glass and steel structure. I pictured everyone on the other side of the black glass nudging their workmates. Look, here comes our saviour. Good God.

The head of Design greeted me in the lobby and led me up to the mezzanine level. Rows of architects and technicians lined the studio floor. Conference rooms overlooked the Chelsea Bridge and the River Thames.

I got the pitch for Ridley and Partners. They were an international practice, responsible for some of the world's most notable architectural projects. I flicked through their photos of glass and steel structures. They required an extremely high standard of visuals to accompany these sorts of designs. I was one of only two people interviewing for the position.

I bullshitted my way through my portfolio and received a thanks as I left.

Feeling a sense of great accomplishment, I decided a reward was in order, hailed a cab to Soho and quickly lined up some crack and heroin. With a chocolate Milkybar in hand, I made my way to the nearest underside of a bridge. The noise of overhead traffic quietened as I slipped inside. The smell of piss thickened. Broken glass crunched under my feet. Old cardboard and newspaper littered the ground. A dozen or so homeless people materialized out of the darkness, some of them asleep, some drinking and smoking. I opened the Milkybar, threw away everything but the tin foil, emptied the drugs into it and sparked up. One inhale and the fear was gone.

The interview had gone well. I came second out of two.

Inspired nonetheless, I continued applying for jobs and was soon hired by a multi-media design company in Sheffield. The owner, Andrew Hockbank, personally called me the day after my interview. The standard of my visuals wasn't quite equal to the best they had seen, but everyone at the interview had concluded I was just the right character to be the overall design manager. This would involve not just producing the work, but managing the projects and building client relationships. They'd throw in a company car. What did I think of starting on Monday? Sounded like a bloody sterling plan to me. It was Friday and all I had to do was quit my job, book the tickets, pack, move and furnish a new apartment before starting work on Monday. Oh, and detox.

I called Chloe first thing. She answered.

"You'll never guess what. I got the job in Sheffield and I'm moving back."

She was elated. I explained about everything I had to do before starting on Monday but left out the part about detoxing from heroin.

With the urgency of an addict who couldn't find his dope, I wrapped up matters at home and caught the next boat to England. The detoxing had begun. Chloe met me at my new apartment and insisted we do a whirlwind tour of Ikea. By the time we got around to screwing the bed and cabinets and wardrobes together, I was falling apart. I couldn't stop my hands from trembling.

"Damn flu," I said, yawning and sneezing. Sweat was dripping off my face and all over the partially assembled furniture.

"Aw baby," Chloe said. "Is there anything I can do?"

There was no easy way to explain to her, no. The aches and pains were deep in my bones. The twisting and wrenching in my guts knew no relief. I did not know which end to place over the shit-sprayed toilet.

With the bed finally made, we got in and Chloe curled up with me in the foetal position. The sheets were quickly soaked with my sweat. I arched my back and scraped my legs together all night, clasping my hands between my thighs. Chloe rubbed me and told me, "My poor baby."

In the morning, I called work and told them I needed an extra day to get set up. Battling the flu had put me behind schedule. My only distraction was a seventeen-inch television in the front room. I curled in front of it and punched the hardwood floor for relief. Can after can of strong lager went down the gullet. I doused my head with mugs of cold water. I was burning with heat and shivering with ice all at once.

Once I had made it to work, over-the-counter pain medication and cold and flu remedies littered my desk. On day five of the detox, I did what any self-respecting heroin addict would do and I joined the gym.

After pumping iron and sweating the last of the drugs out of my system, I left the gym and drove the company car to the nearest country pub. Two pints of Stella and a chicken with chips dinner later, I found myself driving into the city, towards the train station. Near the entrance I spotted a homeless man sitting upright on a flattened cardboard box. One part of my brain said, no, God no, don't do it. The other half said, just one last time, just tonight. After all, you've got a gym membership now.

Long and short of it, I ended up with him and a couple of his homeless mates in the back of my car, cooking up speedballs of crack and heroin and injecting them into gaping holes in their groins. They stunk to high heaven, but I didn't care. I had what I needed.

These blokes became my regular acquaintances, a nightly fix. The cycle continued until I could not. I returned to the doctor and explained my symptoms.

"Fibromyalgia," he told me.

That sounded like a good reason to go home for a few weeks on the Isle of Man. I called the boss from my mum's and told him I was unwell. Within a fortnight I had left the island and was back in the emergency unit at Sheffield. After a series of tests, the doctor explained that my cortisol levels were borderline Addison's disease. Accepting this as Providence in the form of a virus, I returned to the Isle of Man for another rehab. Two weeks later, I called the boss to let him know I was fighting fit and ready for round three in Sheffield.

"I don't think it's quite working out," he said. "We're going to have to let you go."

Stunned, I had a long look at my curriculum vitae. The fake one was incredible. The real one looked like this.

JUNE 1999 – FEB 2001: Creative Director, IDI Digital, Derbyshire.
REASON FOR LEAVING: *Cocaine Addiction.*
APRIL 2001 – OCT 2002: CAD Consultant, Manx Logistics, Isle of Man.
REASON FOR LEAVING: *Heroin Addiction.*
NOV 2002 – DEC 2002: Design Manager, 360 Media, Sheffield.
REASON FOR LEAVING: *Sacked. Heroin Addiction.*

Hell of a soul-searching reflection that one. I talked a crackin' good game, but my follow-through was piss poor. Ruffling bloody feathers all over the show, and a hair's breadth away from flat-lining half a dozen times the way I was battering the junk into me.

I tried to quit. For the life of me I did but the gear well and truly had me by the bollocks.

Having resigned myself to a life of drugs on the Isle of Man, I ploughed through a few more jobs over the following year and soon had these highlights to add to my resume.

JAN 2003 – AUG 2003: Sales Consultant, Viking Systems, Isle of Man.
REASON FOR LEAVING: *Sacked, Gross Misconduct. Heroin Addiction.*
SEPT 2003 – NOV 2004: Interior Designer, Mann Interiors, Isle of Man.
REASON FOR LEAVING: *Sacked. Heroin Addiction.*
FEB 2004 – JUNE 2004: Business Analyst, Royal Bank of Scotland International, Isle of Man.
REASON FOR LEAVING: *Quit. Crack/Heroin Addiction.*

On top of it all, I was up to my neck in debt to Finnegan and had taken to pilfering random crap from my mum's place to make ends meet. Finnegan already had my golf clubs. Heirlooms like a black leather footstool that had belonged to my granddad got thrown into the mix without a second thought.

Once more I was starting to rattle. I needed a fix every hour or so. When Finnegan reminded me of the £1,500 I already owed him, I reminded him of the money Royal Bank of Scotland was supposed to be paying me for being off sick. It was bullshit, but all that mattered to me was that I scored.

Between fixing and contemplating whether to join the local drug and alcohol recovery programme, I got this wild notion in my head that I needed to head to New Zealand. My sister, Sal had moved there, and it was as far as humanly possible away from my current situation. I could get a two-year work visa if I applied before I was thirty.

In anticipation of the long journey, I finally looked into the drug and alcohol programme. The shrink put me on Subutex. It was an opiate substitute that mimicked the effects of the opiate and blocked the effects of heroin.

"You can't take heroin on top of the Subutex," she told me.

I did it anyway and had terrible results. Sent me straight into a cold turkey.

Several months of that shit and I asked about the possibilities for rehab. I knew the rich and famous went for treatment. Maybe I could land in one of those silk sheet joints. That would be the way to ease your detox.

"We do have that facility over at Ballamona," she told me.

The nut house, I thought. Gidawook's old joint. Christ. Not for me.

"There's also Alcoholics Anonymous. It's a spiritual sort of programme. Not for everyone, but it is about God."

I froze.

"You have got to be fucking joking me." As if I didn't have enough shame with this heroin addiction, she was now gonna throw God in to top it all off?

"You need somewhere longer-term, Michael. Someone with your degree of addiction would need at least nine months."

"Nine months? Are you kidding?"

"No. You're still using heroin on top of the Subutex. You've had very few clean urine tests. Plus, we've got you on Valium and sleeping medication. You would need nine months, minimum."

"Nine months at the Priory in London. That'll be expensive," I replied tongue in cheek. The Priory was the first choice for the rich and famous.

She smiled.

On the way out, I checked the brochures in the waiting room. Twelve-step programmes, all of them, all of them dealing with God. Then I found one that wasn't twelve-step.

"Here's one," I said and pointed at the picture of a rustic cottage in the Welsh hills.

"That's a Christian retreat facility," she said.

I threw the brochure on the table. "This is a fucking nightmare."

"There are many types of facilities throughout the UK," she said. "Keep looking. Narrow it down to two or three and go and have a look firsthand. Once you return to the island with a decision, we'll fill out the application forms. Arrange a date and begin your treatment. You'll have to pay up front and once you've completed the treatment, the government will refund a percentage of the overall costs."

I felt absolutely fucking helpless. Sweat dripped from the brow.

"What? I need to go now? Today? I can barely get out of the house, let alone travel to the UK. And I've got no money."

"It's the best we can do," she said.

I left and scored the largest bag of heroin I could afford.

A few days later I learned my mum had taken a job with the church on Iona, a small island off the coast of Scotland. I was left in trust of the house. I had £78 a week to take care of my habits.

First things first, I went down to see the chemist about my Subutex. He was located underneath the Viking Hotel. The way in was surrounded by shops owned by friends of the family. It was a job getting in and out every day without being seen. What would I be doing at the chemist's every day?

Inside, he handed me the tablet. I placed it under my tongue and waited ten seconds, enough time to satisfy him but not enough for it to dissolve. With a nod and a wag of my tongue, the chemist gave me the okay and I left. Outside, I removed the tablet and kept it as an emergency back-up should the heroin dry up.

The social security office was around the corner. I waited in the car, watching the queue of single mothers pushing dual pram buggies, disabled pensioners and other renowned junkies. When it appeared I would be surrounded by the least decrepit of down-and-out souls, I bolted inside, grabbed my cheque and took it to the post office. An old school mate was behind the counter to cash it. She doled out a bit of shame with the cash.

My routine from there was to score heroin and hit the gym. Smoke smack and bench. When all else failed, I called Mum.

She was doing her religious gig on the Isle of Iona. I would call in for another charitable donation, wrapped in my sleeping bag on the sofa, a bottle of cheap whiskey next to me, a box of Marlboro Lights and a roll of silver foil on the coffee table. On the TV a morning chat show discussing such topics as lazy, fat unemployed kids sponging off their parents would drone on in the background.

If ever she wanted to know what the next sum of money was being used for, I'd tell her some shit, like between filling out job application forms, I was researching charitable work in Jamaica. Mum had done voluntary service overseas in Jamaica when she was younger, so I worked that angle.

It might be an opportunity to give back to the community, I would point out, while I was awaiting responses from all my job applications.

"It would cost a few quid, though. I know it's a big ask, but could you help?"

In my head I rationalized the money I owed everyone by saying I would pay it all back one day, especially my mum. It couldn't be much longer before I was off the junk and had my shit together. Then I'd straighten out the rundown house. Fix the cigarette-burned carpets and smoke-stained curtains. Replace the trashed lawnmower I'd thrown off the side of the garden in a rage. Fix the front door I had smashed in when I locked the drugs in the house and myself out. Hell, I'd buy her a whole new house. She and I would travel the Continent together.

During one of my morning slumbers, I heard a knock on the door. That'll be the postman, I thought and stumbled across the room to answer it. Since discretion is the better part of valour, I peeked through the curtain and saw it was the old man. What the fuck's he doing here? I wondered.

With a lick of my palm, I desperately flattened my hair, threw the sleeping bag behind the sofa, tucked the liquor and paraphernalia away and straightened a few cushions.

"Dad, all right, how's it going? Er, come in." I opened the door wider. "What's the craic? You've never been here before."

"I was driving past. Mikey, the grass is a foot deep. You've got the curtains shut. It's the middle of the day."

"Oh, that, I've been meaning to cut the grass," I said, walking into the living room and opening the curtains halfway.

"My God, open the windows. The smell! It's like someone died in here. Is that booze I can smell?"

I opened the window for some fresh air. "Take a seat, Dad."

We both sat. He pointed at my exposed ankles. "What the hell happened to your legs? They're black and blue."

I unwrapped the housecoat and exposed my thighs, then lifted my sleeves. "It's all over me."

"You look like a corpse. What the hell happened?"

"I don't know, it just came on."

I stood and headed for the kitchen. "You wanna cuppa tea?"

The old man followed. "No, I'm not stopping. What the hell's going on?"

I sat on the piano stool beneath the stairs. Tears welled up in my eyes.

"I've been on drugs...heroin, Dad."

He closed his mouth and nodded. I was shocked he didn't stick it to me.

"Thank God for that. I thought it had to be something. I'm so glad you told me. I've not had sense out of you for years. You were drunk and just out there most times you came to the house. It makes perfect sense of everything. What a relief."

"I needed a drink before I came to your house," I admitted. "I thought I was more entertaining. I felt like I was on form if I had a few drinks."

"I just thought you were mental. Your behaviour was all over the show."

Tears ran down my cheeks. Looking at him, I was struck by how his whole body seemed to have relaxed and how kindness and gentleness had come over his disposition. I felt relaxed too, in a way I had not felt since I was a kid.

Suddenly worried that he might shoot his mouth off, I cautioned him.

"Don't say anything to anyone, Dad. I couldn't bear the whole town knowing."

"Mikey, get away from this place. If you can get to New Zealand, go. I'll help you. Sal's there. I had to go to Australia when I was younger. As soon as I was old enough, I went. I had to get away from my home. I couldn't be here anymore."

He shook his head.

"I'm terrified of flying, Dad. I don't know whether I can do it."

"But you were always such a confident traveller," he pointed out. "We flew to Australia when you were five. We've been all over the world. You were fearless, you loved it."

"I don't give a shit about the plane dropping out of the sky. Dying's not the problem. It's losing control in public, people laughin', nowhere to run, enclosed spaces. Public humiliation. Fuck that shit."

He stared at me like I was nuts.

"I'll think about it," I said. "I'll see what I can do. I've got until I'm thirty to apply for a New Zealand work visa."

"That's not long. That's a matter of weeks," he said.

The old man left. A few days later, I filled out the forms and sent off the two-year work visa application. Meanwhile, Mum continued wiring me money from Scotland, and I continued spending it on a gram of heroin a day.

On and on it went, and then one day a near disaster occurred that left me with only one option: to go to the other end of the world. I had taken the twenty-minute drive over the mountain to the dealer's place on the other side of the island. It was a crisp, clear morning. The drugs were wearing off. My body had begun to stiffen. As I closed in on the score, the adrenaline began to kick in. The high was right down the road.

As I pulled to a stop on the opposite side of the road from his house, I found a police van with a cop behind the wheel parked right outside. Logic would suggest that now was not a good time to be purchasing heroin from a well-known drug dealer, but I called to inform him about the cops and he shrugged off my concerns.

The house door flew open and the dealer ran out of the house without a shirt on, pulling up his pyjama bottoms as he crossed the street.

"Are you serious?" I said as he got into my car. I checked the wing mirrors and saw the policeman start his engine in my rearview mirror.

"Here," he said and dropped the heroin in my lap, wrapped in a porn magazine.

"For fuck's sake, it's seven years in the nick for this," I said.

He took the cash and bolted across the road with his pyjamas around his knees. I pulled out with an eye on the rearview mirror. The cop van pulled up behind me with flashing lights. I chucked the drugs out of the window and kept driving until I had found a safe place to pull in. Heroin possession was front-page news on the Isle of Man and the government had zero tolerance. Anyone caught for possession was made an example.

Once I stopped, the cop quickly handcuffed me, squeezed me into the back of the van and went in search of the gear. I had been praying to God when he came back holding something.

Fuck, no. He's found the fucking wrapper.

On the way to the police headquarters, I concluded I was doomed, but once there the cop placed a brick-size block of what looked like charred polystyrene on the counter. I did a double-take. They could not possibly think that was what I had thrown from the car.

I started to detox in my cell. The chills and rattles set in. I nearly lost my guts when they passed some soggy chips through the door. I started to make promises.

"God, whatever the fuck is up there, if you get me out of this one, I'll never touch another drug as long as I live. I'll change, I promise. I'll get away from here and start a new life."

In the afternoon, three officers questioned me. My legal counsel was there. The police thought I had purchased a sizeable amount of crack cocaine from Tommy Kiley, a well-known drug dealer. I was confronted again with the block of polystyrene.

"We can do this the easy way or the hard way, Mr Cannan. Ram through the door to your house or you can give us the keys."

I threw the keys on the table, hoping Mum's Christian literature and religious images would give the house a holy feel.

They took me back to my cell. Hours passed. Finally, I was dragged back into the interrogation room.

"We've been around your house and uncovered syringes, steroids and drug paraphernalia, but no drugs."

They sat back.

"So are you telling us this is not yours?"

We all sat staring at the block of polystyrene.

"Never seen it before," I said, doing my best not to laugh.

All three cops studied my body language.

"Okay, I'm satisfied," one of them said. "Can you help us with our enquiries?"

"Possibly."

"Someone's going to call you later in the week with some questions."

They let me go and I arrived home to find the house turned upside down. Needles, burnt tin foil and steroid packets lay on display all over my bedroom. A cop called the next week asking questions about a robbery. I told him nothing and heard no more.

I was finally ready to ditch it all, heroin, Subutex, the lot. I had lost all hope of carrying on the way I was going but found it impossible to imagine life without some sort of drug. I was terrified either way I looked.

The drug and alcohol team arranged for a nurse to come round every day and check my vitals. I started in with the brandy and bucket detox. The pain peaked on days two and three. I lost count amid my misery, but the agony remained the same. I punched the floor and pulled the bookshelves from the wall in frustration. I was on a mind-numbing collapse with the British equivalent of the *Jerry Springer Show* droning on in the background.

On day five Howcroft walked into the house. We poured a couple of whiskies.

"What are you gonna do next, Fod?"

"New Zealand. I'll go and stay with Sal. Fuck knows how I'm gonna get on a plane, but I've got to go."

"You go out first and I'll come and join you once you're settled."

Sounded like a great idea. The boys on tour again. What could possibly go wrong?

"Come and work for me in the meantime. We're renovating that barn out the North. You can labour. Start whenever you want."

"The sooner the better."

The nurse cuffed a blood-pressure monitor to my arm one day and finally announced that I was normal. I had no idea what was normal, but I went to work for Howcroft a few days later. It was the summer of 2005, and Hurricane Katrina had just slammed into New Orleans. I was recovering from my own state of epic destruction. Fine suits and fine women one day, and here I was, a grunt in the trenches, complete with a farmer's tan.

"Fod, chuck a four to one mix on, yissur," Howcroft shouted from the roof.

The cement mixer whirred to life. I threw in a bucket of water and picked up the shovel: one of cement, four of sand, half of lime, into the wheelbarrow and over to Howcroft.

He laughed. "I've dreamt of this day my whole life – you working for me. Carry on digging the footings for the garage, yissur."

I heard more laughing from up on the roof.

One day, though, I received my ticket out. "Visa came through for New Zealand," I informed him.

"Is that you gone, then?"

"Dad said he'd pay for the flight and give me some cash to take. All I have to do is phone the travel agent. Still not sure, can't stop thinking about heroin, all day, every fucking day."

"While you're thinking, take some tile onto the roof," Howcroft told me.

I loaded twenty Spanish tiles aside each shoulder and walked around the scaffold exterior. It started to rain. I returned the tile to the freshly opened crate. Howcroft came down.

"Rained off. It gets like this as we get into autumn."

I used my free time to call the travel agent and book my flights. December 5. A flight to Manchester, one overnight stay, Manchester to Singapore, five nights in Singapore, then on to New Zealand.

Early the next morning, I heard the front door open.

"Are you ready?" Howcroft called.

I ran downstairs. "With you in a minute."

"Wait, stop, your eyes. You're not…?"

"I'll be gone soon. New Zealand doesn't have a problem with heroin. I'll be safe for now."

A few weeks off detox and I was back on heroin.

Early in December, I met the old man in front of the Isle of Man Bank in Ramsey. He had worked there when I was young. The staff all greeted him as we went in.

In the foyer, he handed me £1,000. "I'll pick you up in the morning."

Back home, I immediately called every drug dealer on the island and scraped together as much heroin as I could find, along with a bit of Subutex and some codeine tablets.

The following morning, Dad drove me out to Ronaldsway Airport. I was already wasted.

"Thanks for the money, Dad, and, ya know…"

What I really wanted to say was, "I can't thank you enough for your tolerance with my bullshit, and for helping me in every way you possibly could. I would not be at this airport if it weren't for you. I love you."

We exchanged a hug. I was choked up but could not cry.

At customs, I stopped for one last check. Heroin concealed in a condom in my mouth; beta blockers; steroids; Ventolin, my asthmatic medication; Klonopin, my blood pressure pills;

Prozac and Seroxat, my anti-depressants; diazepam, oxazepam and lorazepam as tranquillizers; nitrazepam and zopiclone for sleeping aid; dihydrocodeine and Subutex, my opiate substitute, a three pack of Rogaine and a copy of Paul McKenna's *Change Your Life in 7 Days*.

Petrified and sweating like a bastard, I was on my way.

CHAPTER EIGHT

Armed to the teeth and ready for action, I had failed to antici-
pate one thing – actually entering the plane. Now the maw of
that monster was waiting to engulf me just up ahead.

I hesitated at the door, but the force of passengers behind
me kept herding the line forward.

"Welcome aboard, sir," the overly cheerful stewardess said
to me.

Right. I was ready to turn and bolt. My bollocks were up
in my throat.

Breaking out in a sweat, I allowed myself to be crowded
into the tunnel-like space. Fuck, no. Serious sensory overload.
Way too many people. Way too much chatter. Alarms were
going off as I stumbled and bumped down the narrow aisle.

Having found my seat, I quickly shuffled off to the bathroom
for a fix. As soon as I had the door locked, I frantically pulled out
my paraphernalia and lined it up by the sink. A profound feeling
of relief fell over me. Bliss was but a few deft manoeuvres away.

As I sat on the bog, ready to have a boot, I looked up and
noticed the No Smoking sign above my head. For fuck's sake.
What now? I'd completely forgotten the bastards had outlawed
the practice. How the hell was I going to make it to Manchester
Airport without more of the brown to straighten me out?

I slithered back to my seat and somehow managed the short
flight without completely unravelling, only to disembark into the
mad bustle of a large metropolitan airport. I stood there with my

feet frozen to the commercial carpet. A rat in a sewer I was. The flashlights had gone on. My impulse was to scurry for cover.

I made a break for the nearest airport hotel and locked myself in my room. The tinfoil pipe came out. After a good long hit, I raided the minibar and popped a Prozac from its blister pack. A healthy gulp of lager to wash it down. I considered taking one of my Valiums but decided against it. After all, they were addictive. I had the psychological advantage of knowing they were there. Then again, if I took one and it didn't work, I'd be fucked.

I slipped in and out of consciousness all day. Night came. Each time I awakened, I reached for the alarm clock to check the time, then reached for the tin foil. Soon, barely twenty minutes was elapsing between each hit. The effects of the drugs and alcohol were weakening. I knew my heart rate was elevated. I considered taking Valium again.

As if I had not slept a wink, I saw the sky brightening through a crack in the curtains. Time to face the world and another plane, this time for a thirteen-hour flight. After a shower and reorganizing my drugs, I caught a taxi back to the terminal.

On the way, my thoughts flashed upon the dreams of a young lad. The international jet-setter I'd planned to be, travelling the world without a care. What the hell had happened? I now dreaded getting on board. Was I about to lose my mind in public, once and for all?

Boarding the plane, I surveyed all the exit points, on the chance I might need to bolt. Right. Out into midair? I felt everyone scrutinizing me as I came down the aisle. I was a danger to them. They were terrifying to me.

I took my seat by the window and gripped the armrests. A man came and took the aisle seat, blocking me in. After several seconds, I stood up, ready to run. I had to get off the plane.

The man was staring up at me, so I sat back down.

Get a fucking grip.

Still sweating, I wiped at my face and neck. I had thought about taking some drugs before leaving the hotel room, but which ones? And what if they had failed to work?

Either way, I now regretted not taking them.

I was ready to bolt again by the time a stewardess closed and locked the cabin door. The vacuum tube had been sealed. No choice now. The increased whine of the engines had me hyperventilating. In response, I slipped a couple of steroids out of my pocket and necked them. The physical act of putting a pill in my mouth brought comfort.

I opened the book I had brought along. *Change Your Life in Seven Days* by Paul McKenna. He had developed a visualization technique for improving your confidence. Imagine a silver thread coming down from the sky. Now imagine it gently pulling you up from the very top of your head.

Somehow that image had me tumbling out of the plane at thirty-five thousand feet.

My terror reached a crescendo as the plane became airborne. Full panic mode now. The guy next to me kept stealing glances at my white knuckles.

As soon as the seat belt sign went off and the stewardesses came around, I ordered a Singapore Sling and retreated to the toilet. It was to hell with the laws and propriety at this point. I wrapped a few wet paper towels over the smoke alarm, did a nice long rack of heroin, flapped my arms about in there for several minutes, dissipating the smoke, had some bloke knocking on the door by this point and nearly forgot the bloody paper towels but stepped out feeling like a new man. The flight had miraculously become first class.

Thirteen hours later, we arrived in Singapore. A huge notice greeted me as I entered the boarding area:

DEATH PENALTY FOR DRUG SMUGGLING

Painted on the wall. For fuck's sake. I had arranged for a five-day layover in Singapore, thinking it was the drug capital of the world. Instead, they were going to take me out the back and stand me up against a wall.

With the help of Paul McKenna, I imagined that silver thread pulling me up through the top of my head. With feet on terra firma, that much I could manage. I strode through customs with an air of bravado and somehow it worked.

The following five days were spent drunk and stumbling around the back streets of the city, trying to hustle drugs from every stranger I met.

"Nearest bet is the Malaysian border," one of them was kind enough to tell me. "But don't get caught here."

I considered the option but in the end settled on high doses of alcohol and heroin substitutes to sustain me, along with sugar, carbohydrates and fats.

When Sal picked me up at Auckland airport, I was an absolute wreck. The sedatives had worn off and what was intended to be a grand reunion had dissipated into this frenzied aggro inside my head.

At the sight of my sister across the arrivals hall, my mind went into full bullshit mode.

Stay off heroin for the rest of your life. Sorted. Find and maintain a job. Achieve optimum physical condition. Find a missus. Get married. Purchase a home. Start a family.

I'd have that lot checked off in no time. Prove everyone wrong. A month or so and I'd have it all done.

Sal's cheery face darkened at the sight of me.

"Welcome to New Zealand, yissur."

She threw her arms around my neck and stood back to take me in.

"Look at you," she said with a strained smile. "You look great."

I was not convinced. To confirm my suspicions, she tugged at my white t-shirt.

"Apart from these red wine stains all over you. Let's get home and clean you up."

We gathered the rest of my luggage and went out to the front of the terminal.

"Intense sun," I said with a pull at my baseball cap.

"Something to do with a hole in the ozone," Sal said.

"Least of my worries. I feel like I'm under a microscope."

The baseball cap came down even tighter.

At Sal's car, we threw my gear in the boot and drove off.

"You'll be sorted here," she said with a glance my way. "No drugs. There's certainly no heroin in New Zealand."

That was a depressing thought. Sal looked my way again.

"I can't imagine you taking drugs, Mikey. It'll be a new life away from all that crap on the island. A fresh start."

I nodded in agreement. Off heroin straight away. Find a job. A woman. Get married. Purchase a home. Achieve optimum physical condition. One month should do the trick.

"How long have you and Ian been out here now?" I said in an effort to keep up appearances.

"Nearly three years. We're applying for residency."

"And how's everything going? Have you set a date for the wedding yet?"

A look of terror came over her face. "Um, we don't talk about that."

"He phoned me and asked for my permission to ask you," I said. "That impressed me."

"Hey, we're having a Christmas party in a couple of days," she said, changing the subject. "You'll get to meet everyone."

So that's it, I thought. He's keen on the idea and she's having none of it.

No problem. Sal's sick brother has now arrived, providing fresh diversions from the nuptials. It was a covert contract between us, and a hell of a way to rationalize my desperate journey if nothing else.

We drove over the Auckland Harbour Bridge to Devonport, a small arts community at the mouth of Auckland Harbour. Twin volcanic peaks stood as a backdrop. Victorian era wooden villas lined the long road. My heart warmed at the sight of a British-style pub, tucked in amongst all that colonial architecture.

Sal ultimately pulled down a steep driveway and parked in front of a modest clapboard building.

"Your new home," she said. "It's split into four apartments. Ours is the front apartment."

We walked up the stairs and onto a balcony overlooking Auckland Harbour. The city skyline was off in the distance. Ships and luxury yachts were crossing the brilliant blue water.

"Not bad, yissur."

"Not bad. This is a new start, yissur."

She threw her arms around me again. I sensed pity. The charity case. Left unsaid was what she really thought about my arrival, and I was just fine with leaving it that way.

We had dinner with her old man and some friends. The wine took the edge off, but all my thoughts were on getting back to my room alone. I wanted nothing but to be away from all the scrutiny, and as quickly as possible.

With that accomplished, I necked an assortment of tablets back in my room and almost reached the high I was seeking. One check on the calendar. Only twenty-nine days left on my new start in life.

Sal and her boyfriend held their big Christmas party a few days later. I was up on the balcony and already well soused by the time people started to arrive.

Everyone who came in received my offer of a pint of vodka Red Bull. It was my drug of choice that day. I was trying to endear myself and all but had no takers. Single-shot mixers and light ales appeared to be the drug of choice amongst the herd.

The tame pace was unfamiliar territory for me.

Over time, a crowd of people had gathered around the small pool below the balcony. Families and couples. Exchanging pleasantries. My way of bonding was to heckle their conversations. Manx bar room banter. The same way the lads and I had done to each other over darts and pool in the pubs back home.

Again, I had no takers. No one seemed up for a laugh. My efforts were met with awkward looks and people slipping back into the house.

When it turned to evening, Sal came upstairs.

"Mike, you're a bit loud. Can you tone it down a bit?"

"Why? What's up?"

The landlady, who lived in the apartment next door, came alongside the building.

"Come on, Robin, get a fucking drink down you, luv," I shouted, skulling my vodka Red Bull from a pint pot.

"That's what I mean," Sal said, looking distressed.

"I'm just having a laugh."

"Well, no one thinks it's funny."

Her boyfriend, Ian, came up the stairs and nodded. He and Sal convened just out of earshot.

"He's got to go," I heard him say.

With a wary look my way, Ian started downstairs. I caught up with him in the front room.

"Who's gonna make me?" I asked him.

We squared off at six foot three and about five hundred pounds in weight split evenly between us.

Ian backed up against the island in the kitchen. Sal got between us.

"Mike, stop, please."

"I will not be threatened in my own home," Ian said.

I pointed at him and moved closer. He shifted around so that the island was separating us, looking cornered.

"Fuck this joke," I said. "I'm going to Thailand. I've got enough money to keep me going."

Enough for a mud hut and a month's supply of cheap heroin, but I kept that bit of information to myself.

"Mike, please," Sal said in tears.

I pulled her aside.

"You don't understand, Sal. The craving for heroin is monumental. Worse when I drink. I could go right now, fly to another country just to get gear."

Even more despairing now, two of Sal's friends came over to comfort her.

"Mike," one of the women said to me. "Come with us. You can stay at our house for the night."

I left with the party crashed behind me. The festive lights of Christmas were still blinking away. Six days had passed on my new civilized existence. It did not appear I was fit for a normal way of life.

In the morning, I walked back to Sal's house, hungover and still dressed in my swimming trunks. Ian was sitting on the balcony. I reached out my hand.

"I'm sorry about last night. Too much drink, mate. Let's put it behind us."

He nodded without emotion. I went to find Sal.

"Sal, I'm so sorry."

"I was just worried."

She pulled me aside with a glance out towards Ian.

"Listen, the guy in the back downstairs apartment is leaving. Don't tell Ian, but I'll lend you the money. Then you can have your own place. There's another small bedroom in there as well. Ideal for Howcroft if he's coming over like you said."

I had maintained regular contact with the bastard and his plan remained to follow me out once I was settled.

"Thanks," I told Sal. "Best to have some space. I'll pay you back the cash, honestly. Get a job as soon as I can. Howcroft can help too."

"That sounds good, Mikey. I've also booked you an appointment with this naturopath I know. It might help with the cravings."

I laughed. "By fuck I hope she's good."

I went ahead with the appointment. By that point I had been clean from heroin for three weeks. One item checked off my to-do list. One week left to get a wife and house and family.

The naturopath conducted what I thought were a bunch of hocus-pocus tests and then droned on and on about my full body composition analysis, high blood pressure, vitamin deficiency and nutritional guidelines.

"Plus, you're clinically obese," she added at the end.

I leaned forward, my gut lapping over the table edge. "Those machines don't account for muscle mass."

That seemed to set things straight. I purchased some zinc, thanked her for her advice and headed out the door.

Clinically obese, I thought on my way home. What a joke. Anyway, I had bigger worries. I was dying inside. The gates of hell were the postal destination for my soul and the doc hadn't offered any suggestions for avoiding that.

Back at the small ground-floor apartment Sal had rented for me, I got comfortable on the sofa and started flicking through my three TV channels. I had one window and a fence for a view. The place was nearly devoid of all natural light, but I found that comforting.

When I saw bin Laden's mug on the Al Jazeera channel, I turned it up. They were airing the latest audiotape from his bunker. It was the same old shit. Al-Qaeda was making big preparations to attack the United States. I offered a middle finger salute from my bunker to his and nursed a cold lager down my throat.

A moment later, I heard Sal knocking at the door. I called for her to come in. She gave me and the apartment the once-over and handed me Ian's spare laptop.

"Here, just keep this with you for now. You can use it to search for jobs."

I was handed $500. "Here's some money for next month's rent." She pointed upstairs. "Don't say anything. He doesn't understand. He just thinks you're a drug addict and doesn't want me down here."

"He's a fucking arsehole. Anyway, I *was* a drug addict."

"I know. Look, I was speaking to Mum on the phone and it's like we don't have anything to say now that you're not using drugs."

It hit me as we stared at each other. Mum needed me to be sick. Her purpose in life was gone when I was well. Maybe she was as sick as me in this whole drama.

Sal left. I got back to Al Jazeera.

It took several days, and on one of my better ones, I finally pulled together a new portfolio from the Internet. It included three-dimensional renderings, animations and visual effects – what could only be described as world-class work, from leading artists all over the world. Just none of it was mine.

After sending it off to several companies around Auckland, this operation called CADSolutions rang for an interview. Based just four kilometres down the road in Takapuna, they had been my first choice. Sal loaned me their beach car, a 1984 Mitsubishi with faded yellow paint and rusted trim.

Typical luck, Monday morning turned out to be a real scorcher. I was sweating away in my Hugo Boss suit, awaiting the onslaught. People. Interviews. Scrutiny. Terror.

Sal kept the Mitsubishi parked up at the top of our cul-de-sac and facing downhill so any rainwater that accumulated inside would drain off through the large rust holes in the floorboards. I pried open the door, just hoping the beast would start. McDonalds' wrappers, loose change and beach sand made a collage all over the seats and floor. The interior smelled of seaweed and brine.

The battery had lost its charge, so I had to jump-start it. With the ignition on and the clutch down, I released the handbrake and said a prayer. When the clutch popped, the engine came to life. I began wildly pumping the accelerator and working the handbrake.

Lovely way to start the day, I thought. And the ride went beautifully with the Hugo Boss suit.

The door to CADSolutions was next to an all-you-can-eat Brazilian churrascaria. The boss, Alex, greeted me inside. I quickly started piling on the bullshit. Stunned by my portfolio, Alex was offering me the business by the end of the interview. Whatever hours I wanted to keep. His only concern was that the work wouldn't be challenging enough for me. I offered up my team mentality: "Whatever it takes, mate, I'll pitch in."

A week into the job, Alex was still asking me to produce something that lived up to the standards of my portfolio. I had every excuse in the world. I was busy bringing the five staff members on my team up to speed. His PCs were slow and we needed new software. They had just brought out the latest generation. Cheap at $50K. Buy it and I'll happily produce the goods.

The bullshit held up for another week, but just barely.

One day Alex announced a new member to the team. Wary of my authority being challenged – and my bullshit being called out – I watched with subdued menace as this tall, heavyset lad with shoulder-length hair came lumbering in. His cheeks were rosy and decorated with two-day stubble. His three-quarter-length leather jacket resembled a tunic.

All he needs is a few grape leaves on his head, I thought.

"This is Dion," Alex announced. "I think we'll have dinner next door on Saturday. Get to know each other."

Dion made the handshake rounds. I smelled liquor on his breath. He pointed out of the windows at a classic Mercedes.

"Where can I park the old wheels?" he said.

Alex directed Dion towards the back carpark. I was quickly finding ways to hate him and watched with more menace as he crossed the road with large strides, shoulders back, belly out, arms swinging at forty-five-degree angles to his body. It looked like he'd been using the same walking coach as me.

When Dion returned, he took the desk next to mine. I gave him a nod and got back to work. I shot wary glances at him all day. What kind of threat did this man represent? He had wire-rim specs hooked over his ears and his face jammed about three inches from the monitor. His mouse clicks were slow and heavy. His whole head seemed to be following the lines around the screen.

What have we here? I thought. I was hoping his presence to be short-lived.

That Saturday night at the next-door churrascaria, after we had gorged on skewers of beef, chicken and pork, sausages, lamb, ribs and fish roasted over a pit of coals, and downed a boatload of wine, Dion pulled a tube out of his leather tunic coat.

"Care for a sample of our finest New Zealand produce, soldier?"

Herbal ecstasy. And legal, too. I was suddenly quite fond of this Dion character.

After a night of fierce binging, I awoke in the morning with a murderous hangover. Scaling the fence next door in my underwear, I pinched a lemon from the solitary lemon tree in the centre of the empty lot and returned to my bunker. I was settling into a slice of that with a cold Corona for breakfast when the phone rang. It was Dion. He identified me as the squadron leader and asked if I cared for an aperitif.

"Touch of tension in the old head, soldier. Could do with a painkiller."

"What's your choice?" Dion said.

"I got robbed by a psychotic Tongan the other night trying to purchase morphine. Bloody shortage over here."

"What happened there, old chap?"

"Bloody desperate for drugs I was and couldn't score shit in the city, so I bought the newspaper looking for the place with the most murders and shootings. Reckoned that's where you'd find the best drugs, ya know?"

"Sounds like a damn fine plan to me."

"Absolutely. So there was an article about this place up North. Worst street in New Zealand they called it. I headed that way, found the road and took a tour of the place looking for the shiftiest lookin' fuckers I could find. Found one lurkin' in the shadows. That mental Tongan, and before I knew what was what the bastard had me robbed."

"Fucking island bastards. Just so you know, old chap, we do have the same narcotic control laws as Romania and Poland, among other righteous pillars of society. It's not quite Mexico, but you can get a good dose of codeine at the chemist without a prescription."

My first thought every day and all day long was heroin, but codeine was still music to my ears.

"What's the address? I'll be over shortly."

I jotted down the information and rushed through a shower. Pleasant bloke, I thought while soaping down. And there I was, ready to chuck the fucker overboard.

Dion lived with his older brother and two Doberman Pinschers in a colonial style property underneath the Harbour Bridge. His brother worked in the city as a lawyer. A Mercedes, BMW, Range Rover, and Land Rover were parked in the drive. Clearly, the family had money.

The top floor of the house had been converted into a bar overlooking Auckland harbour and the City of Sails. A vision of days ahead quickly gelled in my head: countless hours drinking fine liqueurs and contemplating our retirement strategies. My days with Dion turned out to be a fair bit more sordid than that, but that warm first blush was mostly what I remembered.

In May, Howcroft rolled off the plane. It had taken him three days and five stopovers. He was fucked. Within days, we were both fucked. Then, after an all-nighter at Dion's place, we headed home in the old Mitsubishi. Before leaving, we conducted a field sobriety test and Howcroft won. Claimed he could see at least ten feet in front of him with his glasses on. He could stand up. I gave him that much and let him drive.

Half a mile down the road, the red and blue lights came on, lighting up the black sky behind us. Howcroft got hauled off to headquarters and had to bail his own way out. The cop seized the keys and left me at the side of the road.

Some new start. The two of us had picked up right where we had left off in the Isle of Man, a decadent stew of Ecstasy and booze, only now we threw whorehouses into the mix. Those Kiwis were certainly liberal if nothing else. They had made the world's oldest profession legal.

Our battalion launched a series of debauched escapades, credit cards flying, our fine reputations repeatedly smudged. Howcroft was my wingman. General Dion manned the airborne infantry. I was named the squadron commander and God spare the rest.

Our nightly vehicle was selected from the fleet of cars in Dion's driveway, all depending on the mission. One night I smashed the BMW through the entrance of the brothel. We let the air settle for a few weeks and started right back in where we had left off. It was a merciless mixture of fine wines, glass pipes, bright sun mornings, car horns, retching and paranoia. Every time I turned around there was another $1,800 hotel bill and promises from me to reimburse Dion for his credit cards.

Research on the next new place to run and hide had already commenced. Turn my life around. Dion had mentioned Mexico and their liberal drug laws. I liked that idea. I was looking into it on the Internet one morning when Howcroft walked out of his bedroom dressed in his All-Blacks rugby shirt.

"Love to see this game," he said. "Once in a lifetime opportunity."

He was referring to Australia versus New Zealand at Eden Park. Rugby Union's Bledisloe Cup. It was one of the top international sporting events that side of the world. New Zealand had dominated the cup from the beginning in 1932.

"We'd be lucky to get in," I said.

Howcroft cracked open a bottle in response. "All this way. Hate to miss the opportunity. It'd be a dream come true."

Seeing the disappointment on his face, I gave in. Should have stood my ground. We could have had our feet kicked up with a couple of artisanal lagers, watching on the big screen from a local pub. Instead, we found ourselves stuck in bumper-to-bumper traffic. Howcroft had been to court over that drunk-driving bust by this point and lost his licence, so I was at the wheel, driving his battered old Land Rover, something he had bought for his job as a builder. I pulled over at a bar in Newmarket and we ordered a couple of Vodka Red Bulls. The barman heard our ambitious story and offered us a ride as near as possible.

"The Garden of Eden will be packed. It might be possible to get tickets from a tout outside the stadium, but it'll cost you a bomb."

We declined his offer and set off again on our own.

After much delay, we abandoned the car on a side road and continued on foot. The road was lined with people doing the same. In the distance we heard the thunderous sound of the stadium and started to jog the rest of the way.

The steward at the ticket stand told us, none left. No amount of money could buy one and there wasn't a ticket tout in sight.

"Wait until the match has started. By then I'll know if we have any tickets left."

I walked back over to Howcroft, discouraged. The crowd roared. The match had started. He was on a right old downer. I looked back at the ticket counter. To my surprise, the steward waved me over.

"You're lucky. Two people didn't show up. These are the last two tickets in town."

We ran hard and made the stadium entrance just in time to watch what was called the Haka. The Australian boys were upright, face on. The Kiwi boys started in with their Maori war dance, squatting and slapping thighs, chests puffed out, tongues slashing as they chanted.

Howcroft and I grabbed beers and found our seats. We were doing herbal Ecstasy while the boys on the field beat the crap out of each other.

After a long day of it, we were filing out of the stadium with a crowd when an animated young lad caught my eye. He was spinning a rugby ball a few yards in front of us. A tall lady with long, platinum blonde hair was walking alongside him. She was dressed in jeans and a grey jacket. Very casual and very elegant at the same time.

I offered to catch the ball and the young lad hurled it at me.

"Who are you?" he said as I spun the ball on my finger.

"Michael. Who are you?"

"Dylan. So, what do you do?"

"Professional rugby player," I said with a quick display of my talents.

"So how much do you earn? My dad earned millions a year. Do you earn millions?"

"Nah, not quite that much."

The woman turned and half blushed with her smile at me. She was fine-boned, nice teeth, nice everything.

"Dylan, don't ask questions like that," she said. "Leave the man alone."

I had already guessed the kid was American from his accent. The woman had a touch of European to hers. I glanced at Howcroft. He knew what I was thinking. A woman like that, you had to have her.

I turned back and found Dylan drifting our way.

"My dad's a pro football player. He was quarterback for the Dallas Cowboys and Miami Dolphins. Who do you play for?"

I quickly remembered the name of a team an old girlfriend used to support.

"Bradford Bulls."

If either of them had any rugby knowledge I was fucked but no one said a word.

"So where's your dad now?"

"America. He and Mom don't get along. They split up. He remarried."

"Sorry to hear that, little fella."

"Dad always won most valuable player. Mom's a model."

"Stop," his mother said.

She had come back and gave Dylan a good wrench of his hand.

"Please ignore him," she said with another one of her half-blushing smiles my way.

"She was on the cover of magazines," Dylan said.

That got him another yank. I offered my hand to the woman.

"I'm Michael. He's funny."

"I'm Natasja. And he can be quite a handful."

"That accent. Where's it from?"

"Denmark. But California's home now. That's where Dylan was born. What about you?"

"The Isle of Man."

"I've never met anyone from the Isle of Man."

"That's lucky"

"Why's that?"

"I'm just takin' the piss, luv."

"Taking a piss?"

"Not literally. Joking with you. It's a British expression. Takin' the piss. Making light of something, ya know?"

She laughed.

"Takin' the piss. God, you Brits come out with the weirdest stuff."

"Manx," I corrected her. "Not British. Two different beasts. Mind me asking how you ended up in New Zealand?"

"It's a long story…I needed a vacation," she added when I continued to stare.

We walked along with the crowd pressing in from all sides. Finally we reached the front of the stadium. Natasja started looking for a cab.

"Can we give you a lift?" I asked.

"Sure. We're staying at the Langham."

Made sense. Five-star hotel. The old man made millions. Thank God we brought the Land Rover and not the old Mitsubishi. Nice touch for a professional rugby player.

"Our car's around here somewhere, I think."

Natasja laughed.

After wandering up and down the back streets, I turned to Howcroft. "Where's the fucking car, yissur?"

His eyes were glazed over. No help there. I forged ahead.

"It's around here somewhere," I assured Natasja. "Can't be far now."

A few blocks later, I realized we had been walking around in circles.

Natasja stopped. "Perhaps it's best if I just grab a cab."

We stared at each other with the opportunity slipping away. Have you got the balls, I pictured her thinking. Her beauty and wealth did little for my nerves.

She's out of your league, I thought, but could not let it go.

"Why don't we…"

"Yes?" she said.

"Get a drink or something?"

She seemed both pleased and taken aback.

"Meet me at the hotel then. Just give the concierge my name."

I flagged a cab for her and they left. I was trying to keep my heart and my hard-on somewhat separate.

"Holy fucking shit," I said to Howcroft.

"I have no fucking idea how you do it," he said.

"Fortune favours the bold."

That bullshit had a nice ring to it.

"Just be honest with them, yissur," I added. "The birds love it. Now, where the fuck is that car?"

CHAPTER NINE

Having wandered the streets at length, we caught a cab – and passed the Land Rover a hundred yards later. We looked like a couple of rogues entering the Langham. Five stars was way above our pay grade, but I gave it my best swagger and approached the receptionist.

"Here for Natasja," I said.

"Freeman," he said.

"Could be, her husband's a professional football…" I said.

That struck a chord so he picked up the phone. "And your name is?"

"Michael."

He announced himself and who was waiting. After a moment of silence, he said, "Very well" and hung up the phone.

"She's just waiting for a childminder. Please wait in the foyer."

Howcroft and I walked down some steps into a grand, library style room and made ourselves comfortable in throne-like chairs.

"This is more like it, Howcroft. Civilized, eh? We'll be the new Posh and Becks."

The barman approached.

"Three bottles of Stella. And what do you want, yissur?"

"Same as," Howcroft said, slumped down in his chair.

"You all right?" I asked.

"Absolutely wasted. These tablets are wearing off. I don't think I can do this."

"Chin up, soldier. A few drinks and you'll be right."

We passed half an hour watching well-heeled guests come and go. Compared with birds I'd been knocking about with previously, this was a whole new ball game.

When the lift door opened one more time and Natasja finally walked out, I stood up. She calmly searched the area. A calf-length silver coat concealed her body.

When her headlamps turned my way, I waved and headed in her direction. Bits of advice I had heard over the years about dating came to mind. How to get a woman's knickers off, in ten moves or less. Look her in the eye. Be confident. Cocky but not arrogant. Act as if you couldn't care less if she wants it or not.

Most important, believe you are the prize.

Natasja took my clammy hand. Hers was as smooth as ivory.

We sat down. Her fingers were winking with gold and fine jewels. She smelled of some subtle fancy fragrance, nothing like a ten quid hooker. I was fired up simply by the way she crossed her legs.

"Can I get you a drink?"

"I'll…" she thought for a moment, "take a beer, why not?"

I caught the bartender's attention, ordered another round of Stella and looked into Natasja's striking green eyes.

"So you never finished telling me why you're in New Zealand."

"Oh, I love to travel and take Dylan on vacation."

Staring at me, her mood turned despairing and she looked away.

"Actually, I had to get away from America and the pressure. Divorce. It's been very difficult."

Her face flushed. She paused then continued.

"Look, I really don't want to talk about that, okay?"

The beers came, providing us with a convenient segue from talk of divorce. We toasted. Good health and all that. I was back staring into her beautiful green eyes.

"We went to Buenos Aires first to check on my property," she said with a nervous laugh. "Oh, and I met the All Blacks in a bar in Argentina. They were beautiful. Especially number eight. I figured I'd come get me a rugby player in New Zealand."

We were back to the subject of rugby and my lies. It was my turn to change the subject.

"I admire single women. Really. Take my hat off to you. I don't know how you do it. If I were on the ropes, I'd lock myself in my room. You women are made of sterner stuff."

"Oh, come on, you're a professional athlete."

I feigned modesty, hands up, hoping to God we could skip to the next topic.

"You must know it's hard being married to one," she said. "I was on my own a lot of the time while he was away playing."

I nodded, the friend, the doctor, the psychologist. Not this one, I wanted to say.

Out of the corner of my eye, I saw that Howcroft was staring at the floor.

"So what part of America are you from?"

"Oh, God," she said and laughed. "Rancho del Cielo. It's ridiculous."

The name "Rancho del Cielo" conjured images of old spaghetti Westerns in my mind. Dusty Mexican towns. Decaying churches. Men sleeping beneath their sombreros. Swinging doors and shots of mescal at the local cantina.

Back on earth, I asked Natasja why Rancho del Cielo was so ridiculous.

"Well, the people. You know? It's quite extravagant."

"Oh. Ridiculous in that way."

"Yes. It's one of the more exclusive communities in California. The people are so pretentious. Athletes, musicians, Forbes' wealthiest have homes there."

I kept staring with no display of emotion, playing it cool while I weighed up what all this meant. Was she full of shit? Or full of herself? Or was this finally my ticket to the easy life?

Natasja had a sip of her beer and looked back at me.

"What?" she said. "You can look it up. People get around in golf carts. It's crazy. All these multimillion-dollar homes. The guy across the road just installed a home theatre worth several hundred thousand dollars. The teachers at Dylan's school receive Christmas gifts from the parents. Private air travel, luxury vacations, you wouldn't believe it."

I nodded as if all this was routine to me. "And you were a model?"

"I suck as a model."

"You *suck* as a model?" I said with a raised eyebrow. "Oohhh, one of those kind of models."

That brought on a pause and a flicker away before Natasja looked back with her blushing smile. "Oh God, NO! That's so funny."

She leaned forward and tapped me on my leg. "Oh, I love it when people call me out like that."

I was starting to like what was inside this woman, not just the stunning exterior.

"So, you really weren't any good on the runway?"

"Never thought I was, although I did bring a couple of mil to the table when my ex and I met."

She threw the back of a hand to her mouth with a laugh, as if that was somehow quite amusing.

"What?" I said.

"Oh…just, with the ex making silly money, I used to warn my personal assistant to keep an eye on me whenever I withdrew some funds, just in case I typed in an extra zero."

I stared back.

"Imagine that. Must have been a rough existence."

That comment stopped her dead. Good, I thought. My appreciation for her had rapidly plummeted. Rich bitch, fretting about extra zeroes. And there were me and half the world, living on the breadline.

I was back to scheming over a bit of personal gratification. Then I noticed a dark cloud descend over Natasja's spirit. She smiled, but through a shitload of sadness.

What a turn. In less than a minute, I had gone from a growing fondness for this woman to disgust to now feeling pity.

As I studied Natasja, she bit her lip and shrugged in a way that invited more sympathy.

"It really can be so lonely where I live, you know? This big old house and me all alone in there for the most part."

I nodded and reached out a hand.

"I understand."

"Do you?"

"For sure. Loneliness and me are old friends."

That got me another sad smile, and a reassuring touch from her hand.

Natasja resumed her tale, about being the only woman her age around the neighbourhood and the likes. All the couples were from an older generation, and all the men were rich old lechers. Like that doctor, her one date since getting the divorce. He had driven up in a flashy, rented BMW, as if needing to impress someone. What a joke. Everyone was so phony.

"A pity. Men like that are giving the rest of us blokes a bad name."

The warm look on Natasja's face suggested that she was buying into my bullshit. Maybe it wasn't all bullshit, but enough so to leave me feeling a bit out on a limb.

"Fancy a drink at the marina?" I asked in the lingering silence.

"Sure, I'll just use the restroom."

When she left, Howcroft pulled his head up. "Fod, you're on your own. I'm chucking a whitey."

That was Manx slang for being sick on drugs. I watched him bolt through the reception area and out of the wide glass doors, glad to have him out of the way.

Natasja came back and asked about the missing Howcroft.

"He wasn't feeling so well."

"He didn't look so well."

I laughed. If only she knew the causes. "A taxi?"

"Sure," she said.

We caught one down to the restaurants along the marina. The place was a zoo with rugby fans, mostly Kiwis wearing their All Blacks gear. We sat on a patio outside a bar and talked some more. Out of the blue, Natasja brought up the subject of the universe and asked why I thought we were here.

"God knows," I said wryly.

"Do you believe in God?" she asked.

"No, no," I said, fearing it was a weakness to admit otherwise.

"I've been searching for years," she said. "I've tried all sorts of spiritual practices. I was a born-again Christian, but that got crazy. I found myself surrounded by people speaking in tongues, and that wasn't going to work. Now I go to a church in Los Angeles. Mainly black people dancing and jumping in the aisles. They have the best music and the reverend is just incredible."

"Does it have a white steeple and picket fence?"

She laughed. "No, it's modern. New concept, ancient wisdom. Science of the mind, based on old teachings."

I raised an eyebrow. Bloody cult sounding to me. Definitely leading in the wrong direction. Back to Mum and a lifetime of religious crap. I had travelled to the far side of the world hoping to escape such dreary dogma, amongst other things.

Natasja must have sensed me fretting about hell and the afterlife because she laughed.

"It's spiritual," she said. "Really. It's all about the laws of the universe. It resonates with me anyway. I get so much from it. It's where I find God."

I was still paralysed by visions of the old church on Sunday. Natasja tilted her head to get me out of my spell.

"I'm making you uncomfortable, aren't I?"

"Not really."

"Are you sure? I'm sorry."

"No, don't take it to heart, luv. Let's take a walk."

Seeing her disarmed by my indifference, I doubled down on it. I had her on the ropes and liked that feeling.

We walked across the marina and along the quay overlooking the rows of superyachts and boats docked in the harbour.

Her voice came up out of the silence. "If you could be any animal, what would you be?" she asked me.

Good God, not this touchy-feely new age crap again.

"So, what would you be?" she said again, grabbing my elbow.

"A lion, I suppose."

"What would be your second choice," she asked.

"A silverback gorilla," I said, wanting out of the game. "And you?"

"A bird. They're so free. You know, it's so isolating where I live. I don't see people for long periods of time and I need to be around people."

She was back on that bit, but it wasn't so touching the second time around.

Sensing my distance, Natasja checked her watch.

"I should get back to check on my son."

I reached out my hand, fearing I was about to lose her and everything she represented to me – beauty, sex, the high life with a goddess and a television set with more than three working channels.

She squeezed my hand in apology.

"Sorry, my mind was wandering. A lot going on these days."

I squeezed back and hailed a cab.

"Did you want to come in for another drink?" she said back at the hotel.

"Sure, why not?" I said and paid the taxi driver.

"I'm just going to check on Dylan," Natasja said in the lobby.

"I'll be at the bar waiting. What'll you have?"

"A bottle of Beck's."

Beck's. There was that name again. I strolled through the lobby, imagining the press. Famous wife and her famous athlete husband. A quick nod for the lads and it was off to play polo.

In the bar, I ordered two bottles of Beck's and swiftly consumed mine. I had ordered a second one and was hiding the first when Natasja returned. Things were definitely starting to feel edgy. I'd gone six hours without feeding the beast some drugs.

I stood up and pulled out a chair for her, then helped ease the jacket from her shoulders. Nice touch of chivalry, and a coat of veneer over my deteriorating condition.

I sat down. She remained standing. The curves looked even more spectacular from the bottom side up.

"Everything okay?" I said.

She hesitated, then sat with her arms on the carved wooden armrests. Her fingers were delicately exploring the knobs on the ends. I looked up to find her staring at me.

"Is this an opportunity to fuck?" she said without expression.

With those words, everything pathetic about my existence flashed through my head. Did I want to fuck? Jesus. Do you really know who you're thinking to fuck here?

Under the weight of my blank gaze, she seemed to blush.

"What? I just want to know."

I placed my bottle on the table with deliberate care.

"Well, I'm not saying it would never happen. It's just that I don't really know you that well."

That clearly intrigued Natasja and stopped her in her tracks. Just the reaction I was looking for.

"Actually, just bear with me," I said and went out to the reception desk.

"How much for your cheapest room?" I enquired.

"$300 a night."

"How much per hour?"

I was thinking of my debit card. It was maybe $100 in the black, and that was if my payroll cheque had come through.

"Not this hotel, sir."

"Can I view the room?" I asked.

"I'll have a member of staff take you up, sir."

"No, no need for that. Just give me the key. I'll have a look on my own. See if it's worth the money."

"Sorry, sir," he said and called to a member of staff. "Please show this gentleman Room 328."

The staff member followed me into the bar as I went back to check with Natasja.

"Just going to check out this room. Be right back."

After a quick viewing of the room, I told the young man it wasn't worth the money. We were leaving when Natasja showed up.

"I was just telling this young man I didn't think it was worth $300."

The staff member started down the hallway.

"It looked okay to me," Natasja said.

"I don't mind the money, but I hate anyone taking advantage of me. Any chance we could put Dylan out in the corridor for a few hours?"

She tapped me on the arm.

"Oh, my God, you're silly. I'm going to bed."

She pulled a piece of paper out of her purse and wrote down her phone number.

"Call me tomorrow."

She came closer and stood on her tiptoes to kiss me. She stared into my eyes before she turned down the corridor.

"See ya," I said as she walked away.

I strutted through the hotel lobby with the appropriate swagger. The top banana. Now all I had to do was find some way home. After hitching a ride and walking several blocks, I arrived there and found Dion asleep on the sofa, wearing my jeans and clutching a bottle of brandy to his bollocks. Empty beer bottles were strewn all over the tables, chairs and floor. The room was saturated with burned bacon fumes. I could feel the grease on my skin. From swanky hotel back to my decaying pit of humanity. I checked on Howcroft and found him asleep in his room.

First order of business, I grabbed a cold Corona and turned on the computer. A quick Google search brought up Natasja's ex-husband's name, stats and career earnings. The woman hadn't lied. The lads back home would not believe my good luck.

Second on the agenda was to confirm my own career status. A search of Bradford Bulls Rugby Club revealed basic facts but very few particulars about ex-players. Well, that ought to cover my arse. I'd say I was in retirement. A tough career. Plagued by injuries and leave it like that.

The next morning, I awakened still half tanked up and gob-smacked by what had transpired the day before. Was that a dream or what?

I went straight for another cold Corona in the fridge and used it to ease down four painkillers. Some cut-price tequila scorched my throat and straightened me out. Dion was still asleep in the dim morning light. Al Jazeera was droning on about Iraqi war stories in the background.

I walked back into my bedroom and noticed Natasja's phone number scribbled on a piece of paper. It was real. My urge was to call home. Brag to all the lads. Instead, I busted open Howcroft's door.

He sat up with a start. An open novel flew off his chest onto the floor. He had fallen asleep with his glasses on. They were halfway down his nose and he hurriedly shoved them back in place as I showed him the phone number.

"Hey boy! Did you get a load of that? Look. It was fucking real!"

I went out to show Dion.

"Soldieeerrr!" I called out.

Still half asleep, Dion started mumbling some crap.

"Captain, sergeant, parachute regiment, 8879761524, reporting for duty captain sir, over and out."

He looked at me groggily. Howcroft came into the room wearing his boxer shorts, hanging a cigarette out of his mouth. I started telling Dion about my claim to being a professional rugby player. We had a good laugh.

He stood finally and nodded sheepishly at my jeans. "Crapped my own pants, squadron leader."

He made light work of a Corona and headed out of the door. "Thanks for the hospitality, soldiers. I'll get your jeans back to you tomorrow."

Howcroft sat down with his own beer. "Nobody will ever believe you back on the Isle of Man. You'd better get some pictures."

I called the Langham Hotel, all charged up, but Natasja was out. I left a message and sat down to stare at the clock. Uncertainty crept in with the hours. My cockiness steadily evaporated. The swagger had gone completely out of me by the time Natasja finally called back later in the day.

"Hey, why don't you come over for a swim? We'd love to see you."

And just like that, the show was back on.

"Be right there."

I showered quickly, did everything chemically possible to get my flight path headed in the right direction and borrowed Howcroft's Land Rover.

"Michaaaaeelll," Dylan shouted in the hotel lobby. He ran over and gave me a hug.

"My mom's upstairs at the rooftop pool."

We pushed the button for the lift. It was empty except for the two of us on the way up. Dylan started badgering me with questions.

"Are you really a professional rugby player?"

"No, not really."

"You aren't?" he said, despondent.

"Nah, yeah, of course I am. Just keeping a low profile, you know."

"And you still play?"

"Retired now. That's why I'm over here."

"So what do you do now?

"Computer projects for film and television."

"Like what?"

"Like the new Halo 3."

He formed a gun with his fingers.

"Are you kidding me? I love Halo. That's my favourite game."

God help me if I ever had to tell him the truth.

Stepping out onto the sun deck, I saw why I had to maintain the deception. Natasja. She was lying on a lounger in her bikini, 5 feet 10 inches of heaven on earth.

We exchanged a discreet kiss on the cheek.

"I'll just change here in the locker room."

Inside, I had a look at myself in the mirror and winced. A few flexes of the old biceps did nothing to change things. A life of excess. Part of being a rugby star. She'd understand. I did a quick twenty push-ups. Back straight. Contract the gut. Best foot forward. Fuck it. The emotional turmoil followed me out to the pool.

"You not coming in?" I said.

Natasja shook her head. Dylan was splashing about. To entertain him, I hung onto the railing and pretended to be walking on water. Dylan laughed. I had a sideways look at Natasja. Confirmed. The bonding exercise had gained me serious bonus points.

"We're leaving tomorrow," Natasja said as the day got late. "Why don't you come over and see us off?"

I was gutted to think she was going so soon. A couple of days and I had grown completely hooked.

As requested, I returned the next day and the three of us strolled down Queen Street in Auckland city centre. Close as a little family we were. Not exactly what I had in mind for a send-off, but I played my part.

Amidst our tender little displays of public affection, Natasja window-shopped at all the high-end designer stores dotting Queen Street.

"I really need a new watch," she said with a look in a jeweller's window.

Jesus. The symbols of prestige. The toys of wealth and power. She had said that about the watch as if with a casual flick of the hand. And all I could do was tag along.

The jeweller buzzed us in. Natasja picked through the watches and finally laid one across her wrist. "What do you think?" she said.

"How much?" I asked the clerk.

"$9,995."

I held up my palms.

"What can I do? I earn it, she spends it!"

She shook her head and pointed a finger at me.

"Go on. You can have the watch. You've got the card."

I nodded at the clerk and he buzzed me out of the exit. While Natasja blew ten grand on a bauble, I stood outside with fifty dollars to my name. I had found my role in life. A gigolo.

Back at the Langham, a limo arrived to take them to the airport. Dylan and I said our goodbyes. He got into the long car and watched over the back seat. Natasja pulled me to a spot out of his sightline.

"Don't let him see," she said and kissed me hard. At the end she held onto my bottom lip with hers.

"We'll talk," she whispered in my ear and gave my hands one final squeeze.

I waved until the limo had disappeared out of sight. On the way back to the Land Rover, I puffed out my chest again. Held in my stomach. Back straight. Had to get into that world-class shape. I felt like a million dollars but looked like half a quid.

Over the coming days, a sage observation my dad once made frequently passed through my head. My sister would work hard for whatever she got. Conversely, I would either marry a rich woman or win the lottery. Or be a bum. Well, I now had the winning lottery ticket in my hands, but with the lies I had told Natasja, it was a ticket I wasn't likely to cash.

Desperate as much as I was undaunted, I downed a few beers and several whiskies one evening and gave Natasja a call. I had a whole load of banter about wild sex, first-class travel and fine hotels lined up, but instead she droned on about her busy day. Everything led back to the laws of attraction, universal principles and quantum physics. And God. God, God, God. The mere mention of the word made me squirm. Yet she said she had disavowed Christianity, so what god did she mean? One you could only find in tinsel town?

"All I ask is that you're honest with me," Natasja said as we ended the conversation.

And there you have it. The one thing I did not know how to do.

We exchanged e-mail addresses and Natasja started to send me photos of herself: by the pool, at the Four Seasons in Hawaii, with friends on the beach in La Jolla. She wanted a picture of me. Little did she know that this technological design guru did not own a camera.

I e-mailed her an old graduation photo, with my ex-girlfriend cropped out. The e-mail that came back was on a completely different subject.

"Oops," she concluded. "Where are my manners? Nice prom photo!!!"

Having underestimated my ability to be wounded and completely juvenile, I decided to ignore her e-mail and end the fledgling love affair.

Half an hour later, I caved in and wrote back…

The next morning, I was up the street creaking open the door of the rusted Mitsubishi when the phone rang. It was Natasja.

"How are ya, my lovely? I'm a bit late for work."

"Just missed the sound of your voice."

Elated, I held the flip phone to my cheek and used a McDonald's wrapper to mop the rainwater off the front seat. With the obligatory morning beer placed judiciously between my legs, I turned on the ignition, let off the handbrake and waited for the car to start rolling. Once I got the engine jump-started and the fairground waltzer was under way, I returned my attention to the conversation.

I was feeling particularly stressed out that morning, but maybe Natasja could offer a solution. Help ease the burden of my financial concern. The problem was, a retired athlete of my calibre, with a high-profile film and TV career on his hands, shouldn't have any financial pressure, and not even I could come up with the bullshit necessary to explain that one away.

"Sometimes all I want to do is don a saffron robe," came out of my mouth. "Shave my head and go find myself up a mountain in Tibet."

"Sounds like a great idea," she said.

Too bad. An invitation to America and permanent retirement had been my true hope.

"Do you think people can change?" she asked me out of the blue.

For fuck's sake, I hope so, I thought. Otherwise, once she finds out I'm full of shit, there'll be no cause to give me another chance.

"Yes, I do," I said as I stopped at a busy intersection. "But listen, luv. I'm on my way to work. We'll touch base and put the world to rights later on, all good?"

Natasja allowed me a slick exit, but as I pulled into the work carpark, she was calling again.

"Michael, I just found out my phone bill was over $1,000 this month. How much is it costing you?"

Who knew? I did not have a bill in my name. I had never had a bill in my name. I was buying $20 worth of minutes at a time for my pay-as-you-go flip phone.

Grasping for the latest line of bullshit, I told Natasja I was on a long-distance roaming contract for international calls. I called so many foreign countries as part of my business, it was hard to tell what was what.

Silence met this latest claim. Ah, Jesus. Had I gone too far this time?

"What do you actually do for work now?" she asked me.

"I'm the lead visual artist here. Special effects for film and TV."

More bullshit. What I actually did was take photos, measure the walls, do a sketch and help some merchant obtain a permit for his renovation. I always looked the part, though. Kept up the show: clipboard in hand, pencil behind the ear. Tap the walls here and there.

"Would you mind taking one end of the measuring tape there, Mr Steep?"

A bit of that and I'd hit a bar. Call it a day. My alcohol and drug consumption were now in direct proportion to the scale of my deceit.

I had been awaiting Natasja's response. I was not prepared for the subsequent shocker.

What did I think about coming to visit her in America?

"Uh, sounds like a great idea, but I'll have to check my workload. Everything needs to be done yesterday in this business, ya know? In fact, speaking of workload, I've arrived at the office so I'd better go."

I turned the key, at which point the Mitsubishi shut itself off with a death rattle.

"What was that?" Natasja said.

"Oh, nothing." I laughed nonchalantly. "One of the interns showing up for work. An old clunker for a set of wheels."

"So, what do you think about the trip?" she said.

Game on. I already had Howcroft in the guesthouse. My drinking partner in retirement. Run the vineyard and split time between the Southern California hacienda and the Côte d'Azur.

"Let me check my schedule and I'll get back to you."

"Great. Call me back today if you can. I'm dying to see you."

I hung up in a panic. I could barely afford to speak to her on the phone, never mind plan a trip to the States.

I called Howcroft and explained the situation.

"Getting time off work's no problem, but I'm broke. Every spare penny goes on making the phone calls. How do I get out of this?"

"You're on your own," he said and hung up.

I called Natasja on my first break.

"Listen, luv. The schedule's a bit tight at the minute. Plus the low Bank of England base rates are causing havoc with the payments on my property portfolio."

"I'll pay for the tickets," she said.

I had a sneaking suspicion that might be the case. Just my luck.

"Just go book them," she added, "and tell them to call me to confirm."

"Look, I couldn't accept that."

"There's nothing to accept. It's a gift. Take it and say thank you."

"All right. I'll call you about this later."

"There's only one thing. You'll need to stay at a hotel in La Jolla for the first week. Come for two weeks. Dylan will be at his dad's place for the second week, so you can stay with me then."

A damned hotel? Out of whose pocket? This bullshitting about money was about to drive me mad.

I went out after work to jump-start the car. There was a roadside garage just down the lane. I drove by it every day on the way home. Batteries $25.

Tomorrow, I told myself one more time. Tomorrow I'll buy a new battery.

The gap between my real life and this fantasy one seemed to be growing by the day. Natasja talking phone sex for three hours. Me sitting with Howcroft in our basement apartment with a fence outside the window and the three working TV channels. Have another Corona. Try not to get too close to the truth. Christ, I was broke and owed Howcroft three grand. And my sister the better part of five grand. The whole idea of showing up in California with my bullshit was terrifying.

"I need another grand before I go," I told Howcroft that evening. "I've got to pay for a motel room at the beach for a week. Any chance? Your name's on my guest house. I promise you."

"Okay, but this is the last time," he said. "And anyway, hasn't she had a kid?"

"So?"

"So, it'll be like throwing a baguette down Parliament Street when you fuck her."

"Fucking charming," I told him.

"Just speaking the truth, yissur."

CHAPTER TEN

With Howcroft's money in hand, I went to see a dentist and had the heroin stains removed from my front teeth. The barber was next. A few grey hairs touched up. A few hours in the sun. Add some colour to the cheeks. Then I hit a clinic about the wart-like blemish on the end of my cock. It had appeared without warning a few years back, but I brushed it aside, like most things surrounding my heroin addiction.

The doctor came out looking like Darth Vader in white. The flask in his hand was giving off smoke from the frozen nitrogen. A chemical peel for the genitals.

"Place your penis on the table," he told me.

I did as instructed and waited. He dipped a swab into the flask, pulled it out and branded me like a steer. I winced like hell. He put things away. Two days later, the blemish turned black and dropped off.

I was ready for America.

Natasja called me the night before I left.

"I have one request," she said.

"Anything you like, my luv."

"Please don't drink on the flight."

Not a flinch from me about her request. Thankfully, she said nothing about drugs.

Entering the 747 a few days later, I knew immediately that a few drinks were in order. From there on in, I let my arsenal of drugs take over. I had roughly twelve hours before we landed in Los Angeles. A few breath mints and Natasja would not suspect a thing.

Our embrace in the arrival area at Los Angeles was mostly hips to hips passion, anyway. With the breath mints and a bit of astute bullshitting, I was able to guide Natasja out of the terminal without too many questions.

"You're awfully quiet," she said on our way to the parking lot.

Valium will do that to you.

"Hell of a long flight," I said and threw my arm around her.

Out at her black Escalade, she popped the boot to leather-lined elegance. Like everything about Natasja, it smelled of money.

It was a vision of luxury and ease towards which I had striven all my life, right there before my eyes, mine for the taking, and it scared the shit out of me.

A roughly two-hour journey from LA down to her place north of San Diego followed. Interstate 5 eventually came along the coast, then passed through Camp Pendleton, Oceanside, Encinitas, Solana Beach and Del Mar. At La Jolla, Natasja turned inland and negotiated a winding road up through rolling hills and citrus groves. Eucalyptus trees dotted the horizon like sentinels. The mountains were ahead, the ocean behind us.

Rancho del Cielo had no streetlights or pavements. Equestrian trails lined the roads. All the homes were tucked discreetly back from the street. Natasja explained the protective covenant. A design board made sure that even the biggest buildings blended into the landscape. Spanish, Mediterranean or ranch-style homes were your choices.

It was ten million a pop, and for that you could join the country club.

Natasja drove to the end of a secluded cul-de-sac and then onto a long drive. When we stopped in front of a sprawling colonial revival, Christmas cards with my monogrammed smoking jacket came to mind. Throw in a gold duck's head cane and a brandy snifter. It appeared I might have to ditch the concrete lions on the gateposts, but this Viking had found his home.

Inside, I dropped my overnight bag and received the tour. The open plan layout was gracious, the ceilings lofted. Opulence everywhere I looked. Natasja explained that her hand-carved, Chinese, four-poster canopy bed had put her out the cost of a condo.

Of course. Didn't they all?

We went out of her glass bedroom doors to the back patio. An elevated Jacuzzi overflowed into a deep pool. Sun loungers and hand-painted Mexican pots embellished the stone deck. Eucalyptus trees rustled over the canyons. A brightly coloured hot-air balloon swooped low over the property.

"Why don't you use the pool?" Natasja said. "I'll join you in a minute. There's beer in the fridge."

I grabbed a cold beer and made myself comfortable in the Jacuzzi. Natasja came out of her bedroom doors a short while later in a blue bikini. If she hadn't been crafted by the most skilled plastic surgeons, she certainly looked like it.

When she sat next to me on the ledge, I gripped her ankle and pulled.

"What do you think you're doing, young man?"

"Just very, very glad to see you."

"You can just wait until we've gone to see Dylan playing football."

After a shower, a shave and a wank, we drove over to a nearby elementary school. Dylan was playing quarterback.

"That's Dontrell," said Natasja and pointed at a tall man on the opposite side of the field.

On the next play, Dylan fumbled the ball.

"Damn it, Dylan!" Dontrell shouted out. "Concentrate! What the hell are you doing?"

At hearing his father's disappointment, Dylan's shoulders drooped. He looked like he'd given up. It brought back all that shit with my old man.

The game was soon over and Dylan walked off the field, looking despondent.

I hugged him.

"I hate him shouting at me," he said with a nod towards his dad. "I hate him. Plus, I have to pretend that I like that Wendy he's married."

"I understand, little man," I said.

He did a double-take on my shorts and dropped his head in shame.

"What?" I said.

"They're bikini shorts."

He started off, sulking again.

Natasja choked back a laugh. I called after Dylan.

"Your mother suggested I wear them!"

She had in a way, proposing I opt for function over fashion. To me they were part of a comfortable European ensemble. Who gave a shit if the shorts barely covered my bollocks?

I looked at Natasja. She was still choking back laughter.

"Thanks very much for that, luv."

"Your legs look spectacular," she reassured me.

In trying to manage the tribe, Natasja dragged me after the sulking Dylan and we somehow found ourselves walking past Dontrell. He wasn't happy about seeing Natasja with another man, or about anything that I could tell.

"I told you," she said to me. "Angry man."

"Hey Dontrell, have a nice day!" she called out over her shoulder. He tilted his head back as if to say fuck you. Natasja looked back at me and laughed. "Oh, he's pissed now."

As we approached the beach in La Jolla, my head started to spin. My stomach was churning. Were we headed to a cheap motel or the Ritz? And was Natasja paying? I had no credit cards, and the debit card associated with my bank account wouldn't hold a slot on a campsite.

Pulling up to the motel, I saw Natasja had split the difference. The place was within walking distance of the beach but otherwise your bog-standard lodging.

As feared, Natasja stood back as I checked in. The receptionist gave me a form to fill out and asked for my credit card. I put on a show rifling through my wallet and bag, tapping my back pockets.

"Would you Adam and Eve it? I forgot to bring my bloody credit cards."

"You forgot your credit card?" Natasja said with a look of suspicion.

"Yeah, don't know how that happened. I've got plenty of cash, though."

Natasja shook her head and pulled a credit card out of her purse.

"Here, I've got the cash right now," I said.

"It's late. I'm going home. We'll deal with it in the morning. I'll be over and we'll go to the zoo."

I got a peck on the cheek. I watched her drive off, wounded, feeling I had lost her. This required alcohol at the very least.

I dropped my bags in the room and walked over to the restaurant next door. They had a beachside terrace. Everything from the people to the lawn looked perfectly manicured.

Realizing I was close to Mexico, a prime source of over-the-counter pain medication, I considered making a run to the border but decided against it, called it a night and hit the sack.

The following day, we did the zoo run, then a late dinner at Natasja's house. Dylan went off to sleep. We had a moonlight swim. She held on to the pool's edge and wrapped her legs around me, pulling me tight.

"You want some of this," she said, easing herself out of the pool and leaving me with a vision of her fit arse through a wet bikini bottom.

Women, I thought as I watched her sashay off to the bedroom. When they want it, wherever they want it.

At her bedroom door, I was summoned to the bed with the wave of a finger. I started at the lithe ankles and worked my way up her calf and thighs. It was warm in there behind the wet bikini bottom. With fingernails running down my spine, she pulled at my shorts with the other hand. I helped peel them off at my throbbing cock. As she came at it, I pinned both her hands above her head. There was a scramble to get the bikini off and I was in.

"Do...not...stop," she said. "I mean...continue."

She was using positive reinforcement. Like training a fucking dog. We rolled around for hours. At some point I was accused of taking Viagra.

"It's all your fault," I told her.

She liked hearing that.

Before wrapping up, she went off to the master bathroom.

"Mind if I call Howcroft?" I asked.

"Go ahead," she said over her shoulder.

"What the fuck are you doing phoning me, you crackpot?" he said.

"Just wanted to let you know. It's not true what they say about women with kids. She's been doing her kegels. Nothing like throwing a baguette down Parliament Street."

"Fuck you. I'm sitting here in front of the computer with my pants round my ankles."

He hung up. Natasja glanced around the corner with a smile.

"Everything all right?"

"Couldn't be better."

She went back to humming in the bathroom. I had to pinch myself. Could hardly believe my good fortune.

We did Balboa Park the next day, the beach at Del Mar, meals out in La Jolla and downtown San Diego every night, a personal trainer for our runs through the neighbourhood horse trails. It was decadent and spot on. I began to wonder when Natasja would ask me to move in permanently.

When Dylan left to stay at his father's place, I moved in temporarily to the guest suite.

With me pissed up on booze the following evening, Natasja came around with the phone and handed it to me. "Michael, confirm you're fit to play tomorrow."

"Who's that?" I said, covering the mouthpiece.

Natasja waved for me to get on with the call.

"Hey, it's Brody," the voice said. "Thanks for agreeing to be the guest star at tomorrow's match."

"What?" I said.

"The rugby tomorrow. Natasja set it up so you could be our guest star. What position do you want to play?"

"Oh, aye, right, second row would be my first choice, blind-side flanker."

"Thanks, man. I can't believe we'll have a real pro on our team."

"Looking forward to it, mate."

I hung up with a smile for Natasja. Either she believed me or she was on to my shit.

The following morning, I awakened with a start. Natasja was calling from the other room. "Michael, it's time to go! We need to be there!"

"Be where?" I shouted.

My head was throbbing. I could hardly remember the night before.

"The rugby match! Hurry up!"

"What rugby match?" I shouted back.

Then it hit me. Oh fuck, no. My bullshit was about to catch up with me.

"I'm knackered," I shouted.

"You promised! You can't let them down now!"

Contrary to my every effort, I was soon in the car and on the way to my godforsaken destiny. One of the greatest players of all time, and I had no real clue about the bloody rules.

Out on the field, the players formed a semicircle around me like I was the quarterback. Questions and handshakes came at me from all angles. Again, I was asked what position I wanted to play. I told them second row. I knew that much.

They were all waiting for me to lead the way. I had a sudden inspiration.

"Look, lads, I'm gonna give it a miss. No boots an' all that."

This led to everyone sizing up my feet.

"Size 12," one of them said and kicked off his own boots. "These will fit. I'll sit out the game."

I tried to opt out for lack of a mouthpiece next.

"Wouldn't want to ruin these lovely British teeth."

I forced out a laugh. In response, someone handed me his mouthpiece.

"I don't know where your mouth has been," I said, laughing again.

When all else seemed to be failing, I pleaded my hungover state.

"Look, lads. I had a few too many last night. Not a hundred per cent fit for action, if you know what I mean."

There was grumbling all around.

"Well, can you come and train us sometime?" one of them asked.

"Sure, no problem," I said.

"How about Tuesday?"

"Yeah, that should be all right."

I spent the game alternately criticizing their play to Natasja and yelling corrective encouragement from the sidelines. When my voice grew hoarse, I spotted an enthusiastic young disabled lad amongst the spectators and rolled a rugby ball back and forth with him. Made his day. Set me up as the poster boy for Make a Wish Foundation.

On Sunday morning, I awakened this time to a voice bellowing through the speaker system of the house.

"GOD IS GOOD."

The floor-to-ceiling windows were opened to the pool. The Santa Ana winds were blowing a dry, hot wind through the room.

What the fuck? I thought.

"Who's that?" I called out to Natasja.

The smell of freshly baked buttermilk biscuits followed her into the room. She came in and lay with her arms on my chest.

"That's Reverend Morgan. You're going to love it today. It's choir Sunday."

She went on about the reverend and some fella named Jesse. "Who's Jesse?"

"He's my amazing spiritual director. He just keeps me grounded in truth."

I hated it when a woman called another man amazing. I hated it even more to hear this bloke was Natasja's spiritual guide.

"And he works at this church?" I said.

"In his spare time. He's actually a personal trainer in LA. He trains Alissa Klein."

Alissa fucking Klein, I thought. Now we're talking.

While Natasja named off all the A-list celebrities this guy trained, I was picturing all the introductions. Fuck me. No more looking down my nose at this lot. This was my kind of social circle.

If only we could dispense with the bloody reverend. While Natasja went off to dress, I lay there being browbeaten by his guru status.

"You are a spiritual being, having a physical experience."

Fuck that. I was a bloody Manxman having a murderous hangover.

On the way up to Los Angeles, the reverend continued to berate me. "Align yourself with what is."

Natasja laughed at the look on my face. "It's all working to improve you on a subconscious level."

"Brainwashing is more like it."

She smiled. I didn't. I felt myself being corralled and wanted to bolt.

At the church entrance, we were welcomed by a bubbly, multicultural gathering, a celebrity peppered here and there amongst the crowd, the whole lot brimming with zest for their new world order. Never seen such a diverse bunch, so full of life. My first reaction was discomfort but I decided fuck it. My brain had gone to work. I smelled money and opportunity, somewhere in the thick of this lot.

"Isn't this just amazing?" the mother said.

"Lovely, lovely," I said.

My mind was on the nearest bar as the queue swept us inside.

The place was alive with laughter, bright clothes and extravagant headgear, and every seat taken. We had to negotiate around a camera crew set up in the middle aisle. This was not my parents' church. No hint of fire and brimstone. Not a shrine or cross in sight. I could only imagine my mother's feelings of betrayal.

Towards the front, Natasja introduced me to a man who immediately hugged me. I laughed nervously. Natasja covered her face in laughter. This was not grounds for humour. At every turn, this circus was getting me further and further out of my comfort zone.

While I shuffled my feet, Natasja and her friend chatted on and on about the annual church dinner. The bloke with the hugs thanked Natasja for her financial contribution. It turned out that Natasja had sold a home for several million and given fifteen per cent to fund these bloody bastards.

"At least we've got reserved seats on the front row," she told me.

An odd million quid for a plastic seat on the front fucking row. Charity begins at home, I wanted to tell her. We could have bought a vineyard on the Côte d'Azur and had our feet kicked up with that kind of money.

We took our plastic seats with the choir singing in our faces. The crowd was clapping along and shouting hallelujah. Natasja chipped in that the members of the choir were Madonna's backup singers. I nodded and got on with scanning the crowd. Bloody opportunity everywhere you looked, but one more hallelujah and I was bolting for the nearest bar.

Finally, a man with dreadlocks strolled onto the stage, beaming from ear to ear. "Do we have anyone NEW to Phos?" he said.

Oh, fuck no, I thought. How do I make sprinting for the exit look graceful?

"Come on, all of you. Please stand and identify yourselves."

Natasja elbowed me. I stood up like someone missing his pants in the middle of Main Street. A smattering of others like me popped up throughout the audience.

157

The reverend held his hands wide. "Let's show these people some LOVE!!!! Hold up your hands to the person nearest you."

Everyone turned and raised their hands. The choir resumed and the crowd sang along. Amid the group grope I was thinking fondly of a staid service in old St Paul's Church on the Isle of Man.

The reverend began to preach about gravity and the laws of attraction.

"There ain't no man at the pearly gates."

Bloody blasphemy. I waited for the bolt of lightning.

It dawned on me suddenly that I had never questioned my parents' Christian beliefs. My concept of God was based on lazy, unexamined assumptions. Heaven and hell were physical locations to me. Destinations for the afterlife. Perfect behaviour from here on out would secure me an interview with the Big Guy. A few good politically correct jokes and I'd be straight in through the Pearly Gates.

Or I could go on as things were and keep my appointment with the beast at the gates of hell.

Lost in these reveries, I came back to the extravaganza. When did they pass out the Kool-Aid? Who'll be the first to speak in tongues and roll on the floor?

But audience participation was not required. Things were left at a great stage show, with lots of happy, exuberant people who were perhaps modestly more deluded than me.

When the show ended, the audience stood and applauded. After several minutes of adulation, the reverend walked offstage and came up the aisle. All eyes were on me as the reverend shook my hand. The Hollywood messiah had anointed me.

"What the fuck was that all about?" I asked Natasja as we headed up the aisle.

She was shaking hands with the A-list crowd. I was trying not to look stupid.

"I let the reverend know that I wanted to introduce you, but there's just too much going on. We'll have to meet him and Jesse another day."

Natasja took me for a tour up in the Hollywood Hills. Rising Glenn off Sunset Boulevard.

"I'll live up here one day," I told her with a look back out over the Strip, absolutely convinced that I would own a piece of the place sometime soon.

Two days later, I was on my way back to Auckland and my basement apartment. From chic to shoddy. At least now I could get back to fixing my head properly.

There had been a lot of hugging and promises there at the end. We'd call each other every day. Natasja had plans to visit me soon in New Zealand.

Even Dylan was sad to see me go. He was a load for my addictions at times, but after seeing him rejected by his old man, I felt for the little fella. Maybe I could keep my shit together long enough to actually be worthy of his trust.

As for Southern California, I could not imagine myself living anywhere else in the world now. One taste of the high life and I was hooked. There was no going back.

God help me if I fucked this one up.

CHAPTER ELEVEN

I went on with my crazed bipolar existence, accelerating on its swift descent into hell. I had Natasja and our three-hour phone sessions on the one hand and the reality of my cheap apartment and bullshit job on the other. Natasja thought I had land holdings and an international reputation. What I had was a reputation for being a no-show. On a good day, I made it into work by 11.

"Fucking hell," the staff would greet me and reach for the windows. "You smell like a brewery."

The boss would look up and silently nod.

I'd try making light of my sins, but the joke was wearing thin.

One day my worst fears were realized. Natasja said she was coming to visit, and no subtle dissembling on my part could dissuade her. Bad timing with the job. Critical business deadline looming. My roommate had his mum and sister over staying with us. Natasja brushed aside my every effort and gave me her itinerary.

A week later, I was standing in arrivals at Auckland airport, swinging the keys to a BMW. With Howcroft's Land Rover in the repair shop, I had to lean on Dion for his wheels. Of all the cars to borrow, I thought, remembering the doctor who had rented a BMW to impress Natasja on their first date. But anything to disguise my pathetic state of affairs. A guy with no car of his own, a basement apartment and his sister paying the rent.

I stood there sweating the truth. How was I going to soften the blow? Natasja had asked me for the address and had viewed the property on Google maps. She thought I owned the house and the plot of land. What would she say when she saw my dive apartment and realized I did not own a thing?

There was an alternative plan: tell her the truth. One look at Natasja coming down the gangway, though, and I put that bright idea to rest.

"Aye up, luv," I said, taking her bags.

She was all talk on our way out to the parking lot.

"Where's the Land Rover? Whose car is this?" she said when I popped the boot of the silver BMW.

"The Land Rover's having trouble. A friend of mine let me borrow this for the week."

That was a candid confession, as far as it went.

"Are we going to your house?" she said along the way.

"I was thinking you could settle into your hotel room first."

"I thought your house was on the way."

"Well, we'll get to that."

She shook me by the shoulder. "No, I want to see it."

"Er…All right."

My head raced with a thousand lines of bullshit. I was ready to have a stroke as we pulled into the driveway.

"So this is all your property, right?" Natasja said.

"I'm just down here," I said and led her down the steps to the back apartment.

The end was near. I opened the front door and cringed at the sight. The bathroom door was open. Howcroft had chucked some orange cleanser disinfectant in the toilet, and the green lime scale was showing through. One plate stood washed and erect in the tray. The sunlight glared on the greasy countertop. The place had a middle school locker room feel. You could see the carpet lines from where I had vacuumed earlier in the day. Axe deodorant freshened the air.

Natasja did a 360 in the middle of the room, taking it all in. You could have cut the tension with a knife. I assumed my face was red. I prepared myself for our last goodbyes.

"This is where you live?" Natasja said with a furrowed brow and a look of confusion.

"For the time being," I replied eagerly.

Natasja seemed to accept this qualification.

"Okay, I'm done. Let's go to the hotel."

I tried to make small talk on the way to the hotel. All I got were yes and no answers. It's all over, I thought. Natasja was all matter of fact.

At the hotel on the Devonport waterfront, Natasja checked in and unpacked her bags while I watched.

Out came her camera case.

"Let's go up to Muriwai," she said. "I want to photograph the gannet colony. And I want to view some properties in St Mary's Bay."

St Mary's Bay. The most expensive properties in Auckland, possibly in all of New Zealand. I was included on the journey but as what? The tour guide? I saw no further use for me in her life beyond that.

As we drove up the coast, I heard the rustling of wrappers and looked over at Natasja on the passenger side.

"Michael, Michael," she said with a big smile, her teeth and mouth covered in chocolate. "Give me a kiss."

"For fuck's sake," I said, shaking my head. "No manners whatsoever."

"Oohhhhh, what's the matter? Come and give me a kiss."

She playfully puckered up her chocolate-coated lips. I was punching the air inside. What just happened? Fuck. Who cared? It was still on. It had to be or she wouldn't behave like we were an item.

At Muriwai, she photographed the flocks of birds soaring over the rocky coastline. She was admiring their freedom. I was admiring her.

After some "yeah, stunning, that" comments to appease her, I moved on to seduction. My luck the place was deserted.

We were soon tearing off clothes up on the hillside. The gannet colony was chattering away down below us. Surfers were cutting waves down in the bay. With Natasja submitting to my cock, my lies and pathetic existence faded into the background.

On the way home we got lost and laughed for hours about that. At a pizzeria later on, while we waited to order, Natasja grabbed my hands.

"Remember this day. It will get us through a lot."

Jesus. I felt all choked up. It looked like we were in this for the long haul.

When the waiter asked what we wanted to drink, Natasja looked at me warily.

All eyes seemed to be on me.

"Diet Coke," I said.

Dig deep, old boy. You can get through this one occasion without a drink. I wiped at the beads of sweat running down my face.

"Have you ever thought of coming to the States for longer?" Natasja said around a bite of pizza.

"No. Never really appealed. Well, until now, that is."

Her green eyes came alive with interest.

"Well, you really should. Come for three months. See if you like it. We can travel around a bit."

I nodded, not wanting to jinx good fortune by opening my mouth.

"At least think about it."

"I will."

Natasja left a week later. I got back to my booze and drugs. The long phone calls and phone sex continued.

After one heavy night on the piss, I awakened with an urge to call Natasja and share some experiences from the past few days.

"What the hell do you want?" she said.

Good lord. Full moon or bloody Mercury in retrograde, or some crazy shit.

"What are you talking about?"

"I don't know what you're doing, but I don't want to hear from you. I've got enough to deal with."

"What the hell are ya goin on about?" I said.

"You're cruel. Last night, you were so hurtful with your words. I couldn't sleep. I cried. You told me you hadn't been drinking. I couldn't tell if you had or not, but you were on something. You told me you wanted nothing to do with me. Nothing. Not one thing you said made any sense. It was like another person had taken over possession of your body."

"I think you're overreacting, luv."

"Don't 'luv' me," she said.

In the silence, I vaguely recalled being on a boat in Auckland harbour and giving Natasja a call. I remembered wanting her to share the evening with me.

That was it. What the fuck had I done?

"I'm sorry," I said in vague reference to whatever I had done.

"Michael. You call at all times of the day and night. I love to hear from you, even at two in the morning, but these last few weeks have gotten worse. You sound crazy half the time. I can't tell if you've been drinking. Sometimes you sound the same, but it's…it's like the words of a different person."

Feeling rejected, I resisted the urge to spit venom in return. Must be losing my grip on reality. My mind went scrambling for answers. Amidst my impulse to minimize her claim, it occurred to me that I might drink more tea for the nerves.

"Let's not make a big deal out of it. Trust me. It'll never happen again."

"I've got to get off," she said sharply. "It's too painful. I went through this with my brother. He was an addict and you're starting to sound just like him."

"Don't tar me with that brush. Anyway, you're blowin' this all out of proportion. I just had a few too many. I wasn't even drunk, honestly."

"I know the behaviour. I spent four years in Al-Anon dealing with this stuff. I'm still not sure," she said in frustration. "You sound so normal now."

Normal. That's good. Take the moral high ground.

"I'm sorry," I said, capitalizing on the opening. "Never meant any harm. I just missed you and wanted you near. That's all."

"Michael, just…just, call me later. I miss you, too."

The phone went dead. I seized the moment to reevaluate my disaster protocol. From here on out, leave the bloody phone at home when drinking. Call only after two beers and never after 11 p.m.

That wasn't the only bad news of the day. I got home from work that evening to find Howcroft looking down in the mouth.

"I think I'm headin' back to the Isle of Man, yissur. I've no driving licence. Work is tight and I'm getting skint. My old boss has offered me my job back. I'll be headin' after Christmas."

There went my easy touch. Howcroft had always been there when I needed a few quid. We hung up a few lights for Christmas and a bit of silver tinsel above the window. Bloody splendid it was.

With the new year, Howcroft was gone, leaving me to struggle on my own. I'd have been in America already, if not for a lack of money and no explanation for why this former professional rugby player and computer genius was broke.

In February, I received a call from Mum to say my grandma had passed away. I had thought the world of her and truly felt sad to hear the news, but the sick part of me immediately started scheming: is there any money in this?

There was. £10,000.

I called Natasja first thing.

"My grandma just passed away and left me some money. I've decided to quit the job and travel to America for three months. What do you think?"

Her tone was buoyant, her words precise.

"That's so good. I think it's about time. We'll get you an apartment in Bay Park so you can have your own space."

She must have been keen by the sound of her voice. What a few quid could do. I could see it all right up ahead of me: power, prestige and prescription medication at a glorious postcode. Throw in a hair transplant and I'd have it made.

In April, I quit my job and left for America on a three-month visa waiver. Natasja's face lit up when she saw see me at the airport. That melted me, but I kept up the Viking façade. Not too much emotion. Good to see you, luv. All matter of fact.

There were coy looks on the way back from the airport. Like a game of who had the upper hand. I was definitely getting the better part of the bargain. Chance of a lifetime it was. Connections and opportunity every way I turned. The Viking god Odin had to be smiling on me. No way was I cocking this up.

Natasja kept talking about Dylan on the way down from the airport. He couldn't wait to see me. The old man had abandoned him and Dylan was starting to have trouble in school.

"I really am so grateful that you were willing to come, Michael. Not just for me but for Dylan. He needs a strong male role model like you in his life."

No pressure here then. A father to Dylan; showman and philosopher to family and friends; lover, counsellor and business mentor to Natasja; the ultimate son-in-law to my new mother-in-law. For the life of me I had no idea how Natasja had come up with this impression, but I was willing to give it a go. Whatever it bloody took for her to accept me.

"Michael, Michael, Michael, Michael, Michael, Michael, Michaaaeeeeellll!" Dylan shouted when I came in the door. I let him stand on top of my feet and we walked around the room.

"Mom, I'm going wherever Michael's going. He can stay in my room."

"He's MY boyfriend, Dylan. You get your own friends."

Seeing me distracted with his mother, Dylan darted off through the kitchen on his skateboard. Natasja grabbed my hand and led me off on a tour of the house.

"Take whatever you want to furnish the apartment. It'll be great to use on the weekends. You'll be here most of the time anyway."

"I'll take that," I said, pointing at what I knew was her favourite piece.

"Oh, my God, you've got a nerve. Tell you what: you can have a kettle and that's it."

Natasja went back to the kitchen and began opening wax-sealed envelopes. The cards inside had gold and silver leaf writing.

"To Natasja and Michael," she read from one. "You're invited to the Jamesons' for a Black Tie dinner."

While she read off our invites from the Forbes 500 list, I was speculating about Tijuana and a hoard of prescription medication. When, what time and how quickly could I get to the source?

First things first: fix the receding hairline. As soon as I moved in, I booked a consultation with a hair transplant surgeon. The surgery took place several weeks later. I had been on my best behaviour, but the minute the doctor prescribed Vicodin, all bets were off. One tablet of those opiates and the spell was on. To feel the drug coursing through my veins was to be wrapped in cotton wool. All my pain and confusion disappeared. I felt safe and protected from the world.

Wanting more, I began to stalk Natasja's supply. She was recovering from an operation and had been prescribed Percocet, which was quite a bit stronger than what I had. While she was resting in her room, I used the excuse of needing to piss and slipped into her bathroom. Instinctively, I knew right where to look. That day I took one, the next day two. Soon I had emptied the entire jar.

Fuck it, I told myself. She needs a role model for her son and I need medication to be someone's role model. Besides, she didn't appear to be taking them and the arrangement seemed to be a reasonable exchange from my angle.

Between the vitamins and minerals, high-protein, low-carb diet, and jogging horse trails with my personal trainer, I kept scheming about my crusade to the Mecca of prescription medication, Tijuana. I could not get to the source quickly enough. The thought of it ate away at me every waking hour.

After a couple of weeks of maintaining my façade, I pulled on my gym kit one morning – Nike sports cap, Under Armour t-shirt and matching shorts, Asics Gel Kinsei Trainers – and announced to Natasja that I was headed to the gym. She was relaxing around the pool in her bikini and wide-brimmed straw hat.

"See you, luv. I'll be back in the afternoon."

"Be careful with my car, I'm trusting you," she said, lowering her tortoiseshell Chanel shades.

I looked at her as if to say, I cannot believe you would doubt my reliability.

"I would never let you down, luv."

I kissed her on my way out and was soon headed south on the freeway. The exit for the gym came and went. I had been planning this mission for months and the day had finally come. As I drove, I felt the adrenaline growing with each passing mile. The relief I needed was not far ahead.

Half an hour later, I saw a line of cars stacked up at that no man's land by the border. A large Mexican flag waved against the hazy skyline.

I pulled off at the last exit and found a car park on the American side. A metal turnstile led to the other side of the border. Passing through, I arrived at the main street. Traffic rushed around me. A bus went by belching black smoke. A truck filled with Federales came by bristling with automatic weapons. Every ten feet I was hustled by another street merchant. I found row after row of discount pharmacies. When I saw a sign in the window that read VICODIN, I went in. The woman behind the counter smiled indifferently when I asked for Vicodin.

"Prescription," she said.

When it was clear that I did not have one, she picked up a walkie-talkie and began speaking in Spanish. Her eyes looked me up and down as she did. Convinced that I was being described and turned in, I made a quick exit to the bar down the street. The place had sports memorabilia plastered all over the walls.

"Corona and a double shot of tequila," I told the barman.

Clearly, this manoeuvre was going to require a bit of the old Dutch courage.

My eyes toured the joint and stopped on the glass case behind my seat. There was a signed Dallas Cowboys shirt inside, number 16, Dontrell Freeman.

I raised my drink to Natasja's ex.

"Cheers, yissur."

In better spirits a few minutes later, I entered a back street and found a seedier-looking pharmacist.

"OxyContin?" I asked the man behind the counter.

"What strength?" he said without hesitation.

"What have you got?"

I twitched with anticipation. My palms began to sweat. I had a nervous look over my shoulder.

"20, 40, 80 milligrams," the man said.

"Better make it 80."

"How many?"

"What's the price?"

"$80 for 80 milligrams."

Fuck me. That was steep.

"Just one," I said.

When the man picked up the phone, I was ready to bolt again, but he gestured to stay, so I calmed down. A boy arrived on a bicycle and took the man's order. Off he went down the street. I shifted my feet and nervously paced the store. My heart was pounding. I did not entirely trust that the police weren't involved in this.

Finally, the kid returned with a white paper bag. The pharmacist handed me a container of tablets. I inspected them. It was the real thing.

"And some Vicodin and Percocet," I said, growing greedy now.

Once the man had filled those orders, I bolted from the store.

At the first reasonably secluded recess along the road, I slipped out of sight and chewed down a Vicodin. Desperate for relief, and fearing it would not come soon enough, I took a Percocet. When those two pills did not produce results fast enough, I added half an OxyContin to the mix and sat down with the sun warming my head. Eventually, a trance-like peace spread through my body, a sense of inner warmth and tranquillity. I felt human. Not fully but life made sense. I had a clear vision of the future with Natasja. I would make the relationship happen. I was a good person, not the monster I felt crawling around under my skin each day.

Ready to return home, I stood up and started down the street, hardly noticing the armoured vehicles and traffic racing up and down the road.

At the first street vendor, I stopped and pointed at a wooden bird. "How much?"

Natasja will love it, I thought. Then I realized it would raise all sorts of unsavoury questions and sacked off the idea.

"The border," I said to the man. "How do I get back?"

"Can take hours on foot, señor. Busiest border crossing in the world. Catch the bus. It takes you straight to the front. No lines."

He pointed up the street. "This way, señor. You are going all the way to the top to find the bus station."

I walked along until I found the bus station and caught a bus. A few minutes later, we arrived at the border and were met with the monumental lines of traffic, just as the man had described it. The bus driver skirted off to one side and cut to the front, also as the man had described it.

When we arrived at the customs building, the driver stopped and everyone filed off the bus. I went in through a side door and showed my visa to a customs officer. He waved me through without a question.

Once I was safely through the gates to the US side, my gait quickened. My mind started scheming. I had my fix and an unlimited source at my disposal. Bi-weekly shuttles from Rancho del Cielo to Tijuana and back. An hour, tops, I imagined.

A warm wind blew through the car as I drove north on Interstate 5. The stereo was blasting. My being was infused with euphoria. It was the counterpoint to the drive down. Would I get the drugs I needed? Would I get caught? Would I end up in a Mexican prison? Now I was home free.

But into that brief moment of exhilaration, new feelings of uncertainty began to creep. I remembered Natasja. Christ. Could I even make a relationship with her work? In my state, she was likely to call me out so I started rehearsing a speech, intended to counteract any suspicions.

On and on it went, as if I thrived on chaos and drama.

Back at Natasja's place, I found her laying out rows of filet mignon in the kitchen.

"Long workout?" she said, eyes narrowed slightly, a hint of suspicion.

"Got chatting at the gym, ya know."

"We've people coming over later for the barbeque. You did remember?"

"Of course. I'll get showered up."

"Michael, I don't want it ending up like last time. You were telling stories to everyone one minute and then you just passed out."

"Mind if I grab a beer? Just the one."

Judging by her look, she did. I went for the refrigerator door anyway. As I was opening it, Natasja abruptly announced.

"You know, I remember seeing my dad have a beer once. Other than that he never drank."

Once? I thought. Must've been rough.

"All the rest of his time he was angry, though."

I paused with the bottle in midair.

"Goddamn it, how did we get onto him?" she said. "I just don't want to talk about it."

171

I placed the unopened bottle down on the counter and gave Natasja a hug. Whatever had prompted that ugly memory, I did not want to keep encouraging it.

When I returned from my shower, the bottle was still standing there, beading up with moisture. I needed that beer desperately and began to reach for it, then stopped. Natasja was staring at me. She knew the results. I knew the results. She knew that I knew that she knew the results. We said nothing. Without another word, I grabbed the bottle and placed it back in the refrigerator.

At least I had the pain medication. I sat on a sofa by the pool, eyes closed, stoned. Natasja was soon flipping filet mignons at the poolside barbeque.

When the guests arrived, I played host and got them all a drink. Several of them congregated in the kitchen, where gift bags were stacked all over the island.

"So you must be the professional rugby player we've heard so much about," a woman said.

I felt heat flushing behind the smile.

"Let's all go out to the poolside," Natasja said.

She gave me a sidelong glance as she passed. Had she figured me out? From the dive apartment to the lack of a proper credit card, I had left a trail of deceit. Why did she even keep me around? I wasn't sure, but a look at the bar prompted a longing to pour myself a stiff drink. I needed a bit of reassurance. Just a few swigs to go with the pain medication and everything would be right.

I glanced in Natasja's direction. She glanced sharply back at me. I abandoned the idea of a drink and took my place on one of the padded loungers. Neil Young *Rockin' in the Free World* played over the exterior sound system. The smell of steak and coconut suntan oil filled the air. Several hot air balloons passed overhead in the warm California breeze. I saw a man waving from one of them and I waved back. I had it made, so fuck you to every teacher, employer and bloody drunken bastard who had ever questioned my ability to succeed.

Three days later, I was back down in Tijuana, and three days after that. On and on it went, sometimes daily. Each sortie was like a secret mission for me. I was constantly tempting fate, addicted to the adrenaline as much as I was to the drugs.

I quickly found a café away from the bustle of the main drag and established a system. Order one beer. The waiter, my new friend, would return with the beer and my supply of OxyContin in an ashtray. After downing the beer, I would jog to the bus station. On a good day, I had the grab down to two hours, from start to finish.

If the trip turned into any kind of saga and I was delayed, I would head to the Bay Park apartment and call Natasja.

"Just need some time to myself," I'd tell her.

Eventually, she started to get on my case. You've been gone for hours, she'd complain. What can you possibly be doing down at the gym?

When she no longer bought my story of bonding with the lads, I threw the indignation card at her. Can't believe your lack of trust. I hid at the apartment and sulked. Fuck you. If I'm to suffer, so will you. I had my OxyContin to smooth out any rough edges that came along.

One night when I was hammered on the usual chemical cocktail, I decided to stay at the apartment. The evening grew late. The apartment backed up to the train line, so I always spotted transients coming and going along the tracks. One of them had converted the pampas grass in my back garden into a split-level development, with a mezzanine. I had seen rugs and pots and pans. He had more furniture than I did.

I was thinking of him and the easy life when a knock came at the front door. It was Natasja. I heard her call my name. I lay on the bed smoking a cigarette. The knock came again. I went on smoking in silence.

"Michael, please. Open the door. I know you're in there."

Question my integrity, will you? Let this be a lesson to you.

There were more knocks. When my phone rang, I turned it off. She finally left.

The following morning, I shaved, showered and took enough OxyContin to act like a reasonable man. When I returned to the house, Natasja was going over the books with an accountant. My smile and hug met with a cold response.

While I retreated to the guest room, I heard Natasja and the accountant go out of the front door. I moseyed into the kitchen, scratching my nuts and stealing glances at the stacks of paper on the kitchen table. Pretending to enjoy the scenery outside, I walked past several times. It appeared to be a list of assets with the corresponding dollar amount. Back and forth, back and forth, but it was hard to make out the exact figures without a closer look.

Ah, fuck it, I said finally and leaned in closer. When the finches chirped in their luxury cage, I jumped. I expected Natasja to walk in on me at any second.

When the columns finally came into focus, I nearly shit my pants. Home, condo, land, investment accounts. I saw $3m, $4m, $1.2m, $800,000, $500,000, $250,000. And this was just page one of three.

Fuck me sideways. I'm rich.

Suddenly beneficent at heart, I saw Alejandro, the gardener, struggling to remove a tree from the ground and went out to give him a hand. No one in this world was ever going to struggle again. Not if I could help it. My mind went to work on various philanthropic means to distribute Natasja's wealth.

She came back in with Dylan shortly.

"Michael, Michael, Michael, Michael, Michael, Michael, Michaaaeeellllll!" he called out and wrapped his arms around the top of my legs.

I looked over at Natasja with a grin. Dylan was my trump card. There was no getting rid of me as long as Dylan was around.

"He's been waiting for you to take him golfing."

"Well good, let's go grab your clubs right now, little man. You know my fellow countrymen practically invented the sport."

Off we went to the golf course, with me the strong male role model, rendering the sage advice of a self-made man.

Upon our return that afternoon, Dylan bolted off on his skateboard.

Natasja was still fuming over my vanishing act down at the apartment.

"I get so mad at you. Then I hear you singing Lionel Richie songs as Kermit the Frog and hear Dylan laughing and I don't know what the hell to do."

She shook her head and wandered off without another word. I knew I had about two minutes to break her down and make her laugh.

With a cheesy Barry Manilow tune still echoing in my head from the stereo, I chased after Natasja and started whistling *Copacabana*. She didn't flinch. I tried singing a verse but basically murdered it.

"Natasja, she was a showgirl, yellow feathers in her hair, and her dress cut up to there."

I ran a hand up my leg, indicating where her dress should be.

Natasja stared at me in silence.

"You're having none of it, are ya?"

Still nothing. She did not look the least bit impressed.

I parted her arms and started kissing around her heart. Then I sniffed her armpit and cringed.

"Ugh, you smell."

"You think this is appropriate, Michael?"

I tried another smile. She almost smiled in return.

"You idiot! I know! I don't smell too good!"

I tried reassuring her with more kisses. She continued her discourse as if I wasn't there.

"God, my old relationship was fuelled by anger, but you don't engage. You just make me laugh when I'm angry. It gives me permission to be softer and more feminine. I like that."

Thank God for small mercies. Mission accomplished.

Natasja and I went to settle scores in her bedroom. Every problem we had was settled between the sheets, or anywhere else we could arrange sex in the house. It settled very little, but it did conveniently put things off for another day.

With my three-month visa waiver about to expire, I made another run down to Tijuana. I had heard that all I needed to do was cross the border on foot and get it stamped. With my usual supply of drugs, I queued with the long line of immigrants at the border. The smart ones had a cardboard box to shelter them from the sun. The really smart ones had a few cold Coronas. Six hours later, I finally stood before a customs official and placed my passport on the counter.

"Visa expire, renew," I said.

He chuckled and looked at his fellow customs official. "Where did you hear you could renew your visa here?"

"Common knowledge. Are you telling me I can't?"

"Yeah, I'm telling you that you can't. You have to return to your port of origin."

Well, fuck me, I thought. That meant to maintain my legal status and position as lord of the manor, I had to book a flight back to New Zealand.

Later that day, I explained the problem to Natasja. She was baking in the kitchen, making the room smell of warm bread. I sloppily prepared myself a peanut butter and jam sandwich.

"Look at that mess," she said, laughing. "He's a caveman. That's what I tell all my friends when they ask."

"Not a Viking?"

"Whatever you are, you're so basic, like a Neanderthal!"

We both started laughing as the contents of my sandwich spilled out the sides and onto my hands.

"A work of art," I said.

When the laughter stopped, I found Natasja assessing me.

"You all right?" I asked while lapping up the loose peanut butter and jam with my tongue.

There was a coy look away on her part and back.

"Are you in love?" Natasja asked out of the blue.

"What sort of question is that?" I asked once I had cleared my throat.

"I want to know," she said with a laugh, blushing.

I pulled myself together and paused.

"Oh, you want to know, do you?"

"Yes," she said. In the ensuing silence she gestured as if to prompt me.

"Yes," I replied.

"Good," she said promptly. "Because I feel it."

"What, and that's it?" I asked.

We both start laughing.

"Go on, you can do it, Natasja."

"I looovvve you, Michael. Oh, my God, I am so red."

I made her abandon the baking for the moment and we walked up to the meditation garden overlooking the canyon. It was quiet at the end of the day and we sat silently together.

Eventually, Natasja waved her hand over the property. "I just want to share all this with someone."

"And who might that be?"

She laughed.

"Okay. You, Michael."

And there I stood at the crossroads of my depravity and the land of make believe.

So why not a family together, I found myself thinking? Certainly I could do a better job than my parents had.

Giving in to long-abandoned hopes and dreams, I asked Natasja if she would ever want more children.

"Oh, I would love to," she said. "I just loved being pregnant. But life changes. It's not something you just do. Everything would have to be right."

I grabbed hold of her hands, the reassuring lover and counsellor again, only meaning it sincerely this time.

"Michael, if I ever got married again, I would like it to be alongside the Dart River in Queenstown, New Zealand. Reverend Morgan could do the service. I would fly all our friends and family over. Wouldn't that be spectacular?"

Jesus. I felt a bit choked up over her gesture. Spectacular, all right. I pulled her close and we watched the dying day.

"I have to go back soon," I reminded her.

She nuzzled her head against my shoulder and looked up tenderly.

"I'll take care of everything, Michael. Will you promise to come back to me? All well? So everything will be perfect?"

I nodded. I did want the marriage, and all the security it offered, but God, what a burden. For richer, for poorer? In sickness and in health? Faithful to one woman for the rest of my life? Till death do us part? And all done under the scrutiny of God?

Fair to say that Natasja was getting the rough end of the stick on that deal and I would be building up more points on my one-way trip to hell.

That night, lying alone with my thoughts, my mind began to assemble a plan of action. Return to New Zealand with a handful of 80mg OxyContin. The reduction schedule would be a half tablet three times a day for the first two days, and then a quarter tablet three times a day until it was gone. The codeine would bring me down from the OxyContin. Then I'd drink my way down through the remaining withdrawal. By the time I returned to America, I'd be a new man and ready to begin a new life.

CHAPTER TWELVE

Natasja saw me off at the airport three days later. I returned to Auckland to find my sister had moved into her own place across town. The boyfriend was history. I ditched the basement apartment and moved in with Sal. I could always rely on her to lift my spirits. Full of life she was. Took me as she found me and never judged.

Within the week, I was down to the drinking stage of my reduction schedule. Natasja had been calling me daily, wondering why I didn't simply turn around and come back to America.

"Don't pressure me," I said the next time she called. "Don't you understand how difficult this is for me?"

"What's so difficult about it? Just organize your visa and come back. Trust in God," she added before hanging up.

An e-mail followed:

I've been working on a poem that starts off, 'I'm not crazy but my boyfriend is.' I think it would make a great song, and since you never cease to inspire the lyrics, I'm planning on making a whole album just based on that one line...

Natasja called again later that night. "You know Jesse, my spiritual director?"

"Yeah," I said warily.

"Well, I'm going to have him give you a call and pray with you. I think you should look into doing a course at Phos."

I did not tell her that the insanity in my life was caused by drugs. I needed them. Lots of them. They terrified me, but I had no idea how to live without them.

The next day, Jesse called. I listened and sipped on a cold lager while he prayed for clarity and direction in my life, and for my safe return to America.

"Michael, do you want to be in control?"

"No," I said.

That was a famous one, as lies went. I wanted to control everyone and everything but assumed saying no was what he wanted to hear.

"Then let go and let God."

An invitation to the Phos University of Transformational Studies followed. Attending would help smooth out my visa. With mixed emotions I agreed.

"You're gonna LOVE IT!" Jesse said.

The bloody Christ is Right Academy, I thought, hanging up the phone.

Still, the call came in handy. When I finally got around to tackling my visa application, I was confronted with a section that read: What is your reason for requesting the visa? I entered: I want to travel to America to further my spirituality. Attending the Phos University of Transformational Studies will be part of that plan.

I called Mum, who was now working at a Christian retreat house in Cyprus. She wrote me a reference letter, complete with the *Diocese of Cyprus and the Gulf* letterhead written across the top. It was a nice touch for a lad hurtling towards hell. To show my financial clout, Natasja transferred $15,000 into my account.

On every level, I knew that a return to the States was potentially disastrous for me and talked my sister to death about whether or not I should go back at all. It seemed much safer and easier to stay in New Zealand, away from temptation, but Natasja had bought a plot of land in Hawaii and had tasked me with flying back and forth to manage the project. Help install the infrastructure for several homes and sell off the individual plots.

There were worse ways to spend my time and a voice kept telling me to run with it. Things will be different this time. All I had to do was stay away from the Mexican border.

A week later, I returned to a passionate reunion. Within days I was back at the border. By now the cab drivers knew me by name. I had to wave them off. Even to me, making a deal in a yellow cab had the aura of a setup.

Back on the street, I headed over to see my main contact. He spotted me from the balcony of a second-floor bar and waved with a hard pull on his cigarette. I started up the stairs. An old man sat slumped on the first-floor landing, shooting up heroin. His dog was by his side. By the time I got to the top, my good friend was waiting for me. Otherwise, the bar was empty.

I ordered a bottle of Corona and a shot of tequila. A pipe full of something white and illegal sat on the bar mat. The barman rubbed his fingers together.

"Where?" he said in his heavily accented English.

I handed him $140 that I owed him.

"I was out of the country. Any crack?"

He pointed at the pipe. It was meth.

"Heroin? Oxy?" I said and gave him more cash. I needed the heroin and oxy to balance out the intensity of meth, along with the abrasive come-down. I couldn't do one without the other.

He left and returned with the heroin and OxyContin. Then he loaded the pipe from a black bin bag filled with several pounds of white crystal. We passed the pipe back and forth, our faces contorted like we were sucking lemons.

"Eees good, eees good," I said in a high-pitched voice.

I lost track of time. The meth started wearing off. I took another hit and noticed the bartender chopping lemons and limes with ever-greater ferocity. His eyes darted around the room. His body was twitching and jerking like a marionette.

I offered him the pipe.

"No more," he said, crossing himself.

I headed for the toilet to have a blast on the heroin. The only access was through a narrow passageway at the side of the bar. I broke out the foil, took a hit and held my breath until the heroin smoothed my body to velvet. With the next deep breath, I got a taste of the stale piss and shit lingering in the air. The place was foul around me. When I returned, the bartender was still twitching and slicing lemons.

Over the course of the next hour, I ran back and forth, smoking meth at the bar and smoking heroin in the bog. Things were getting more mental by the moment. The meth imparted a sense of invincibility and bravado, such that I was compelled to scrounge more and more of it from the bartender.

When I came back one more time, he turned and drove his knife into the countertop. His fingers rubbed together. He wanted more money. I had maxed out my daily limit on the debit card and what money I had left was just enough to get me back across the border with some measure of sanity.

"Back down tomorrow," I said. "Pay you then, si?"

The bartender stared at me, thinking. I had nowhere near enough cash to cover the meth I had smoked, so flight was increasingly an option.

While we stood there, a man and woman climbed into the bar via the fire escape. The woman wore red lipstick, but a good portion of it had missed her lips. The man kept nervously looking over his shoulder while ordering two beers. The barman had a final look at me and pulled the knife out of the countertop.

"They've got the place surrounded," the man said to me. He looked like he was nuts.

"Who?" I asked.

"FBI. They've been following me for weeks."

Or maybe they were following me. Damned drugs. They were driving me crazy.

The woman gave a knowing look to her partner and whispered in his ear. He whispered back and they both looked at me.

"You're fucking FBI!" he said and bolted for the door, pulling the woman with him.

I used this opportunity to make an exit down the fire escape. There were paranoid looks over my shoulder for the bartender. I worried about the FBI too as I hustled down the narrow street. The meth was wearing off, adding to my growing madness.

The road was lined with street vendors, the stalls divided by a sheet and covered with canvas. I approached a man selling sunglasses, lighters and souvenirs.

"Heroin?" I asked him.

We both stood back as a police truck rushed by.

"Wait out back," the man said and took my money.

I did as instructed and sat smoking a cigarette to take the edge off the meth comedown. A fleeting thought of Natasja met with the depravity inside my mind. How far would I go before all this ended in catastrophe? When the man came back, I inspected the black tar heroin. It was good.

"Crack," I asked him.

He pointed up the street.

"El Zoco."

"I can get crack in there?"

He nodded.

I walked up to El Zoco and went in for a drink. The strippers scattered around the bar came to life. One of them approached and squatted up and down in a suggestive manner. I waved her off with my hand. While I was getting my measure of the place, a blonde slut with fake tits came up. She seemed friendly.

"Crack?" I asked.

She nodded at the front door.

"We have to leave to score crack?"

She nodded again, so I necked my drink and we left.

Down the back streets, we came to a stall with several rough-looking characters. It was a collage of hoodies, bandanas and tattoos. The blonde signalled that I was okay, so they waved us through to a cobblestone lane. An open sewer ran down the right side. Cubicles with wooden doors lined the left. The blonde unlocked one of the doors into an unlit eight by six room with a worn mattress and a pile of dirty clothes.

Fucking dump, I thought to myself.

The blonde closed the door and started to undress. I gestured for her to stop.

183

"Let's get one thing very straight, luv. I do not want to fuck you. Where are the drugs?"

"Drugs," she said and rubbed her fingers together.

"Crack," I reminded her when she took the money.

She went out and closed the door. I sat there with my heart pounding. It had the smell of a mugging and the only way out was the way I came in, past a gathering of gangbangers.

Relieved as hell I was when the blonde returned alone and with the drugs. Not crack, but meth. I didn't give a fuck about the type of drug by this point and smoked until it was all gone and sent her off again. She let it be known in a pleasant way that I was a wreck. I didn't argue. I just sent her off for another load. Anything to stop the menace inside my head.

After the third trip, she started to feel me up. I protested but was too intent on smoking the meth to put up much resistance. Before I knew it, she had my fly down and my cock in her mouth. Very good technique, I must admit. When I stood up, she stood too, my cock still held in her hand. In the heat of the moment, I reached down to hold her crotch and found half a fucked-up cock in place of a crack. I jumped back.

"What the fuck?" I said.

"It's a ducky."

"A fucking ducky, my arse. You're a bloody bloke."

And by God it was. An effeminate young man dressed up as a lady. I had half a mind to land a knuckle on his chin but decided against it. The hour was late and it was getting time for dinner.

With the money I had saved for the bus fare, I had blondie go buy me one more pinch of meth. He escorted me out. I did my best to keep the raw sewage away from my Prada sports sandals.

The gang gave me the once-over as I walked back out to the street. I recalled news stories of headless bodies being found in oil drums down in Tijuana. Tourists went down there and did not come back.

Hoping to look tough, I put my shoulders back, chest out, stomach in.

I heard one of the gangbangers snigger and intuitively checked my face in a passing storefront. The blonde bitch had left lipstick all over my cheeks.

As soon as I was out of sight, I broke into a run for the border. The drugs were already wearing off. Queued up with a long line of immigrants, my body was twitching like that bartender chopping lemons. Fear and anxiety ate at my core. The windows of several pharmacies lined the opposite side of the street, but I had no money left to change the way I felt.

I made it to the border and was home in time for dinner. While Natasja spoke, I stared at the ground or walls. Every look in her eyes brought me shame and discomfort. I wasn't sure how, but I made it through dinner without a complete mental breakdown.

Alone and at the poolside bar the next day, sampling a lunchtime cocktail, an international number flashed up on my phone.

"FINNEGAN"!

It was my oldest friend and partner in crime from the Isle of Man.

"Bloody hell, what's happenin', yissur?" I said.

"I heard you were in America. Howcroft put the word out. Big gossip round here. They reckon you're with some rich woman. I just got back from South Africa."

"What were you doing there?"

"I was in rehab for three months. I'm back in the UK and all I want to do is shoot smack. I can't stop thinking about it."

"So rehab didn't work? Where are you?"

"I'm in Wales. If I go back to the Isle of Man, I'll end up back on the gear. I was told to reach out to other addicts for support. What's happenin' with you?"

"Well, I'm sat at the poolside bar having a cocktail. Packed in the drugs," I added, hoping to save face and spread the word that I was no longer a junkie all in one swoop.

The conversation quickly dried up and we rang off, but he had me thinking. Maybe rehab was an option. Three months of peace and quiet.

Before it came to that, I just hoped to take a shit without it being agony. When you eat painkillers all day long, every day, taking a shit becomes a major problem. Clogs you up to the point of sickening abdominal pain. After four or five days of that, you might smash out a few rabbit pellets, if you were lucky. Strong coffee and cigarettes had no stimulating effect at all. I was down at Walgreens buying stool softeners and laxatives by the case. Eating them like candy I was. Stuffed a suppository up my jacksy for good measure. Game for a damned enema by that point.

After an hour or so that day, my guts began to growl. Thank the Lord. I roamed the house and picked a toilet where I thought nobody could hear or smell the potential aftermath. I dropped my kecks, crunched into a ball and sat there with a grimace like I was squatting five hundred pounds.

A dribble turned into a torrent as days of compacted faeces piled the pan. The end game scenario was like shitting a pineapple sideways. Relief like no other.

I flushed and watched the water rising up the pan. Fuck no. Crap was spilling over the lip. Across the pebbled stones on the bathroom floor and out into the conservatory. I grabbed a bunch of paper towels and watched the crap overrun them. I grabbed some larger towels and threw those on the floor. The water and shit spilled out into the conservatory, up against the floor to ceiling windows and into the kitchen.

Christ, no. The bastard finches were chirping away in their cage. Had never heard them so cheerful. I was down on hands and knees, six towels deep in shit and water.

Natasja appeared.

"God damn it, Michael! You idiot! Why do I find this so funny?!"

I looked up at her from my hands and knees.

"What did you do or not do? Those toilets are designed not to block."

"Well…what I did was…"

She laughed.

"That polite British accent. Oh, God save it. Dylan!" she shouted. "Come and take a look at this, and bring my camera!"

"Look, listen, what I did was…"

"Why won't you ever just do as I say?"

"That wouldn't be any fun, would it?"

"God, you drive me crazy!"

In the days ahead, rehab was back on my mind, but before any of that assumed serious proportions, I found a dealer on my side of the border. Whatever I wanted, he had – morphine, Dilaudid, OxyContin, Vicodin, tramadol and Percocet. We'd meet in downtown San Diego. Back at the house, I'd wait until late at night. I had given up the apartment, so there was no other way to hide my habits from Natasja. I would be up smoking into the early hours of the morning and explaining away my habits when I got up at noon each day.

I thought I was fooling Natasja, but she had seen it all before. Her brother was an addict and she knew the nightmare.

"You walk around the house at seven a.m. making wisecracks to yourself. It's as if you're permanently intoxicated. I've seen all this before, Michael."

Dear God. Why didn't she just come out and say it? Then I could try to defend myself. Instead there were these knowing looks.

Maybe she was rewriting her own childhood. Or just keeping me around for the drama.

After being cornered by her like this for several weeks, I had this wild notion to come clean.

"Look. I've been taking painkillers."

"I know, you stole mine."

"Oh, the Percocet. Yeah. Sorry about that. I only meant to take one."

"And what are you taking now?" she says.

"OxyContin."

"How much?"

"About 180 milligrams a day. I break it up, though, not all at once."

"Oh, my God," she said.

She had her head in her hands and looked back up.

"Michael, you have to go. I cannot have you here anymore. I won't have addiction in my life."

She went on about her brother destroying himself. I told her she was overreacting, but she was done.

"I've spoken with your mum and sister. It's over, Michael. You need to go."

Spoken with my mum and sister? What the fuck?

Faced with her icy wall of spent emotion, I packed my bags and checked into the nearby Holiday Inn. The only money I had left was the $15,000 Natasja had transferred into my account, minus about $10,000 I had blown on drugs.

Having nowhere else to turn, I considered calling Mum. She had always offered to help me with treatment, if and when I wanted it. I picked up the phone and dialled. Strategy in place, I already had a silk sheet joint in mind, something proper in the way of a treatment centre, where I could socialize with the celebrity female clientele.

Once I heard Mum's voice on the phone, I was choking back tears.

"I need to get help."

"What is it you're doing?"

"What isn't it?"

I explained everything that had been going on and that I really wanted help.

"The rehab facility needs to be twelve-step," she said.

I knew she wanted me to find Jesus. She wanted Him to save me.

"I'll do anything. Twelve-step. Whatever."

"All right. I'll do what I can to help."

"Thanks, Mum. I'll start looking for a place straight away."

I hung up and went down to use the hotel computer. Prospects in Malibu came up straight away. Celebrity endorsed. Hot tubs, swimming pool, massages. Thank God for you, Finnegan. You were on to something, old boy. A couple of weeks of that should do the trick. I could not believe I had failed to think of this sooner.

I called Mum and passed along the contact info. She called me back a few minutes later.

"It's $35K for thirty days. I just can't afford it. I'm living off my pension and the work I do is for charity. They've put me in touch with their sister clinic in Los Angeles. They might be able to do a deal. I'm waiting for someone to call back. As soon as I know, I'll call you back."

"Do not tell anyone, Mum. I don't want anyone knowing I'm going into rehab. Do not tell Dad. I don't even want Sal to know. If word got out, it would ruin me."

I Googled Prospects' sister clinic in Los Angeles and was greeted by the image of a plush Swiss-style house.

The clientele should be up to my standards, I assured myself.

It occurred to me that I should go up and repair things with Natasja before I went to treatment. To better communicate my good intentions, I drank a few lagers and smoked a cocktail of heroin and meth. After a cab ride up to Natasja's place, I took a few deep breaths and knocked at the door.

Dylan looked out of the window and then answered the door.

"Michael! She's mad now, but she'll calm down. Please come back. I miss you."

"I miss you too, little man."

Natasja appeared and moved him to one side. She was filled with anger.

"I'll call the police if you do not leave right now."

"I'm sorry. Please give me a second chance. It'll be different, I swear. I'll stop the drugs. No more drinking. I'm getting help."

"Look at the state of you. I've got your plane ticket to Hawaii here. That's wasted. I've got to check on the land and the development. I've got to have the infrastructure put in. I needed your help. We had plans. All a waste."

She went to shut the door, but I blocked it with my foot.

"Natasja, give me a chance to explain, please. I'm gonna get help. I'll go to rehab. Thirty days and I'll be sorted out."

"You're drunk now. You're out of your mind. I told you never come here drunk ever again. MOVE YOUR FOOT!"

"One last chance. Natasja, please."

"MOVE YOUR FOOT!"

She slammed the door. I loped off down the road. Foolishly, I had told the cab driver to go on his way.

The front desk had a message for me from Mum when I got back to the hotel. Prospects' sister ship had given her a special rate. A technician would come by the hotel to pick me up on October 15th.

The night before treatment, I did enough drugs to kill a horse. While I was at my peak, I made my way down to Bloomingdale's in Fashion Valley for a black Armani shirt. Natasja had paid for it with a credit card a week earlier and it was waiting on hold. I had to look my best for our supervised meals at the Chateau Marmont.

I was asleep with my head hanging off the bed when my wake-up call came in the morning. I thanked the clerk and surveyed the room. Empty Corona bottles, sheets of burned foil, cigarettes, Valium and tramadol containers scattered around the bed. I found a piece of foil with heroin on it and took the last hit. It was 8:10. The technician from Prospects was scheduled for 8:30. I ate half an 80mg OxyContin to make sure I was in top form for the journey.

When the technician arrived, he helped me into the back of his minibus. Along the way, I saw him repeatedly checking me out in the rearview mirror.

"So, dude, what are you hoping to get out of treatment?"

"It'd be good just to get the thirty days under my belt. Be nice to know I'm not dependent on the drugs, ya know. Stick to alcohol after that."

I didn't share the monthly plan I had envisioned once I was clean. Choose one drug to have on the last weekend of each month. Maybe twice a month on special occasions. I would be back playing sport by then. It would be after the football match on a Saturday, with me having scored the winning goal. The wife and kids wouldn't miss me for a few hours. Nobody would suspect a thing. A small heroin/crack wind down before I returned to my 9–5 job at the bank on Monday morning.

The technician smiled like he knew it all, but fuck him.

Arriving in the Los Angeles area, he turned off the freeway and into a suburban jungle. I smelled poverty. We came to a couple of shabby wooden buildings and the driver pulled in. There was a woman's shelter right next door. Across the street I saw a building that vaguely resembled the image on the Internet, but where we had stopped was without doubt the wrong side of the tracks.

You have got to be fucking joking me. This is not Malibu.

The driver led me into a site administration office attached to one of the wooden shacks. The shack next door was identical, aside from the administration office.

A female aide appeared with a clipboard and medical questionnaire. "And you are in here for?"

"Mainly painkillers. I've been taking a few too many."

"Well, if you have anything to add to that list, let me know."

She pointed a Polaroid camera at my face. I tried to give it the old handsome look. No worries. I'd be tanned with piercing green eyes and a big white smile in thirty days' time.

While the aide filled out her form, I watched the Polaroid develop opposite me. Dear Lord. A face strained with the unknown and a grin that had come off more as a grimace.

"We have strict regulations on clothes," she went on. "No short shorts, no singlets, no fitted t-shirts. We expect you to be appropriately clothed at all times."

I looked down at my sports bag. Half the contents had been rendered useless.

"And no exposed flesh either. Do you have a phone?"

"I've got a mobile here."

"I'll take that. No mobiles. Communication is by payphone and limited to a set time each day."

With a glance I saw there was a text on my phone from Dad. *Tried calling. Will keep trying. Hope you're OK. Luv ya, dad.*

Christ. He never texted. He didn't know how. And "luv ya". He'd never say that sort of thing in a million years. I immediately suspected my mother of shopping me, and the old man's new wife of writing the text.

A 400-pound black man entered the room as I passed off the phone.

"This is Tyrone," the aide said. "He's in charge of all the men. First thing, he'll need to do a strip search."

"How are you doing?" Tyrone said in a Barry White voice. "Follow me."

He waved me through to a back bedroom. "Take off your clothes," he said from a safe distance, arms folded, a big smile.

"What's all this toe-touching stuff? What's the deal here?"

"Compulsory strip search. Get on with it."

While I stripped, Tyrone searched my bag and did an inventory.

"One hundred 10mg Valium. And tramadol," he said, holding up the containers. "Are these prescribed?"

"Er...no."

"These will be disposed of. What about these?" he said, holding up my anti-depressants.

"They're prescribed."

"They will be given to the on-site doctor, who will administer them each morning."

Tyrone had not found the one Valium I kept wrapped in silver foil in my wallet. It had been there for years. I had the psychological advantage knowing it was available, if and when I could get at my wallet again.

Tyrone tucked my toiletries away into a locked storage area.

"This is your room," he said. "That's your bed."

There were twin beds, the one next to mine was empty. I had noticed two other bedrooms on the way in, one of them with two more twin beds, the other with a single bed. I sat on mine. A big blue book titled *Alcoholics Anonymous* rested on the bedside table, along with a notepad.

While Tyrone explained that we all shared one bathroom, the kitchen and a TV in the living room, a stocky black lady with peroxided hair stuck her head around the bedroom door.

"Michael, I'm Jaz, your counsellor. You'll be answering to me, mister."

She laughed with a big grin.

"Come on, I'll introduce you to your fellow inmates."

We popped into the single room first. "John," Jaz said. "Meet Michael."

John nodded from his bed. Short and red-faced, he was not much for cordialities. I nodded back as Jaz dragged me down the hallway.

"In treatment for the twenty-second time," Jaz whispered with a shake of her head. "Has a penchant for suicide."

Jaz gave me a look. "By revolver. Apparently he's a lousy shot."

We popped into the other room with twin beds. Jaz introduced me to Maxwell and Tony. Tony was dressed in black, cloaked in chains and had a ring through his nose. He pointed in the direction of Maxwell.

"Fucking faggot porn star meth head. Watch out for him. Stick with me."

"Now, now, gentlemen," Jaz said with a shake of her finger.

I made a quick exit. Jaz went off down the hall towards the front.

"You're on your own until tomorrow morning," she said over her shoulder.

Before I could duck into my room, Maxwell came out and pulled me aside.

"Keep away from that devil-worshipping bastard, Tony. He's homophobic."

I got lost in Maxwell's sallow green complexion while his rapid-fire speech continued.

"Had to get his big famous cousin to pay for his treatment. Thinks it gives him special privileges."

With the speech at a stop, I excused myself and continued towards my room.

"Hey," John called out from his bed. I stopped to look in.

"What's up, mate?"

"I'll bet you Jaz told you my story."

"Not really. Just the odd bit."

"Yeah, I used to spend hours with a revolver in my mouth. Teeth to metal, you know? I shot my ear once."

"Right. OK…"

I lay on my bed and stared at the ceiling. Am I really here? Is this really happening to me? It was hard to believe I had fallen so far.

On a positive note, a doctor came by and dispensed some drugs to control my withdrawal. The afternoon and evening passed in reasonable comfort. With the drugs, my detox was mild and I slept.

At 6:30, I was awakened and told to clean my room. Meditation was at 6:45, breakfast at 7:25.

The day was split up into private time and group sessions. The inmates would be taken to a twelve-step meeting outside the treatment centre that night. I was relieved of participation for a few days while I detoxed.

While the other patients went off to a group meeting next door, I found some suntan lotion in a cupboard and made myself comfortable in the sun.

Jaz looked back from the driveway. "Michael, put some clothes on! You've read the rules! No exposed flesh! Don't let me see you like that again!"

Miserable auld bitch, I thought.

After a few more minutes with my flesh exposed, I threw my shirt back on. I was piss bored and walked over to the building next door. They were holding their group meeting inside. I looked in and saw the Twelve Steps and Twelve Traditions on the wall. I did a quick run through of the steps. One – powerless over alcohol. Check – I'm certainly not an alcoholic. Two – I read the word insanity in there. Harsh, certainly not applicable to me. Three – Turn my will and my life over to the care of God – That must be all the Jesus stuff, I guess – Check. I'm a good Christian boy and all that. In rapid succession I completed them all in my head and felt ready to leave.

By the end of the day, the only entertainment I had was with my cock. With the bathroom door not locking properly, I had to get creative, one foot on the door, a hand on the wall for balance and reverse hand grip while I leaned over the toilet.

On day three I heard a ruckus and went out the front to observe. A slick Italian looking man was stumbling around on the driveway, babbling nonsense and pleading with the staff to let him in.

"Vincenzo, you know the drill," Tyrone told him. "Payment first, then we let you in."

"But I am super alcoholic."

I left them to fight it out amongst themselves. From my bed I heard Vincenzo claiming his father would get them the money. He sounded desperate.

Maxwell stopped by my room to give me the inside scoop. Vincenzo had been in and out of the place more times than you could count. One day you saw him in all the gossip magazines, full of coke, birds hanging off his arms. Gold dealer, amongst his other businesses. Connected to the Mafia. Then he was back out there on the driveway, drunk and pleading for help.

After more commotion, the staff escorted Vincenzo into my room. Christ, I thought. Thankfully, he curled up on the other bed without a word. I saw him trembling and shaking out of the corner of my eye. The staff eventually sedated him and he fell asleep.

I lay there with thoughts racing. Why are we here? What's the point? What is the meaning of life?

Not finding much in the way of answers, I reached for the blue book on the nightstand. AA – Alcoholics Anonymous. That wasn't me. An alcoholic was someone with a bulbous red nose, pissing his pants and drooling on himself at the bar.

Not me, I reassured myself again with a flick open of the cover. The publication date was March 1976 – the year and month of my birth. Some joke, I thought. They've had it printed up especially for me.

The cosmic signs were everywhere, right under my nose. I had a plastic card for the Automobile Association of the United Kingdom in my wallet. It read: AA – Breakdown Recovery.

At 3 a.m. I was wide awake, writing on the notepad. I had no idea what I was trying to say, but it seemed business critical.

In the next room, I heard John screeching – like a wild animal being slaughtered – then commotion and strange noises emanating from Maxwell and Tony's room. The following morning I caught a glimpse through a partially opened door. Maxwell and Tony's room was covered in white powder.

Maxwell pranced out of the door and past me.

"That devil-worshipping bastard doesn't like gays, apparently. He started throwing baking flour all over the room in the middle of the night. Trying to raise the dead. Figured they'd come back and kill me because I'm gay."

"Fucking faggot," Tony shouted. "Get out of my room and stay out."

With a pouty look, Maxwell thrust out his hip.

"I think he likes me."

Good God, tell me this isn't happening.

I queued up for the mandatory morning medication, did a sleight of hand with the anti-depressant and pretended to drink it down with a glass of water. No need for them anymore, I thought. If I'm going to do this, I may as well do it properly.

Most of the other patients were sitting at two tables between the wooden buildings, all of them slumped over, elbows on their knees, drawing hard on their cigarettes. Vincenzo appeared from the back door and sat next to me. Soon, I was hearing tales of his playboy lifestyle – a penthouse apartment at the Peninsula Hotel, cocaine and alcohol addiction.

"So why couldn't you afford to get in here?"

"Blew it all, my friend. Some of it was robbed."

He looked over at me ominously.

"Yeah, big trouble. One day I was driving down the 101 in Los Angeles. A motorcycle pulled up alongside and robbed me at gunpoint. Took millions. I'd just done a big deal and now I owe the Mafia a ton of money. That's where the gold came from. I had shops all over California, making millions. Millions! I had it all. Then I had to go into hiding. They found me in a hotel and tied me to a wheelchair. Hung me off the side of the roof. Either get them their money or they throw me off. I told them to fucking kill me. I didn't care anymore. I'm a super alcoholic! Now I need $200,000 to get more gold and get back on my feet."

"And I might just have the solution," I said.

"Really, you have the money?"

I nodded knowingly and gave him a story about the Isle of Man. An old friend had come by with a suitcase full of drug money. Stashed it in my back garden. Don't know but it might still be there.

It was bullshit. I knew the suitcase was long gone, but it looked like rehab was a good place to spin a yarn and I was all in.

Vincenzo left and Maxwell took his place. Three days sober and you couldn't shut him up. He had the look of a meth freak. Incessant chatter, this time about needing a plot of land. He had big hotels and golf courses in mind. I offered up Natasja's plot of land in Hawaii.

"Sound any good to ya, mate?"

Maxwell was on. Christ, what a dream team. A grand total of eight days of sobriety between us, not a pot to piss in but there we were, thick in the gold trade and making multi-million dollar real estate deals.

Back on form, I finished up with the twelve steps. Clearly, I had underestimated my entrepreneurial skills. Time to get out of this joint and back in the real game. Little did I know, my life was about to change beyond all comprehension, from which there would never be any turning back.

CHAPTER THIRTEEN

Jaz dragged me into her office later that morning, pitching me on the idea of completing the full thirty days.

"I appreciate the opportunity and everything, Jaz, but it's just not for me. I'm finished with the twelve steps. I'm good to go."

Jaz sat there nodding her head. "Making excuses already, eh?"

"No, but these lot are nuts. I'm not."

"Don't leave before the miracle happens," she said with a smile.

Miracle? What the fuck does that mean? I turn into something like the camp meth freak and the gothic wonders back there?

"I'll give it another day," I said. "After that, I'm done."

"Your call, but it's the end of your detox period, so you'll be going with Tyrone and the boys to an outside meeting today."

Next thing I knew, I was being crammed into the back of a white minivan with eight other inmates.

"Change of plan," Tyrone announced along the way. "We're going to a different meeting today."

The others started grumbling, but the news meant nothing to me.

As we drove along, the neighbourhoods progressively deteriorated. The houses had caged entrances and iron bars over the windows. I might have been geographically lost when it came to Los Angeles, but I had seen my share of Ice-T gangster films and Dr Dre videos and knew South Central LA when I saw it.

We pulled up to a recreational centre where two Afro-American teams were engaged in a pickup game on the basketball court. The game stopped to watch nine honkies disembark from the minivan.

"Look at the peckerwoods," one of the black fuckers said.

There was laughter.

"What the fuck are you peckerwoods doing here?"

"Hey, Vincenzo," I said. "Is this like the Crips and the Bloods?"

"Ssshhh," he said in a full state of paranoia. "They'll blow your head off."

I liked my head, so I shut up.

We were led into the recreation centre, down a hallway and into a small room. The walls were painted apple green. The black to white ratio was about six to one. The meeting started. Literature was read. My mind drifted far away from South Central.

"Is there anyone here from outside the Greater Los Angeles area? If so, please identify yourself so we may get to know you better."

"Michael, addict, Isle of Man."

Heads turned.

"'I love man'?" an old black bum said from the seat in front of me.

He turned his head. Maxwell gave me the camp once-over. Jesus.

"Isle," I clarified in my best BBC voice. "Isle. Not I love. Isle. Isle of Man. It's a place near Ireland. Off the coast of England."

Every face was still turned and staring at me in silence.

"Welcome!" the leader of the meeting said.

I caught Vincenzo staring at me.

"Mate, this is not what I had in mind when I signed up for treatment."

"You'd better get used to it. This is you for the rest of your life."

"Are there any newcomers with us today?" the leader asked.

Vincenzo stood up. "I am Vincenzo, super alcoholic."

I shook my head. Super alcoholic. What the fuck was this compulsion to supersize his disease?

Vincenzo sat down and nudged me. "Look," he said and nodded towards a black guy with a feather in his fedora. "The feather. That's how you know he's a pimp."

And that summed up what I learned at my first meeting.

That night, back at the treatment centre, Vincenzo offered me half a sleeping pill. I took it, but as I lay in bed, I was still unable to sleep. Finally, around 3:00, I grabbed my pad and pen and went to sit in the backyard. Quotes from Shakespeare and the Bible were running through my head. I scribbled them down. All the world's a stage. The truth shall set you free.

Suddenly, I had an "ah-ha" moment. All knowledge and truth throughout the ages was a metaphor for some greater, universal truth. God had sent me here to translate it for Him. I thought it was a bloody marvellous idea to start rewriting the Bible.

Flush with euphoria and the clarity of the ages, I walked back into the shed. A heavyset black man sat in front of the television set. He introduced himself as Reginald and said, "What's up?" without looking at me.

"I get it!" I told him. "That's what's up! I fucking get it!"

Reginald laughed and nodded at the television. "Have a seat. *X-Files* is coming on."

Not entirely deflated, I went back to lie on my bed, the truth pounding in my chest. I understood everything now. Jesus Bond, special agent. That's who I was. Come back to save the world and all that. The bible had promised a second coming and I was it. Why didn't everyone else get the message?

Christ, I was losing it.

The next morning at breakfast, I learned that wildfires were threatening Malibu Prospects. Natasja's home in Rancho del

Cielo as well. Further proof. Another sign of my calling. I had been saved from the fires of hell. It was now my duty to rescue everyone.

"All the residents at Malibu Prospects are being evacuated," Jaz announced. "They'll be staying at the main house."

At afternoon group therapy, we split into groups of four and acted out a sketch from our drug-using days. While the others busied themselves with critique, I was off rescuing Natasja and saving the world in my mind.

Later, I met with Jaz for an individual session. She suggested I invite Natasja down for group therapy. I had already attended one of those, with a wife wounded by her husband's drinking. They had it out in front of everyone. Then she stormed off in tears and he was left there red faced.

Jesus Bond had not signed up for that kind of public humiliation.

"Natasja is coming nowhere near this place, Jaz. Of that you can be certain."

Jaz confronted me with Dylan, and the idea that I did not want to be a father to someone else's child. It was the truth, but I did not like being confronted with it. Still, I held out hopes of being with Natasja.

A few minutes into our session, I slumped over on my knees, straining on a cigarette. One of the twelve steps came to mind, about making amends. I excused myself and ran off to the payphone in a mad rush, copious amounts of change inserted into the phone. After several rings, Natasja answered.

"Natasja, it's Michael. I just want to let you know. I'm a master manipulator and a liar."

There. It was off my chest. All settled. Natasja could finally trust me with the keys to her home. But instead of welcoming arms, an angry voice came through the phone.

"What are you saying? I don't hear from you for over a week. I have no idea what's happening and you call me to tell me this. What the hell? Where —"

The phone went dead in mid-sentence. I furiously inserted more money and punched in her number again. No tone. I tried again and again and finally heard that the lines were down.

I slammed the phone into its cradle. They kept telling me I was powerless. Fucking bullshit. How could that be? I was Jesus Bond.

A delusional state of euphoria hung over me for days. My body constantly shivered, raising goose bumps on my skin. I could not sleep. While Reginald sat there watching late night television, I was out there under the stars, writing down the keys to the universe.

The following day at my individual therapy session with Jaz, I told her again. "I get it."

"You get what?"

Certain this was a test, to see if I was worthy of being welcomed to the enlightened side, I kept my cards close to my chest. A bit gutted, too. I had yet to be congratulated on my revelation. What was wrong with these people?

"How are you getting on with this Higher Power business?" Jaz asked me.

"I get it," I told her again. "I never understood the Bible was a metaphor, but everything's making sense now."

"And what about the steps?"

"I'm good to go on that front. Done. Completed."

"You need to get a sponsor. Someone who can take you through the fourth step. The inventory."

"I've done it." I told her.

She reached into her folder and pulled out a worksheet. "Here, Michael. Answer the questions on the sheet."

I read through the columns. How much money have I spent on drugs, alcohol and women? Have I ever been with a prostitute? How much money have I spent on prostitutes? How much money do I owe?

Fuck this, I thought. Jesus Bond has far more important things to be doing.

The next day, I talked to Mum by phone.

"All I want to do is be a personal trainer," I told her.

"That's great, Mike. You really know what you want to do with your life."

"I just want to help people. It feels amazing."

At that afternoon's group session, Jaz popped her head into the room and signalled for me to follow her.

"Natasja's been evacuated from her house in Rancho del Cielo. The fires have spread and are threatening her property. She's gone to a hotel. You can call her later."

Jaz took the opportunity to ask me again. "Any problems with alcohol, Michael?"

"No, I'm an addict. Never had a problem with alcohol."

Her head bobbed and weaved while she retained eye contact. She seemed sinister suddenly. Her coarse black skin and tightly curled bleached blonde hair gave off an otherworldly appearance.

She was an alien!

Terror gripped my body.

"So you've never had ANY problems with alcohol, Michael?"

So that was it. Addicts and alcoholics are alien life forms but from different planets. Jaz was testing to see which side I was on. Next step, abduction.

Get a grip, for fuck's sake. This is not happening.

At a meeting in Santa Monica that night, I heard a man sharing up front.

"When I first got sober, I thought I was being abducted by aliens."

Everyone laughed but me. This was no longer funny. Something major was happening. An aligning of the stars or something.

The following morning, I asked for acupuncture, to no avail. I was exhausted, elated, confused and terrified. The taste in my mouth was metallic, so I walked outside to spit. Just then a female patient emerged from the back shed and called over to me.

"Michael, your mum is on the phone from Cyprus."

Almost simultaneously, a patient emerged from the front shed and shouted:

"Michael, your dad is on the phone from the Isle of Man."

I dropped to my knees on the driveway, unable to take the calls. Vincenzo walked past me, shouting the twelve steps in Italian.

"Go see Dr Clark," he whispered.

Dr Clark was the centre's psychiatrist. Each new patient was offered one free meeting with him upon entering rehab. I get it, I thought. He was the one who had the next clue, the directions I needed to complete my Jesus Bond mission.

I got up off my knees and went to see Jaz. "I need to meet with Dr Clark."

"It'll cost you $400, Michael."

"What? I thought we got a free visit."

"No, your mum bargained for a reduced rate. It did not include the free doctor visit."

Jaz nodded knowingly. Outside in the yard, the other inmates gathered at the picnic tables, scribbling away as we spoke. Clearly, they were listening to our conversation, gathering information on me.

"I know the truth about what is happening here," I said.

Jaz played dumb.

"I fucking know what is going on here."

She was the chief alien of the alien addict race. She was testing me to see if I belonged.

"What do you know, Michael? What?"

It suddenly came to me. Reverend Morgan, the head of the spiritual centre Phos. It all started when he walked off the stage and shook my hand. It was the signal to start the mission. He knew where my journey was leading. I had to speak with him.

"I need to speak with Reverend Morgan," I told Jaz.

"What?" she said.

"Reverend Morgan. He's at the top of the chain."

"What are you talking about, Michael?"

"You know Reverend Morgan, don't you?" I asked.

"I might. Why?"

"I knew it, I knew it. I need to speak with him."

"Why do you want to speak with him, Michael?"

"You know why, Jaz. Now, could you get him on the phone?"

"I go to Phos, Michael. What do you want with him?"

"Just get him on the phone," I said with more force.

She walked into her office and picked up the phone. I saw her talking but could not hear the words.

She came back outside. "I've left a message that you want to speak with him."

"Good."

I walked back to the driveway and dropped to my knees, staring at the concrete. I was overwhelmed and terrified but on my way.

The bitter metallic taste was back in my mouth. What the fuck is going on? I began to spit uncontrollably. I laughed at everyone watching.

"Jaz," I said, back in her office. "What do I have to do to make this stop? What do I have to do before you tell me the truth of what is happening here?"

"Has anyone given you drugs?"

She must have known about the sleeping tablet Vincenzo gave me. This was merely one more test, but I confessed.

"Okay. Vincenzo gave me a sleeping tablet."

"Oh, he did, did he? Well, thank you for that."

She stormed off. I returned to lie on the bed. Vincenzo stormed in a moment later.

"You're crazy. You cannot be trusted. She threatened to throw me out. You're crazy. You are on their side."

He slammed the door. I lay there reflecting back on my life, clearly seeing the signs that had brought me to this point in time. Diabhal, the devil for introducing me to heroin; Mum, the virgin birth, like Mary, with her spiritual awakenings; meeting Natasja, Eve in the Garden of Eden; the fires representing hell, ironically burning both from where I had come, Natasja's house, and where I was going, Prospects in Malibu.

I was the second coming. The Messiah. The chosen one. Jesus Bond. The new, hybrid, special agent messiah superhero. I knew the truth and had to save the planet. The first assignment was to save Natasja and Dylan from the fires.

When one of the male nursing aides pulled into the driveway on his BMW motorbike, I walked over and told him to get off the bike. We fought over the helmet.

"Dude," he said. "What the hell?"

"Get off the fucking bike."

As we struggled, I heard Jaz shouting. "Michael, what the hell is going on?"

I laughed in her face. The bitter metallic taste had returned to my mouth. How did I get this all wrong?

I walked inside the building. John was watching television. My body felt hot. My face was burning. John laughed at the sight of me.

"You're bright red. You look like you're having a heart attack."

Vincenzo must have heard the discussion and came in for a look of his own. "Yeah! The air is FREE!" he shouted.

The air is free. It was the biggest revelation of my life. It was the punch line to 31 years of chasing after money, power and prestige. My whole life had been like *Groundhog Day*, a 31-year-long episode of *Punk'd*.

I walked back outside and sat down at the table. A biplane passed over. And then again. *Groundhog Day*. I am on the motherfucking *Truman Show*. The buildings and cars and trees became two-dimensional, like theatrical scenery in a stage play. I felt a sense of weightlessness and a loss of separation between myself and the other objects.

I saw clearly the vastness and simplicity of the universe and felt repulsed by manmade objects. I was back at the beginning of time. Nature provided everything I had ever wanted or needed – water, food, shelter. What else was there? To test my theory, I began to eat the shrubs. No longer needing clothes, I began to shed them.

Jaz, Tyrone and a doctor rushed over to stop me. I surrendered and sat inertly as they spoke. They were aliens, examining me. No sounds came out of their mouths. The tinny aluminium taste was back in mine.

All three of them were staring. The doctor ran off and returned with a pill. Jaz stuck her tongue out, coaxing me. They were testing to see if I still needed medication. I refused.

All the while I saw their mouths moving and heard noises, but none of it was coherent to me. Everything they said came out muffled.

Eventually I was led back to my room. I lay there, spiralling back through time, to when I was a baby, then back in the womb. Now I was dying. My heartbeat seemed to have slowed to a few beats a minute.

I was preparing to cry out to God for help when the door swung open and several firemen dashed into the room, theatrical-style, complete with Fire Department badges and walkie-talkies.

Their acting seemed subpar – lots of exaggerated movements and over reaction.

I shouted, "Oh, my God! What!? What!?"

The heat of my skin was unbearable. My heart felt as if it had stopped.

One of the firemen leaned over me and held the defibrillator pads to my chest. Another one strapped a blood pressure gauge to my arm and began pumping. They both look at the reading with concern. All three of them shook their heads.

"Is this a fucking joke?" I said.

I kept expecting someone to burst out laughing. Gotcha!

Two cops came in with similar expressions on their faces. It was a joke. I felt certain it was a joke. At any moment, someone was going to say. "All right. He's on to us."

Instead, one of the firemen called out to get me on a gurney. I was wheeled from the room and down the short corridor, past the other patients. It was dark outside. The gurney was rolling swiftly. The Santa Ana winds blew hot and dry.

I was rushed to a waiting ambulance at the bottom of the drive. The neighbours were all out, watching this reality TV episode unfold.

Jesus Bond: Survivor.

Meanwhile, I was lined up at the back of the ambulance and hoisted inside. The doors closed and I was left there staring at the ceiling. The sterile, clinical scent made me feel all the more uneasy.

With the back window of the van above my eye line, I was unable to see my reflection. A thought occurred to me. Am I still alive? I started to raise my head to confirm this but was stopped by a sense of sheer terror. What if I saw the white hockey mask of Hannibal Lecter staring back?

While I was praying for this movie to stop, the ambulance pulled away. The city lights began to pass by outside. With each thrust of the gears, I expected the ambulance to blast off for the mother ship.

Twenty minutes later, the ambulance stopped. The back doors opened. Orange and yellow spotlights glared from the back of a building. We were still on terra firma.

I was wheeled into something very much resembling a hospital. Ceiling tiles and fluorescent lights flashed by overhead. People surrounded me, coming and going, stopping to analyse. I was sure they were the aliens, preparing to dissect and dismember me.

Rolled into a cubicle and lifted onto a bed, I had a view of the reception area. People were standing around in white gowns with clipboards. Do I get them before they get me? Kill them all now? I bolted upright in the bed. How could I escape?

A woman was wheeled into the cubicle next to me. I could not see her face but she was shrieking.

"Cold coffee!"

Again and again. Demonic it sounded.

Sickened, I turned the other way. A TV was blaring. I stared, trying hard not to lose control.

The Late Show was on. David Letterman was playing along with the script, pretending that nothing was wrong. I was on the show, screened live to the world.

Suddenly it dawned on me. I had been trying for years to fix myself: drugs, alcohol, women, starvation, sex, steroids, surgery. All I had to do, really, was kill myself. Then I'd be free. The show always came to an end anyway. The prospect of eternal life was calling to me.

I noticed a security guard filling the corridor across from me. He must have been seven foot tall and 350 pounds. Plus, he was carrying a gun, his hands clasped on it in front of him, his eyes staring over my head. He would not make eye contact with me. I had an impulse to take his gun, put it in my mouth and pull the trigger. Then it would be over.

Jesus died to save the world. As the new world saviour, now it was my turn.

But what if I was wrong?

A voice kept telling me to do it. Take the fucking gun and blow your fucking brains out, you fucking pussy. Only, in this scene, a flag will pop out of the end with "bang" written across it. The director will shout "Cut".

I lay back down, petrified. The woman behind the curtain was still shrieking. While I lay there, a group of people formed a semicircle in front of me. I recognized my black travel bag on the floor beside the bed. How did that get here? I stood up and looked inside: blue jeans and a black t-shirt. No wallet, no money, no phone. I recalled that I was in LA. I could head for Skid Row.

"Fuck this, I'm going," I said.

When I reached for my pants, a young man dressed in a white shirt and black trousers stepped forward. He began to read from a piece of paper. His hands were shaking. I hardly understood a word. Something about an involuntary psychiatric hold. I laughed.

"That's terrible!" I said. "He's a terrible actor. He's giving the game away. Look. He's shaking. I knew it. A setup. Fuck this. I'm out of here."

When I made a move towards the door, the security guard forced me onto the gurney and pinned me down with his hands and knees. While I struggled, he and three other men strapped me to the bed, my arms and legs in four directions. I had no fight left in me, except for a violent spit in the face of the guard.

My track pants had been pulled down around my shins in the struggle. Two men were moving around me, adjusting the equipment. Then they simultaneously inserted large needles into both biceps and depressed the plungers. Everyone else stood and stared. Letterman was still offering comedic relief in the background. With the fluorescent lights, the scene was growing surreal.

I was suddenly desperate to shit and asked to use the restroom. A nurse left and returned with a cardboard bedpan. She pushed it into the leg of my boxer shorts and underneath my arse, completing the degradation. I expected the Letterman show to turn the cameras on me. Mum and Dad will see me, pants down around my ankles, restrained to a bed with a cardboard tray beneath my arse, my public humiliation complete.

Reginald appeared out of nowhere. "Did you want to tell me anything?"

"Like what?"

"We told you from the start of treatment to be honest. You've not been honest, never told the truth, have you?"

"About what?" I said.

He started to leave. "You know where I am when you're ready to talk."

He reappeared a few moments later. "Are you ready yet?"

He left and came back several times. Finally, I forced the words out. I was morally and spiritually incapable of telling the truth. My entire lifetime.

Reginald took a seat at my bedside. The gold boxing glove around his neck was hypnotizing. "Start with the drugs," he said. "What drugs have you done?"

Preparing to die anyway, I decided to purge my soul. "Heroin," I said.

"Good, keep going. Did you shoot up?"

"Yes."

"Coke?" he said.

I nodded. "And crack."

"Keep going."

"Cannabis, Ecstasy, speed, meth, ketamine, acid. I also injected Ecstasy."

"Anything else?"

"Steroids."

"You ever done mushrooms?"

"Everything apart from PCP."

"Prostitutes?"

"Yes. And I'm not a professional rugby player."

Reginald looked perplexed by this last admission so I went on to explain about Natasja.

"You owe a lot of money, don't you, Michael?"

I nodded, yes.

"You've hurt a lot of people, haven't you, Michael?"

"Yeah."

"You've been a liar all your life, haven't you?"

"Yes."

"See, man. Now don't you feel cleaner inside?"

My ego was in shreds, I lay naked before the world, but aye, I felt real clean.

Reginald left me alone and the ordeal had soon put me to sleep.

I reawakened to find myself still shackled to the gurney. Shell-shocked like nothing I had ever experienced. At least the paranoia and delusion from the previous night had vanished. Now it was just one continuous nightmare.

A nurse's aide came in to check on me. I was trying to count the days and establish coordinates and felt encouraged to learn my location was Santa Monica. One step up from East LA but the involuntary psychiatric hold was not to my liking, nor was this four-point restraint business. Hard to kick off under the circumstances.

An ambulance team arrived to move me a short time later. With my arms and legs released, I was placed on another gurney and wheeled outside. It was daylight now. Traffic was rushing by in every direction. That seemed to be the only normal thing left in my existence.

Two men lifted me into another ambulance and I was back to staring at a ceiling. One of the ambulance crew members appeared over my head.

"How do you feel, Michael?"

"All right. I'm good."

"We can let you out of these straps if you're going to behave."

"No fighting, men. The last thing I want is a fight."

He unbuckled me.

"Maybe my mum," I said. "And to go home."

He smiled. "There you go."

"Where are we going?" I asked.

"The hospital's in Glendale."

I felt him lock the gurney into position in the ambulance.

"How long's it going to take?"

"Forty-five minutes to an hour, depending on traffic."

The van doors shut and I instinctively revolted against the enclosed space. The ambulance crew laughed and joked along the way. They had plans for the evening: finish work, meet up with friends, have a few beers, shoot some pool and watch the game. It all sounded so normal. I couldn't remember ever going out for a few beers. It might start with a beer, but that always led to drugs and whores and chaos, more and more of everything, until days had passed and the money had run out.

The same crew member turned to check on me. "Everything still all right?"

"All good."

He gave me a thumbs up. "The place we're going is better than the other option. I think they even have some sort of… er…pictures on the walls."

Pictures on the walls? Where the fuck are they taking me? A brothel?

212

CHAPTER FOURTEEN

We pulled into a driveway and stopped outside another decaying wood-clad building. A small yard was enclosed by a fifteen-foot fence, capped with barbed wire.

What the fuck? I thought I had just escaped this place.

Somebody with security told the crew to go around to the back of the building. Once we had stopped, I was wheeled from the van and assisted to my feet. My legs struggled to maintain balance.

The crew led me to a steel door with several locks. An '80s era surveillance camera pointed down at us. The entire setup looked dated. A nurse opened the door and let me in. She thanked the men and they left. Locks and bolts slammed shut behind me. I spied another security door up ahead, and my claustrophobia started growing.

The nurse led me to a room about the size of a two-car garage. Two lost-looking men and a woman sat in flimsy chairs at a white plastic table. They were playing some kind of card game. When two matching cards slapped onto the table, the two men said, "Sssssnaaaaapp."

Where this was going, only they knew.

The card game stopped while the nurse introduced me. All three of them said "Hiiii" and stared through glazed eyes. I smelled urine, wheat biscuits and cigarette smoke. Their short sleeves displayed blood-stained bandages on forearms and wrists. All three were cut to ribbons. Amidst the wounds I saw tattoos.

"This is the Coliseum unit, Michael. Please have a seat. And remove your shoelaces and drawstring belt."

This was to prevent suicide by hanging, I presumed. I sprawled out on a faux leather couch, doing my best to look calm and relaxed. The nurse did a double-take but kept filling out forms.

The feel of the room was somewhere between a primary school classroom and a prison ward. The nursing station in the corner was protected by a chain-link cage. Games were scattered around the room. The options included pushing beads around a metal frame and an abacus. Otherwise, you could have mistaken it for a World War I lunatic ward. Everything smelled of stale cigarette smoke. The walls had yellowed with time.

The nurse came out of her cage and waved her clipboard in my direction. "Somebody will be along soon to check your vitals and ask a few questions. Just remain seated."

I did and studied my sedated brethren. They seemed comfy in their pharmaceutically induced comas, safe from society, safe from themselves.

A Grizzly Adams look-alike nodded at me. His hair was wild on top of a voluminous beard. He was wearing a blue checked shirt.

"I'm Monty. What you in here for?"

"I have no idea. I'm meant to be in Hawaii."

Why I bothered to bullshit anyone now was beyond me. I had just come clean with Reginald a few hours ago, and already I was spinning new lies.

All three of the inmates were staring as if they could not care less what I said, or comprehend it.

"Join us for cards?" Monty said.

"No...really...thank you."

I heard a shriek from down the corridor. Eyes fixed on a 15-inch TV, I considered my exit strategy from the faux leather couch. The final game of the 2007 World Series was on. The Red Sox and Rockies. Fenway Park. It's *One Flew Over the*

Bloody Cuckoo's Nest. I felt a twinge at remembering Natasja's 42-inch HD plasma.

"Michael!" a nurse called.

I raised my hand. She came over and took my blood pressure. With that done, she crouched down and looked into my eyes. "How are you feeling?"

She had said it slowly as if speaking to the retarded. Her look of pity triggered an old reaction. It was my mum when I was a sick little boy. Pity was another drug for me. Lethal. A soul destroyer. But seductive.

"Excuse me," I said. "If you have a moment, I really shouldn't be in here. I'm sure this was all an overreaction to yesterday's events. I'm actually meant to be in Hawaii. I'm wondering if you can possibly find out how I can get out of here. And soon. When am I likely to be leaving?"

"No time soon, Michael. You'll be here three days at the least. And you'll need to be seen by the psychiatrist. They're the ones who make the decisions. Unfortunately, there are no psychiatrists available until tomorrow. Don't keep to yourself. It will look better if you join in with the other patients. Play a game."

No way did I wish to bond with the other patients. I would be deemed guilty by association, like admitting I'm sick. So I was damned if I did, and damned if I didn't.

"Your behaviour last night was quite serious," the nurse continued. "And unfortunately, we don't have any contact numbers or medical records to establish your background or condition. We're working on it."

I stared, my mind a blank.

"Also, we have an isolation room, so if you show any signs of abnormal behaviour, you'll be back in five or six-point restraints."

"This is ridiculous. What's considered abnormal behaviour?"

"If you try to destroy hospital property, try to injure yourself or others. Or if we find any other medical or psychological grounds for doing so."

She tried to soften the insult with a smile.

I rolled my eyes and exhaled. "Anything else you can throw at me?"

"ECT," she said.

"What the fuck is ECT?"

"Electroconvulsive therapy."

The nurse went inside the nursing station and returned with some forms. "I need you to fill these out. We need a detailed medical history."

With 16 years' worth of doctor's visits, treatment, surgeries and therapy, most or all of it stemming from my drug and alcohol abuse, I had to manipulate the forms quite a bit to make myself look less despicable. An hour went by. When it came to signing each page, I struggled to do so legibly. My mouth gaped open as the pen scrawled across the dotted line.

When I finally handed the forms back to the nurse, she handed me another one.

"I also need you to sign this. It says you agree we can use restraints and ECT should they become necessary."

Shit out of ideas, I signed it.

"Oh, and this," she said.

It was an agreement to pay for the treatment.

"I have to pay for this? What about National Health Service?"

"You can claim back on your insurance."

"I don't have insurance. Well, I have private health care in the United Kingdom."

It was another lie I'd have to square with Reginald and the world.

Glancing through the payment form, I saw the costs detailed. $900 for each ambulance journey. $700 for emergency hospital care. $850 a night to stay in this dump. An itemized list of doctor's fees, examination fees and lab tests followed.

"Excuse me, sorry to trouble you, but it says here that it costs $850 a night to stay in this place."

"That's correct. It's for the extra nursing care. We have to monitor you continuously throughout the day and night for your own safety."

"And you have to keep me here for 72 hours?"

"That's right."

Mum had just shelled out $20K on the treatment centre. I quickly added up the ambulance rides and other entertainment in my head. By the time my 72 hours were up, we would have topped the five grand mark.

"Do excuse me. When did you want this money?"

"You have an extended time period to pay."

With no intention of paying anything, I signed the forms.

Grizzly Adams came through and called out to me. "Fifteen-minute smoke break in the yard. Are you coming?"

"No, thanks."

"I'll make you a roll-up."

I waved him off. No way was I going to be spotted by surveillance cameras with that lot.

A couple of hours passed. I was offered pizza and chips. I said no to the comfort of food. The only thing I had left to control was calories.

I sat and stared at the television set until my room was ready. I could not recall the last time I had gone to bed without drugs or medication. Making a request for medication was imperative. I tried a few pitches in my head. The idea was not to appear too desperate. Reverse psychology. If the nurse declined, I had to take it in my stride.

At the first sign of a nurse in the cage, I called over and pretended to focus on the TV first. "Excuse me. Sorry to trouble you but would it be possible to get something to help me sleep this evening?" I threw in a smile with my glance over from the TV.

"No," she said.

My foot and leg twitched. "Okay. No problem."

For fuck's sake, I mumbled to myself.

Eventually, a nurse escorted me to one of the six bedrooms. It was the first time I had seen a bed, sink and toilet moulded to the floor. The only way to hurt yourself was to throw yourself at the walls. The room had a solitary plastic window with steel bars and a wire mesh window guard. The orange glow of sunset lit up a distant mountain range. It could have been Mars.

I lay down on the bed, scared and alone. Did anyone know I was here? Did anyone love me?

A shriek rang out from the isolation room across the corridor. I pictured a naked woman, hung by her wrists, electrodes strapped to her neck and extremities, hair on end, piss dripping from her toes.

Cruel fucking mind. If only I could turn it off.

Evening passed. The room turned dark. I was alone with my thoughts. I twisted and turned on the thin, piss-proof padding, a scratchy rug clenched to my chest. The foetal position was best though nothing brought me comfort. At fifteen-minute intervals, the night nurse opened the door and shined a light on my face.

When the door opened again, cold fluorescent light flooded in from the hallway. Dawn was peeking through the bars on the window.

Moments later, I heard frantic movement out in the corridor, then screaming and shouting. A nurse closed the door.

Later I heard a knock and said, "Come in."

A well-dressed young man came in. His nervousness was forgivable. "Hi, I'm Stewart. Dr Kranzler's assistant."

"Hello, and how are you?" I said, skipping the joke about how I intended to eat him.

"Good, thank you. I'm here to evaluate your case for Dr Kranzler. Do you feel up to telling me a bit more about what happened?"

"Sure. Dr Kranzler?"

"The psychiatrist who will be taking care of you. He's back at the office, but he'll be along as soon as he can. I've got your case notes here."

Stewart unzipped a brown leather portfolio. "Did you want to start from the beginning?"

"Absolutely. By the way, have you any idea when I can get out of here?"

"I only take notes and then brief Dr Kranzler. He can make a decision on what to do once he's seen you."

I began to recount my medical history. We talked for over an hour, during which time I provided a fairly honest and sincere account of recent events. Stewart even laughed at a couple of my jokes. I reckoned I'd be out of this place in no time.

"How long before the psychiatrist arrives?" I asked again.

"I don't know. He's taking a while. Can we talk a bit more about your substance abuse history?"

I became tired of the conversation. My mind switched back to escape routes.

"I hope you don't mind," Stewart said. "But Dr Kranzler suggested you would be a good case study for my Ph.D. thesis, so I'd like to get as much information as possible."

Weary, but realizing this interview might put me in good favour, I confessed to my steroid use.

Stewart laughed. "You've done steroids?"

I nodded. "Grew a set of tits for my troubles."

"Tits? Really?"

"Yep. Had them chopped off on the National Health Service. Indian doctor. Not what I would call the most finely tuned procedure. The doctor walked in moments before the anaesthesia, slapping a silver spatula in his hand." I went on in my best Indian voice. "Now, what are we doing today, sir?"

Stewart laughed.

"And that was that. I woke up in more pain than I can ever remember. Didn't tell the doctor I was taking opiate blockers. Ashamed I was. Needless to say, the post-op morphine had no effect. Shed a tear or two, I'll tell ya. Hackled like a slaughtered beast. Not the most fun I've ever had. No feeling in my chest for a year!"

Stewart sat there speechless.

"Are you taking notes, fella? It shrinks your bollocks too. Then you have to inject pregnant women's urine to get everything back to normal. Get that down."

Stewart resumed writing. "So, about these steroids..." Stewart said, looking up.

"Stewart, can I, er..." I nodded my head at the door, "Can I go?"

"Um, we need to wait for Dr Kranzler. Can you tell me some more about the steroids?"

I gave him the science master class. Anabolic steroids, androgenic steroids, compounds, testosterone levels, molecular structures, physiological effects, psychological effects, supplementation, diuretics, oestrogen retention, amino acids, pre-competition water expulsion, diet and nutrition. I had it all covered. Most of it was completely irrelevant unless Stewart suddenly had a yearning to flex on stage wearing a thong. If nothing else, he looked duly impressed with my professorial acumen.

"You seem stable to me," he said. "Once Dr Kranzler gets here, he can review my notes."

Dr Kranzler eventually arrived with a "hello" and a handshake. He looked the part: portly, dull clothes, glasses, a beard and carrying a leather briefcase. Stewart debriefed him. The doctor listened with a look of concern. With my future in his hands, my stomach was in knots.

"From what Stewart has told me, you seem to be doing well. I've reviewed your case notes, so now I need to hear your account of the events. Then we'll go through a standard screening inventory to diagnose your condition."

He pulled out what I now knew to be the *Diagnostic and Statistical Manual of Mental Disorders*. "So, tell me about your experiences with depression and drug or chemical abuse."

Convinced that the full story would ensure my being locked up here for a very long time, I prepared an edited version. I had never told a doctor the full truth, and I did not intend to start now.

"Any suicidal tendencies?" he asked me.

"Er, no, not really."

At his prompting, I recounted the events of the past few days, somehow drawn towards complete honesty. There were fluctuations in mood, morbid thoughts, severe anxiety, periods of euphoria, giddiness, irritability, auditory and visual hallucinations, thought disorganization, sensory integration issues, manic behaviour, sleep disturbance and grandiose delusions.

I stopped, suddenly concerned that I had served myself up as a nut case.

Dr Kranzler seemed unmoved. "You do score high on the list for Bipolar 1 in a number of areas," he said, "but low in others. I'd put you between a Bipolar 1 and Bipolar 2 diagnosis."

"What's the difference?"

"Bipolar 2 is characterized by episodes of major depressive symptoms, with less severe manic symptoms than in Bipolar 1. Bipolar 1 includes at least one manic episode or symptoms of mania and depression at the same time, with the symptoms being a lot more severe and lasting several days."

Good thing I had not included my Ecstasy-induced psychosis experience at age 18. I would have qualified for the Bipolar 1 poster boy.

Dr Kranzler tapped his fingers, looking baffled. It was not surprising. I had sugarcoated the truth with an abundance of bullshit. I half expect Kranzler to shrug and say "fuck knows", but deep down inside I felt relief. There was freedom in knowing the truth. A few tablets and I'd be right. I was that close to a solution. Of course, who the fuck wanted to be diagnosed with a serious mental illness? It screamed of embarrassment, humiliation and shame.

My head was oscillating between admission and denial.

Dr Kranzler continued. "Of course we need to get you on the correct medication. It's critical. You should never have been taking anti-depressants for this condition. A person exhibiting your mental phenomena can experience suicidal tendencies and manic episodes. You must have been tortured."

"On the odd occasion," I said with just a hint of sarcasm.

The pill-popping part of me was scared as fuck. I had visions of Dr Kranzler dispensing some rocket-launching medication and getting me hooked anew. The dying part of me was screaming inside.

"Get some help, you proud, stubborn fuck!"

I settled somewhere in between. We'd accept the drugs and deal with the addiction part later on.

"In any case," Dr Kranzler was saying, "you certainly seem okay, so I'll arrange to have you moved to Nine West later today. That's our dual diagnosis unit."

Assuming the existence of God, I thanked Him. "So, what exactly is the dual diagnosis unit?"

"We treat for both bipolar and addictions there. You'll get treatment for both."

Another scream echoed down the corridor. Dr Kranzler stood up with a flat smile and shook my hand. Stewart did the same and they left. I lay back down. The screams continued through the course of the morning, reminding me of where I was.

Sometime in the early afternoon, a nurse came to collect me. My walk down the corridor went haltingly. Something had gone wrong. The stress of the past few days had affected my ability to walk. Basic locomotion was on the level of a stroke victim: left leg and arm forward, right leg and arm, my movements akin to a drunken puppet as the nurse escorted me. Each step sent a jolting shock to my head, causing me to tense and flinch.

Outside, I winced as the sun hit my face. The air felt raw against my skin. We walked amongst the lush botanical gardens. Small wooden cottages were grouped together along the pathways. The famed Nine West, Dual Diagnosis Unit, was up ahead.

"There are twenty-five acres of botanical gardens," I was told. "The psychiatric hospital itself is over a hundred years old. We have detox facilities, rehab, residential treatment, hospitalization and of course outpatient services."

"A one-stop shop for every mental illness," I said.

The nurse smiled. I smiled.

"The facility is well known for housing the rich and famous," she went on. "The Gables residential unit was named after Clark Gable. Marilyn Monroe was seen doing cartwheels through the gardens. Rumour has it that the hospital was the inspiration for the Eagles song *Hotel California*."

I was growing winded from our stroll through the botanical gardens but encouraged. Soon I would be rubbing shoulders with the rich and famous. I pictured silver plate dinners delivered by black-tie waiters.

My elation was short-lived. We passed a combined tennis and basketball court, then a rundown swimming pool littered with dilapidated chaises longues. The main building was straight ahead. Nine West, it turned out, was just that, the west wing. It was also another lock-down unit. I was escorted through a secure door and into an elevator.

The nurse offered me a tutorial as we waited in the lift. Nine West was a mixed unit; there were thirty rooms on each floor, men and women on both floors, with each person assigned a room according to their condition. Depressive alcoholics were on the first floor, drug and alcohol users with severe mental disorders were on the second floor.

The elevator stopped at the second floor. The doors opened onto a long, narrow corridor. The feel was that of an older, cheap motel: worn carpets, paint peeling from the walls, derelict-looking people wandering the corridor. Things actually looked out of level. The place had definitely gone downhill since Gable and Monroe. I smelled Clorox and Lysol, sickness and despair.

"This way," the nurse said. "We have it all in here, you know. Schizophrenics, bipolar, personality and obsessive compulsive disorders, mental retardation, generalized anxiety, anorexia/bulimia, along with a mix of crack, heroin, meth and alcohol addicts."

That would be me, I thought.

As we approached the nursing station, I tried to put on my best swagger. The usual claustrophobia had sucked the air right out of me. I was at least reassured by this knowledge. If the clean life failed me, that nursing station up ahead had enough drugs to sedate an empire.

A young kid with his cap on backwards and his pant waist down around his scrotum came by. "Hey, whassup? I'm Justin."

What's up? I'll tell you what's up, you little fucker. Every fucking thing I have ever dreaded has come to pass. I don't know a soul in this fucked-up country. Nobody knows where I am. I've been in the same filthy, shit-sodden clothes for the past few days. I've never felt so ashamed, terrified and alone in my entire life. That's what's up.

In place of my diatribe, I nodded and responded, "Just checking in, man."

At the nursing station, a nurse took my vitals and went through yet one more induction process. From there I was escorted down a corridor to the manager's small office. His bookshelves were littered with literature on addiction and mental illness. A couple of tubs of protein powder sat on a table beside his desk.

I took a seat and waited. A few minutes later, a tall, well-groomed and thick-set man came bounding in.

"Heyyyyyyyy, I'm Ryan, the unit manager. Welcome to Forest Hills Hospital."

He came off like an AM disc jockey. I shook his hand, considerably less enthused about Forest Hills Hospital. Ryan quickly informed me of the rules and regulations. His eyes focused on the wall directly behind my head. I did a quick double-take around the room. It felt as if he was talking to someone else. His lack of eye contact did nothing to instil confidence.

"So, I got a brief history of what happened at Prospects," he went on. "No need to be afraid. Bipolar is serious, but I'm considered bipolar too. We just need to manage the symptoms and your lifestyle to prevent a relapse or psychotic episodes. If you do everything prescribed, it's possible to have a fairly normal life."

He removed his glasses to clean them and I saw that he was cross-eyed. The glasses went back on. He gestured a hand at my upper body.

"You clearly work out. Are you an athlete? Play any sports?"

"Not at the minute," I said with an ever so faint flex of my biceps. "Used to play professional rugby but haven't worked out for a while now."

Another lie. Why did I keep doing it? Whenever in doubt, pull out the old rugby story. Hope the recovering athlete bullshit leads to preferential treatment?

"Okay, I'm going to get you a good room. Something with a stable roommate."

Justice.

Ryan handed me another copy of *Alcoholics Anonymous*. "This saved my life," he said and stood up.

I was glad for him. My copy was headed for the first rubbish bin.

Out in the corridor, we turned a corner and found 5 feet 10 inches of physical perfection coming at us, all big brown eyes, luxurious brown hair and rose petal skin. Justin appeared to be attached to her left leg.

Shoulders down, chest in. Stomach out. Shit! Wrong way round.

She went by without a word and hardly a look.

I'd not worked out for the last five days. Clearly, that's why she ignored me. Top priority was to find a gym.

My room had two single beds, with a chest of drawers alongside each one. The thin carpet was worn and brown. The window was embedded with wire mesh. It looked like someone had shot a couple of bullet holes into it.

"Settle in," Ryan encouraged me. "Someone will be around to move forward with your therapy soon."

I settled into doing absolutely nothing. After staring at the ceiling for a while, I noticed the books on top of my chest of drawers. A small book had *Daily Reflections* written on it. The other one said *Twelve Steps and Twelve Traditions*.

Along with the book Ryan had given me, I tucked them out of sight in the top drawer of the chest. No more shame for me.

Exhausted but in need of a shower, I entered the bathroom. The dilapidated toilet, sink and bath/shower combo were all crammed into a six by five space. Everything metal was rusting. There were no toiletries provided and I had no clothes, so a shower was pointless. I twisted the small shower handle and a stream of cold water dribbled out. I threw some water on my face and dried it with my t-shirt.

I looked in the mirror above the sink, afraid of what I would see. It was the first time I had seen myself in days. The harsh lighting revealed a man with dark circles under his eyes and deepening crow's feet. A few dishevelled hair transplants were sprouting along the receding hairline. The face was covered in stubble and greying at the chin. I was looking at the problem: me.

I tensed my biceps, exaggerating my declining physique. Shoulders back, chest out, stomach in.

Dear God.

An attractive lady entered the room, surprising me.

"Good afternoon," I said, coming out of the bathroom.

She had ironed blonde hair down past her shoulders and a fitted sweater that clung to her pert breasts. Her tight skirt sat above the knee.

"Hi, Michael, I'm Dr Anderson, a psychologist. I work with Dr Kranzler."

We shook hands. She sat on the bed.

"Let's see what we can do about making you feel better."

In the abyss of my perverted mind, that involved pulling the sweater over her head. Instead, she pulled out a book entitled *Bipolar Survival Guide*.

A bit disheartened, I listened absent-mindedly while she stressed the need for medication, therapy and education.

"I'll just pull that door shut," I said.

No need for anyone else to hear this. I had experienced enough shame on all fronts by this point.

"Michael, bipolar is not curable," she went on, oblivious to my vanity.

Considering where I was, it was laughable to think that pride was even on my agenda.

Her dissertation droned on. I needed to be aware of my energy, mood, sleep and eating behaviours. Lifestyle management was paramount. A steady routine was required, regular sleep, a sober and healthy lifestyle. Keep stress levels low. Regular therapy. When she got to the part about psychiatric monitoring and medication, my leg twitched. We were back to a life sentence of drugs.

"Your treatment will involve a new anti-psychotic medication," she said. "Dr Kranzler has prescribed Seroquel, a sedative to keep you stable until he arrives on Monday. At that point, we'll address a proper treatment for your bipolar condition."

"Can you call Mum?" I said. "Let her know where I am. Let her know I'm okay."

Dr Anderson left the room and returned several minutes later.

"We finally located the information for your mum in Cyprus. Here's the number. You call."

I did and waited while the phone rang. She finally answered.

"Mum, it's me."

"Oh, Mike, I'm so glad to hear from you. I've had Prospects on the phone, the doctors, and Natasja."

All these bloody people in the mix, discussing me, the basket case.

"What did Natasja say?"

"Oh, no need to worry about that now," she said.

"Is there any chance you can fly over to America?"

"Absolutely, I'm leaving. Get off the phone. I'm on my way. Consider it done."

The medication hour was at six o'clock. The queue started forming in front of the nursing station at five-thirty. Patience soon turned to violence, multiple personalities with multiple disorders beating on the bulletproof window, threatening bodily harm to the staff and themselves if some fucker did not open up the fucking window and give them their fucking drugs.

Inclined to observe the call to arms from afar, I noticed that same bit of elegance and perfumed hair and took my place at the back of the line. Justin was still attached to her legs.

"Sophie C," she confirmed when it was her turn at the window. The nurse reached for the Tupperware container filled with the medication.

"OxyContin, eighty milligrams," the nurse said. "This is your third dose of four. Sign here. Here's some water to wash it down."

A girl after my own heart. My head began processing a well-worn tape. Two for you, two for me. We would move in together, con a doctor for more. Somehow we would taper down, get clean, save the money and start a life together.

Sophie took her drugs and drifted down the corridor, my imagination following her.

When it became my turn, I was administered a dose of Seroquel, to be taken four times a day. Twenty minutes later, I was in a trance that kept me safely integrated with the pace of the unit, shuffling, giddy, muttering obscenities and chain smoking.

The nurse shined a torch on my face every thirty minutes throughout the night. Somehow I slept and awakened at dawn to find my roommate kneeling at the end of his bed, muttering the Lord's Prayer.

Has he no shame? I considered making a break for it, but in my condition, that was out of the question. I thanked the Lord the man was leaving today.

Dr Anderson dropped in after breakfast with a razor, toothbrush, deodorant and some clothes from Target. Her choice of multicoloured shorts and green crew neck tops wasn't mine, but fresh clothes were fresh clothes.

After a shower, it felt luxurious to pull on unsoiled cotton for the first time in four days. The white sports socks were for comfort, not looks. The first person I walked into was Sophie.

I acknowledged the encounter with a tug of my t-shirt.

"It's not mine."

She clearly could not have cared less and kept going. Justin was now attached to her like a shadow.

I was busy trying to keep Gidawook out of my thoughts, that old nutcase back on the Isle of Man. Drooling and mumbling to himself. He had become the benchmark between sanity and madness for me.

I recalled one time when the local kids were taunting Gidawook, and Finnegan had uttered a profound statement through all his dyslexia.

"Don't mock the afflicted 'cos you're temptin' the probable."

Immortal line that one. For once, the truth had departed his lips with complete clarity.

Well, never again would I be mocking anyone's ailments. Karma's a bitch.

CHAPTER FIFTEEN

With the morning meds in me, I settled in to observe my fellow patients. Shannon looked like Malibu Barbie. She was currently appearing on a Friday night reality show, channelling Anna Nicole Smith. Sean was a ringer for Gary Busey and our Nine West village idiot. I heard him around every corner long before I saw him: a loud, argumentative, complaining, swearing, sometimes humorous, meth-smoking paranoid schizophrenic. I watched him all day, both troubled and perplexed that I had ended up in here with the likes of him.

On Saturday night, I received a message that Mum had left on a flight from Cyprus to Los Angeles via the United Kingdom.

A nurse found me in the television room. "Phone call for you, Michael."

"Who?" I asked.

"Natasja."

I picked up the phone and took a deep breath. Even with the sedatives to calm me I was trembling like hell.

"Hello."

"Michael, it's Natasja. How are you? Where are you?"

"In Glendale. I'm hanging in there, but I've seen better days."

"I'm coming to visit."

"No, Natasja. I don't want you to see me in this place, please."

"Michael, I'm coming. I need to know you're okay."

"Listen, give me a few days. You can call anytime. I just need to get my shit together."

"They said you had a complete breakdown. Your mum's been on the phone. I've spoken to your dad. Nobody knows what's happening."

"Natasja, I don't want you seeing me in this place."

"Well, I'm coming. Early next week."

I got off the phone, filled with fear. Mum was fiery as hell about her religion. Natasja was just as belligerent about her spiritual stuff. The two of them would be petrol and matches together. I couldn't risk having them in the same space.

After fretting over things for twenty-four hours, I received a call from the nursing station late on Sunday night. Mum was in the ground-floor reception area. She'd driven straight over from the airport. My mind scrambled for ways to get the drooling patients out of the corridor. A moment later, I heard the lift stop and saw Mum walk out. She looked white and drawn. Her eyes seemed twice their normal size. Who could blame her? It must have been soul destroying to see her son in such a place.

"Sorry about this," I said, ashamed but trying to make things appear as normal as possible. I glanced around at the babbling patients. Why couldn't they just fuck off for half an hour?

"Different," Mum said.

"To say the least."

When we hugged, I felt her shaking. A tear trickled down her cheek.

"It's all right, Mum. I'm all right."

"Okay," she said. "I'm okay now."

"Unbelievable you got here so quick."

"Yep, last flight out of Cyprus to Newcastle. Newcastle to London, connecting flight to Los Angeles. I just drove straight from the airport. I've not checked into the hotel yet."

"Let's go into my room, eh?"

She walked along beside me. Despite my best efforts, the medication had reduced me to a shuffle.

"I'm so glad you came," I said with my eyes on the floor. "I can't tell you how much it means to me."

"It wouldn't matter where in the world you were, or where I was, I'd be there. I would just do anything for you kids."

I glanced over. Her lip was trembling.

"I really don't know what to say, my boy. It might sound like a silly question, but how is everything?"

"Well, it's not exactly plan A. I'm all right, though. I could do with getting out of here. I'll apologize in advance for the residents."

We talked for a while, but it was already late.

"I suppose I should get on to my hotel for the night."

Our walk down the corridor turned into a guided tour of the unit. She was clearly in shock over where life had led me.

"I'm just down the road, and I'll be here for ten days, or for as long as you need me. I understand you've got stuff to do during the day, but anytime you want, I'm here. You just let me know."

I thanked Mum again and watched her leave.

Alone in my room, I wanted to cry but couldn't. How could I do this to Mum? She'd been through so much heartache already.

Dr Kranzler arrived Monday morning and reviewed the notes on my stay so far.

"We'll get you started on Abilify," he said, coming into my room. "That will treat the bipolar and keep you stable. You'll take your first dose at lunchtime."

At the appropriate hour, I headed over to the nursing station, received my first tablet and washed it down with water. A case worker appeared and pulled me aside for another medical assessment. We sat in a window seat overlooking the gardens.

"How are you feeling?" he asked.

"Tired."

"Tired is not a feeling. It is a biological condition."

My expression went from blank to slack-jawed.

The questions continued. After ten minutes, my mouth grew dry, but not from talking. I felt increasingly agitated and started to sweat. The tension in my neck quickly turned into a cramp and spread from the back of my right ear to my right shoulder blade. My head and neck were twisting involuntarily. I fought body convulsions and focused hard on the questions. When the cramp pulled my head back, horizontal to the floor, I stood up. I had to get out of there before someone diagnosed me as sick. I sat back down, still convulsing.

"Everything okay?" the caseworker said.

"I've gotta go."

I stood up and walked to my room. On the bed, I twisted and convulsed. Sit up. Sit back down. Must save face and stay out of sight. I went to the bathroom to check my face in the mirror. It was ashen, harrowed and twisted brutally to one side. Somehow I had developed a double chin.

Shaking and sweating and in complete confusion now, I blocked the door to my room. Then I felt an impulse to leave. How to do so without being seen?

I pushed my neck into some socially acceptable angle and reassured myself that everyone in here was so fucked, they would never notice my condition.

Out in the corridor, I checked the lift. It was locked. The only exit was over a secured fence. Not much hope there. I had no idea where I was going anyway.

I walked into the TV room and took a seat. Aware that patients were staring at me, I left and circled the unit. An impulse to hide took me in and out of toilets.

Deciding that contrary action was the way to go, I headed down the stairs. I'd show them nothing was wrong. A group of inmates was gathered on the grassy backyard, enjoying the leisure hour. They spotted me.

"Come on, join in."

One of them was Sophie. Christ.

"You have a choice of tennis, table tennis, basketball, colouring or the bongo drums," a counsellor told me.

I thought it prudent to skip all competitive sports, including the bongo drums. The group started out on an escorted tour of the botanical gardens. I followed a few strides behind Sophie. Damned neck. I decided to strike up a conversation anyway.

"Hello. How's it going?" I said in my best British accent.

"Hi. Are you British? I love British accents. I'm Sophie," she added with her hand extended.

"Michael, lovely to meet you."

I grabbed my neck and winced. Best to get the elephants out in plain sight.

"Is everything okay?"

"Bad neck. Must have slept on it awkwardly."

At the tennis courts, I picked up a racket and tapped the strings like an old pro. Doubled over at the hip, touched my toes. Ouch. Flexed at the knees and was ready to go, nearly.

"Game?" I said with a few forehand, backhand swipes of the racket.

"Sure," Sophie said and bounded elegantly to the other side.

A basketball from one of the other patients bounced my way. I hurled a shot at the basket and missed the backboard entirely. Thankfully, Sophie failed to see it.

I held the tennis ball aloft, signalling the first shot. "Ready?"

Sophie showed her racket. I launched the ball high and took a swipe. The ball bounced by my side.

"Practice stroke!"

Sophie showed her racket again.

After a few more futile swipes, I drove one into the net, then three more. I looked at the racket. Bloody thing. Finally got one over the net – and the back fence.

"Your serve, luv," I said and threw Sophie the ball.

Luckily, she wasn't much better.

My neck continued to contort. I couldn't take much more.

With the sun out, I removed my shirt. Every movement I made was to announce that I was fine when I wasn't.

Our Gary Busey ringer peeled off his shirt and swung it around his head. Mad laughter followed. My neck kept contorting. I thrust it back and all around. Look at me, I'm okay. Sports injury. Fucking Christ, this is brutal. Nobody must know what's happening.

I had one last go with the basketball and cleared not just the backboard but also the back fence. I did my best "face-saving" swagger off the court and kept going.

Back in my bedroom, the contortions continued. I stood. I sat. I lay there twisting with my eyes fixed on the ceiling. It felt as if my head was trying to unscrew itself. Hours had passed since the contortions started. It never occurred to me that I might be having a reaction to the drugs. Thought I'd caught a dose of cerebral palsy.

Finally, I headed down the corridor and collapsed on the restroom floor, my jaw hard on my right shoulder, my face twisted up to face the ceiling. My pulse was racing. I had broken out into a cold sweat. Trying to ease the tension, I got up on all fours and moved with the contortions, like a dog chasing its tail.

Someone knocked on the door, bringing me back to planet Earth. A fucking queue had formed out there. I was trying to keep this one on the down low. Chin up. Chest out. Shoulders back.

Oh for fuck's sake, God, please fucking help me.

I heard a voice inside as if one of the boys was calling me back home on the Isle of Man.

"Hey Wally, get off the fucking floor and go and ask for help, youuuu cunt!"

I stumbled out of the door and past the patients. At the nursing station, I grabbed my neck and tried futilely to hold back the contortions. The nurse inside slid open the security window.

"What the hell is happening to you?"

"My neck," I said, shaking, unable to face her.

"What medication are you taking?"

"Abilify."

"And this has just started?"

"Yeah," I lied.

"Well, I'm glad you came right away."

She pulled out a tub of blister packages and broke a small tablet free.

"Here, take this. It's an antihistamine. And do not take Abilify again."

While I continued contorting, she called for extra medical care.

"Help's on the way. Wow, I've not seen this for years. It's a rare side effect of the medication called NMS. If left untreated, it can be permanent or fatal."

I sat down and bent over on a plastic seat. "Nothing's happening," I gasped.

"Here, you might need this as well."

The nurse passed a second tablet out of the window.

I took the additional medication and sat there trying to hold back the contortions. Several patients had come to stare. Now I was the sickest of the sick.

After several minutes, Dr Anderson arrived. "Let's go to your room, Michael."

I soon was sitting on the bed, gasping and hyperventilating.

"Focus on your breathing, Michael."

Fucking brilliant, I thought. You try to focus on your breathing under these circumstances.

Over the next hour, the symptoms finally subsided. I explained to her what had happened. Dr Anderson thought the timing was right to deliver a poignant statistic.

"The number of people choking to death in restaurants has increased considerably in recent years, simply because people are ashamed and run to hide in the bathroom with their condition. Shame is a killer. You can't save your ass and your face at the same time, Michael."

Brilliant.

After a knock at the door, Mum came in.

"I called to tell her what was happening," Dr Anderson said.

Mum looked sharp in a tight-fitting jacket and trousers.

"Hi, Mum," I said.

"Why don't you look at your mum when you say hello, Michael?" the doctor asked.

"He's never looked me in the eye. Not since it all happened."

"Since all what happened?"

"The separation with his dad. I know how it affected him."

"Do we have to fucking do this now, for fuck's sake?"

"Michael, look at your mum when you speak."

"Any conversation we had was around a corner, through a wall or with him hiding up the stairs. We never communicated face to face."

"Do we have to do this now?"

"Look at your mum when you speak, Michael."

"I am."

"No, you're not. Look at your mum when you speak."

"Okay, what am I supposed to say?"

"Tell your mum how you feel."

"I don't know how I fucking feel."

"Michael. Look at your mum when you speak."

"I am."

"No, you're not. Tell your mum that you appreciate her coming over."

"She knows I do."

Mum stared silently.

"Well, tell her."

"For fuck's sake! Okay! Mum – "

"Look at her when you speak."

I looked up. "You know I appreciate you coming."

"Look your mum in the eye, Michael."

"Fucking hell! Mum, I appreciate you coming."

"And what else, Michael? Do you love your mum?"

"Of course I do."

"Well tell her. Look her in the eye."

"Love you lots," I said.

"Start with 'I', Michael, and look at her when you say it."

"I…love…you…Mum."

"I just love you so much," she said in return.

When Mum left an hour later, I was still inflamed by the experience. I wasn't sure why saying "I love you" made me feel so humiliated, but it did.

After all I had been through that day, I could not wait to get to bed. I took my increased dose of Seroquel at the nursing station, had a quick snack and headed off to my room. I was quickly asleep.

Moments later, I awakened with my stomach growling. I had an appetite like nothing I had ever experienced before. The patients had warned me.

"Seroquel. Expect an increase in appetite."

Fucking hell. I was turned on by the thought of fats, sugars and carbohydrates.

I hurried to the nursing station, knocking. A nurse slid open the window, looking disgruntled. "Can I help you?"

"I'm starving. Can I get some food, please?"

"What do you want?"

"Peanut butter with jelly. Honey Nut Cheerios. Ice cream. Bread. Any chocolate?"

The nurse reached for the industrial-sized tub of peanut butter. I watched with an open mouth.

Next thing I knew, I was staring at the ceiling. I heard the nurse scream.

"Call an ambulance!!!"

I tried to move and saw a face come into focus above me. A piercing white light surrounded it.

"Stop!" a voice said. "Please stay still!"

Something sweet was oozing down my throat. I touched my face.

"Don't do that!" the nurse shouted.

My vision cleared and I noticed red on my hand. A crowd of patients had gathered around me for round two of the Michael spectacle. I should be selling tickets to this show.

"I can see his gums through his face," one of them said.

I felt the nurse applying the blood pressure band to my arm. "Michael, can you hear me? Your blood pressure is dangerously low. I need you to stay still and breathe."

"Sixty over thirty," she said to another nurse.

"What happened?" I said.

"One minute you were standing there. The next minute you just dropped out of sight. You smashed your face on the metal guide rail going down."

While she spoke, the familiar metal frame of a gurney came flying through the doorway. The ambulance crew looked like they were doing a Laurel and Hardy sketch.

Soon after, I was horizontal and racing along beneath fluorescent lights again. Outside, Laurel and Hardy managed to smash my head into the ambulance door frame as they hoisted me in. Apologies came flying, followed by one blaming the other. Under most circumstances, I would have laughed. All they needed was a change of outfits and Max Sennett to direct.

At the local hospital, emergency personnel quickly surrounded me.

"Why the hell is he not in a neck brace?" the head nurse shouted.

Laurel and Hardy looked at each other. Laurel was ready to break down in tears.

"He has a head trauma," the nurse shouted to no one in particular. "Get him in a neck brace immediately."

I was wheeled off for an MRI. Laurel and Hardy got a verbal thrashing.

After abundant tests and scans and a bunch of stitches in the face, I was back at the nut house. The state or somebody was out another three grand.

The next morning, I sat on a bench in the backyard, the war wounded. Sophie came over and sat down next to me.

"So, are you from around here?" I asked.

"Santa Clarita. I live with my parents. Whereabouts in the UK are you from?"

"The Isle of Man. What are you in here for?"

"Alcohol, depression and chronic pain."

Justin appeared through the door and hovered in the background. What a pain in the arse.

"What have they got you on?" I asked Sophie.

"OxyContin. I've been prescribed it for a while now."

"That was always my first choice."

"I need it," she said without smiling. "I'm off drinking, but I can't stop taking those. I'm in too much pain. I just started working for my dad's construction company. As a secretary. Just a few hours a week. That was before I ended up in here. My back hurts too much for me to sit and concentrate."

"I understand," I said, sympathizing. "It must be difficult. I was unable to work because of chronic pain. I was unable to do anything because of chronic pain."

Still no smile.

"Now I can't work because I don't have a work visa. I need to get sponsorship from an American company. I was hoping to use my skills in computer-aided design. It's what I did before leaving New Zealand. So what sort of work does your dad do again?"

"He has a big construction company. They do really well."

"Oh, right. I was actually working for construction companies in New Zealand."

"You should come to work for my dad then."

"Ah, what a kind offer," I said with a tilt of my head. "Thank you, but I couldn't do that. Wouldn't want to put you out. Lovely thought, though."

"No seriously, you could come and stay with us!"

Nothing like familiar territory. The schemer in me playing coy while I worked on a back-up plan for my departure.

"You're so kind, and it sounds like a fantastic offer, but I wonder how your dad would feel about it."

"I leave in a couple of days and I'll ask him, but I'm sure it'll be okay."

"What's most important is that you're okay when you leave, and especially that you have a network in place to help you keep sober."

I was parroting what I had learned about recovery so far in an effort to be valiant. Sophie certainly seemed touched by it. Justin not so much. He turned and bolted back inside. Sophie checked to make sure he was gone and turned back to me.

"All he does is follow me around," she said in a whisper.

"I've noticed. He's obviously quite keen on you."

"His family abandoned him, so he's stuck here. If he leaves, he'll go straight to prison for various felonies. He's been in here for several weeks and no longer has insurance to cover his stay. He'll be leaving two days after me. Somehow he's gotten this idea that he's coming to stay with me."

"Just be careful and keep your distance. If he gets to be too much of a problem, you can come and find me."

"Oh, thank you," she said, obviously relieved. "Here, put my number in your phone."

Once she left, I reflected on our conversation. My default behaviour was to manipulate and find whatever angle was necessary to get my way. Obviously these old ways were going to take some time to unlearn.

That afternoon a bag filled with my clothes and belongings arrived from Prospects. On the handmade card inside, all the patients had written me a personal note, wishing me well. I wiped at tears and felt emotions I had not experienced in years.

The day Sophie left, I gained a stalker. Justin started shadowing me everywhere I went: waiting around corners, listening to my phone calls. He sat staring at me. When I looked at him, he looked away. I thanked God that all the sharp objects had been taken from us. Justin had nothing in his quiver but a plastic fork.

Sophie called every day to talk with me at the unit. Justin was always hiding around the corner, trying to listen. After a couple of days, Sophie returned for a visit. The safety and security of the unit was a big factor pulling her.

"Why didn't you text me?" she asked.

"I looked one day and your number had been deleted from my phone, along with all your texts. I suspect it was Justin."

"Oh, my God," she said. "He's been making crazy phone calls to my house at all hours of the day, professing his love and pleading with me. He's devastated and accuses me of wanting to be with you instead."

"I'll handle it," I told her.

Justin had been circling us the whole time. Once Sophie left, I cornered him.

"Have a seat, mate. What's happening?" I said with a look of concern.

"Nothing much."

He looked so down, I felt sorry for him. He went on to explain about his situation.

"You know you can talk to me if you need to, don't you?" I said.

"Yeah, I guess," he said.

A nurse came by and said Justin was my new roommate. I explained the predicament and she agreed to assign him a bed alongside Sean, the worst insomniac, paranoid schizophrenic we had on the floor. My empathy and compassion for Justin soared to new levels as he left.

I mean, he couldn't do anything for me, but I still felt for the poor kid. Maybe my moral compass was shifting in the right direction. That was definitely new behaviour. I could not recall the last time I had sincerely cared about someone else's feelings. I was always motivated by what was in it for me. Some sort of decency did seem to be emerging from my darkness.

CHAPTER SIXTEEN

The Crosby-Gables residential treatment complex was tucked in amongst the botanical gardens. It would be my address for the final twelve days of my thirty-day treatment programme. The security policy was more relaxed there: no bolts on the doors, no perimeter fences, less nursing staff. The patients looked a bit more coherent. They were clothed and exhibited far less drooling.

Crosby was a single-story, five-bed house, primarily used for housing female patients. It also housed the nursing facilities. The Gables was a collection of Swiss chalet-style dormitories. My room was in the Gables, possibly Clark's old room. The back door definitely faced into Marilyn Monroe's rose garden. I pictured her fresh from the set of *The Seven Year Itch*, cartwheeling across the tightly cut grass, propped up with phenobarbital. You couldn't beat a bit of Hollywood.

Most patients at Crosby sat around watching television. Most were in long term. Several were equipped with GPS units strapped to their ankles. I spotted a familiar face, Monty from the Coliseum unit. He sat at a table drawing with a ballpoint pen.

"Monty!" I called and walked over to him

"Ah, oh, heeeyy," he said. "Hey, Michael."

"How the hell did you beat me in here, mate?"

Residential treatment was the last stop before you were deposited back into civilization, and the last time I saw Monty he was in no fit state to be in anything but four-point restraints.

"Oh, they said I had to leave Coliseum. My insurance had run out. The bastards won't give me any medication."

He lifted his head to reveal a harrowing sketch of skulls embedded with knives, surrounded by a high chain-link fence. Heads were impaled on the barbed wire, their spines exposed from their bleeding necks. All in vivid detail.

A nurse passed. I caught her attention, pointed secretly at Monty and mouthed the words in silence: "You might want to keep an eye on this one."

I went over and sat next to Timmy. He was our resident child pornographer. Slightly built, glasses, his nose constantly twitching to keep his glasses up. The police had discovered a considerable amount of that junk on his home computer. It would be nine months before he could go skulking about again.

An impeccably dressed young man sat on the other side of me, hair gelled to one side, his skin ethereally pale. I had tried to strike up a conversation, but all I got was a vacant look. There was truly an embalmed quality about him.

Timmy explained that Alan was on Thorazine. It was the equivalent of a chemical lobotomy. A few days of that and everything one associated with humanity was lost: love, concern for others, rationality, judgment, creativity and concentration, to name a few.

Alan's family owned several internationally renowned businesses. After a bout with depression a year back, his family had dropped him off at the unit. The shame of being committed was too much for them to bear. He was welcome back whenever he had learned to function in society again. How removing his higher functions through the use of Thorazine could ever return him to a happy, rewarding life, no one had explained.

Julie sat across from us. I had no idea why she was here. She sat with a furrowed brow, her legs crossed, arms folded tightly across her chest. One hand managed to hold a cigarette. She had red streaks in her blonde hair, lots of piercings and looked angry – really fucking angry. Any attempt to endear myself met with a draw on her cigarette.

A tall, elegant frame passed through the room. Milena had dark almond-shaped eyes and high cheekbones, of the sort I associated with Eastern Europeans. With her long brown hair and lithe frame, a model came to mind. She had taken her first drink only a few years back. Pity. She'd hardly had a chance to enjoy herself.

I put so much thought into what I was going to say to her, I said nothing.

Over the sound of the TV, I heard an upper-class British accent thunder through the house:

"I WANT MY FUCKING LITHIUM!"

Music to my ears. It sounded like a young Queen Elizabeth II.

I quickly rounded the corner and found a young lady with matted blonde hair standing at the nursing station window. Her hair rose at right angles to her skull and concealed her face. She was insulated in several layers of clothes: shirts, thick jumpers and a baby blue dressing gown, topped off with a fur-lined parka.

"From the UK?" I asked.

"Yeah, Chelsea."

Chelsea girls had quite a reputation, the cream of London high society.

"What about you?"

"Isle of Man."

"How the fuck did you end up here?" she asked.

"Chasing the dream, ya know. You?"

"Come with me," she said

We left Crosby and headed through the gardens past my chalet. Molly introduced herself along the way. She was holed up in some prime real estate, a corner unit, her own two-bed-room suite. The inside was not high society but high in com-fort: fluffy duvets, several large pillows and blankets. A table was covered with M&M's, Marlboro Reds, biscuits and luxury chocolates.

"How the fuck did you end up with this?" I asked.

"I demanded it," she said with a grin. "But really, the in-laws came. One in particular. They rolled out the red carpet."

"Why's that?"

"Anneka Tryst."

"Serious?"

Oscar-winning actress and Hollywood royalty.

"You don't do things by halves."

"I married her brother."

I nodded at the colourful cocktail dress and red stilettoes on the floor. "Came prepared, then?"

"That's what I arrived in."

"Bloody Chelsea birds. What happened?"

"Overdosed on Tylenol PM. Couldn't do it anymore."

"Was it, like, a serious go, or…ya know, 'somebody help me' sort of thing?"

She shrugged and shook her head. "Oh, I meant it. The divorce. Life. Alcohol…My dad killed himself."

A framed photograph stood on the side cabinet, a profile shot of an attractive girl staring out to sea.

"Who's that?"

She looked me hard in the eye.

"Me, you fucker."

"Oh, sorry, luv."

The girl before me looked exhausted. Dark rings under her eyes, hair all over the place. She and the photograph were the before and after faces of addiction.

"So where did it all go wrong?"

"Michael, let me explain. This disease is a fucker. It's true what you hear all the time in meetings. It's cunning, baffling and powerful. I was sober for eighteen months. The promises came true. I was happy, joyous and free. Now look at me."

"Why? How?"

"Putting other stuff before my recovery," she said.

I pointed at a photo of a young girl. "And who's that?"

"Gracie, my daughter."

She turned on the kettle. "Cuppa tea?"

"Love one. And you've got proper tea-bags."

She dropped PG Tips tea-bags into two cups.

We sat on her patio overlooking the botanical gardens.

"Did you see the unit over in the back corner?" I asked her.

"Oh, that's where the proper basket cases go. Have you seen those zombies?"

"In person. I was one of them."

"You are fucking joking me. You were in there?"

I nodded and she burst out laughing at my fate.

"Seriously? How on earth did you end up in there?"

I shared my story without any edits or attempts to impress. Looking back, the shameful parts seemed to be the funniest. There was no judgment on her part. She understood. She had been there too. I felt better able to breathe when I was done. There was a comfortable silence. For once I did not feel the need to pad out the story with bullshit.

With the help of the meetings and therapy, I developed a habit of sitting beside a large oak tree each morning in prayer and meditation, fascinated with nature and the intricate details of life: the trees, the animals and all living organisms. I seemed to be participating in the ecosystem for the first time.

I had been in my world of increasing inner comfort for several days when I received a text on my phone from Sophie.

Hey! Is it OK to come and visit?

Sure, I wrote back.

I considered the options to improve my appearance: Timmy's cheap aftershave, my trousers and shirt immaculately pressed by Alan, roses from Marilyn's garden. I settled for a change of underwear and pulled on a cap.

A couple of hours passed. Another text appeared from Sophie.

I'm in reception.

My stomach fluttered at the prospect of opposite sex interaction without alcohol or medication. I saw it in Sophie's anxious face too. She had gone to considerable lengths with her makeup. Her hair was groomed.

We hugged and I felt her trembling. Her hand shook when the receptionist asked her to sign the visitors book, to the point that her writing was illegible. The receptionist looked concerned. I gently took the pen from her.

"Here, let me. What's your surname?"

"Dolby."

I wrote the name for her and we went outside.

"I'm still sober," she said. "I've not drunk, but it's a real struggle."

We walked through the botanical gardens to Crosby. Inside, a few patients recognized her. The group atmosphere seemed to break the tension.

We sat on a bench outside my room, overlooking the rose gardens. We were alone. Sophie sat close. We made small talk, but a strange tension stifled the air.

Sophie went off to use the restroom and returned smelling of alcohol. It was intoxicating. I could practically taste it. Afraid, I stood up.

"Let's go," I said.

We walked to the common room adjoining the Gables. A couple of patients were using the kitchen facilities. I invited Sophie to sit with me in front of the TV. She tucked up close, her thigh pressed hard against mine, her face turned towards me. The other patients grew uncomfortable and left. Fuck. There went my backup.

Sophie pulled out a brown prescription container filled with 80mg OxyContin and began to empty the tablets into her crotch area. She ate one and looked down at the rest, nodding. Her hand rested seductively on my thigh. I was gripped with fear, terrified of drugs and alcohol, terrified of being out of control, terrified of slipping back into mania, terrified of bipolar, terrified of losing my mind, terrified of being thrown out, terrified of being on my own, terrified of dying. It was all a universal conspiracy to test me. How could I honourably kick her the fuck out?

"Sophie, please. It's just not for me."

I stood and left her sitting there as I headed back to my chalet. Halfway there, my conscience got the better of me and I turned back. I found Sophie sitting on a step, visibly upset. A counsellor came by and reminded us that visiting hours were over. I walked Sophie to the reception area and waited while she called a cab.

As soon as she'd left, the counsellors called me in for questioning. Some of the patients had smelled alcohol on her. Having told them the truth, Sophie was barred from the facility. For my honesty, I was rewarded with a pass out of the joint, to be used at my discretion.

Gold's Gym it was then.

A taxi arrived to take me on my first journey into the outside world since my sobriety had begun 21 days earlier. Outside the perimeter fence and abundant tree cover, the light immediately seemed brighter. The sound of traffic thundered sharply in my ears. A passing car stereo made me jump. My senses were alert to the slightest movement. The brightly clothed citizens were captivating.

It was a new world.

I sprang into the gym and hit the bench press machine first thing, going light. Best to ease into things. Next to me, a young black man had taken the opposite tack. He had enough weights on the bar to lift his arse right off the bench. While he grunted, I smelled the alcohol oozing from his pores. This wasn't leftovers from last night's piss-up. He was flat-out drunk.

Without prompting, he looked my way. "I can't train without a drink."

"Mate, I understand," I said with complete sincerity.

Later, two men stopped by to introduce themselves. "Not from around here, are you?"

I gave them the Isle of Man thing and left the rest to mysterious circumstances. They seemed to enjoy the accent. Great with the birds. Next thing I knew, I was invited to a big party on Saturday night at the V Lounge. Lots of women, I was told.

I immediately saw the drinks and drugs awaiting me. It was on the tip of my tongue to announce my sobriety, but I remembered anonymity and used another badge of honour.

"Too old to carry on like that, lads."

They kept pressing. It appeared that my British accent was their ticket to getting laid. My mind started to play with some tempting scenarios. I could do this. What the hell. One night on the town. Who would know?

Finally, enough was enough.

"I don't drink, lads."

"That must be boring!" one of them said.

They both got a big kick out of that. I didn't. It had struck me. Without drink and drugs, I might never have fun again.

I grabbed my towel and headed for the showers. It was a good time for me to make a safe exit.

Back within the safe confines of Crosby-Gables, I added the first notch on my sobriety belt. How could such a simple expedition be so exhausting? Envisioning my life ahead, I was only able to see that sort of brief sortie out into no man's land. A horrifying thought occurred to me. Once they let me out, where would I find sanctuary?

At 4 a.m., I shuffled out of my chalet and headed for the nursing station. Opening time. I saw the queue ahead already lined up for the first round of medication.

"Hey, tosser," I heard from behind me in a posh British accent. "Wait for me."

I turned to find Molly coming up the pathway, dressed in her usual four layers of clothing, a fag hanging from her lips and a baby blue dressing gown and parka to top things off.

"Look at the fucking state of you," she said. "You loser."

"Says who? You look like a fucking bag lady."

"You've got your shorts on back to front. Jesus, you look rough."

"Yeah, well, it's the blind leading the blind here."

"From now on, if you wake up first, come and wake me up so I can get my sedatives."

"What?" I said. "You want me to wake you up so you can go back to sleep?"

"Nooo, if you think I might be asleep, you wait outside and let me wake naturally. When I wake up you can walk me down to the nursing station."

"What, all forty yards of it?"

"Yes, that's your instructions from now on."

She pretended to knee me in the thigh, then wrapped herself under my arm. We entered Crosby in this pose and passed Monty scrawling another picture at the table.

"Early start, Monet?" I said.

"Yeah, they won't give me the meds."

He had been scribbling furiously over the same spot in ink until the paper tore.

At the nursing station window, Molly took her meds from the nurse. It was a handful of pretty colours.

"You must be really, really sick, you nutcase," I said.

"Coming from you, Coliseum boy. They'll have you back in restraints before the day's done. Zappin' you with the electric, they will."

"You're fucking charming."

"He's acting strange," she said with a nod at the nurse. "Very erratic."

"Fuck you."

Molly laughed, but just as quickly tried to stop herself, like she shouldn't have been doing so, given the current state of affairs. When she snorted again, it became all the more endearing.

Same drill every morning, we sat on the patio outside Molly's room and watched the treatment centre come to life. Like *Groundhog Day*, the same people performing the same routine at the same time every day.

The first patient up was a young lady at the soda machine. She saluted us with her Diet Pepsi. "For the vodka," she shouted.

Patients began to jog through the gardens. An old lady hobbled past with a walking cane, impeccably dressed, her hair and makeup looking glamorous.

"Awww," Molly said. "She's so cute! I wanna take her home with me."

"I wonder where she's going. Think maybe she's got an old boy tied up in one of those cabins? He'll be sunk to the nuts in a few minutes. Can you see them?"

We both cringed.

"Lucky bitch," Molly said.

Her phone rang. "The lawyers from Europe," she said.

I listened while she barked orders at her lawyers, trying to coordinate a divorce and child custody battle from seven thousand miles away.

An aide walked past and signalled it was time for breakfast. I walked off with a final wave to Molly, rubbing my stomach.

"Go on, you fat bastard!" she shouted without covering the phone. "Go get yer Jell-O with the rest of them! You know you love the texture! And bring me something back!"

"Yeah, I will! Jell-O!"

I returned a short while later with a tray of eggs, bacon, potatoes, sausages and half a dozen pancakes with several packets of syrup.

"Cheers, tosser," she said, grabbing the tray.

She sat with one leg under her arse and the other one swinging back and forth from the chair. She was clearly very deep in thought.

"Don't say a thing about this, tosser, but I just got news about my inheritance."

"Our inheritance, that is."

"Put it this way: I'll never have to work again."

"Really, we don't? Bloody marvellous!"

She punched me in the arm.

"I've no idea what's going to happen when I get out of here," I said.

"You're moving to the Valley," she said. "That's where I'll be. If things were different at home, with the divorce and my daughter, you could come and stay with me, but I can't have someone else in the house at the minute. The ex would use it against me in court. Especially if it's a man."

"I need to get something figured out. I was in a hotel before I left San Diego."

"The Valley's the place to be for recovery. Twelve-step meetings all hours of the day and night. I'll introduce you to people. I'll make sure you're all right."

"I got a message from Natasja yesterday. She'll be here this weekend. I'll introduce you."

"Hmm," Molly said with a wary look.

That afternoon, Molly's friend Carry stopped by with her daily supply of cigarettes, food and clothing. Carry was an American actress and singer, with a son fathered by a rock legend. They chatted away about their experiences with addiction and bipolar. I listened and marvelled at how many people were fucked.

Given their laughter, I finally opened up about my own fears and uncertainties. It was a relief to feel human and heal. The humour began to outweigh the shame. Getting sober was starting to look bearable.

"Get a sponsor, straight away," Molly reminded me for the fourteenth time. Carry echoed the idea. I had been hearing the same mantra for over a month now. "Go to twelve-step meetings. Put your recovery first. Take the meds and see your psychiatrist. And work with others."

They laughed.

"We don't do any of it, though."

"Apart from the meds!" Molly added.

"Do as I say, not as I do, is it?"

They both nodded. I headed back to Crosby for my afternoon meds. The place was frantic with activity. I saw Monty wheeled away from the unit on a gurney. He had slit his wrists with a snapped-off pen. He survived and they deposited him back at the Coliseum. Christ, this thing was serious.

I decided to go for a run. I hadn't done so in quite some time. The botanical gardens offered a scenic circuit. I did a few hundred yards, then hid behind the back of a building to catch my breath. Keane was pumping through my headphones. For the first time in ages I heard the lyrics.

You hide the cracks, the facts will find you, Turn your back and leave the lonely days behind you. All the things you took for granted, Hit you like a bullet in the gut, You can't get up, Well are you gonna even try? 'Cos if you never even try, Time will pass you by.

Thought I was gonna burst out bloody cryin'.

I noticed some staff coming and jogged around the next corner, where I again had to stop and pant. My limbs were cold. My hamstrings were already aching. I retreated out of view behind the nearest hedge and bent over, sucking in air, holding back vomit. What have I done? My plan was to impress the induction nurse at Coliseum. She was an athlete and all that. Now they'd probably wheel me past her on a gurney. Some things never die. Like bullshit.

I half jogged, half stumbled back to my room and quickly closed the door behind me. After a stint of being buckled over on my bed and a couple of blasts from my inhaler, I lit a cigarette and sat there with it hanging from my mouth.

Mum called to say she had spoken with my psychiatrist and would catch up with me after my men's stag meeting. Her meeting had been an effort to understand my condition. My meeting was group therapy for inveterate wasters. Basically, everyone sat around swearing and making sexual references. The occasional glimpse of truth emerged.

"Forest Hills takes you through the first three steps of recovery," the group counsellor said once the meeting had begun. "These are designed to reconnect you with God, as you understand God. Spiritual, not religious. Let me be specific about that. It's a God of your own understanding. It can be anything, so long as it's not you."

I was good with that. After my experience at Prospects, I was 100% all right with a God of my own understanding. That word no longer kindled memories of walking into our local church as a boy. Everything there had been designed to scare the shit out of you. Getting nailed to a cross. Suffering. That was religion to me, which was separate from the spiritual in my mind.

"Let's talk about God," the counsellor went on. "Let's hear your experiences."

We went around the room. Eventually it was my turn.

"My name's Michael, and I'm an alcoholic."

It was the first time I had identified as an alcoholic in public. I had been identifying as an addict. That seemed more socially acceptable. Alcoholism still conjured up visions of old men with brown paper bags, passed out on the street, pissed pants and a red, bulbous nose, but in fact alcohol had been the bookends to all my drug use. Everything started and ended with a drink.

"I grew up with this concept of God from the Old Testament. He was some all-conquering barbarian that loved me but wanted to kill me. Then this whole scene went down in the last treatment centre. I don't know where it came from, but the experience gave me clarity to really understand the metaphors of the Bible. I'd taken all those stories literally. That concept has gone. I think God's everywhere. In everything. Nature, people. The universe an' all that, universal forces, laws of attraction, they were all things that I never considered, just taken them for granted. My life depends on them. Someone walked past me in the last place and said, 'The air is free' and I flipped out. It was so obvious. It was like someone snapped their fingers and said, 'Awaken'. Lost my mind, I did. The whole thing was like an exorcism. I even had the symptoms of exorcism, spitting, talking garbled crap and stuff. Although the demon, I now realize, was not some beast, but false information. The lie. I was possessed by my very existence – my life myth. It must be my creator sustaining my life. Why would He want me to poison myself with alcohol and drugs? Without sounding like an old hippie, it's all about love. I feel completely connected to this higher power, although I don't understand any of it...And, of course, all that ended me up in a set of restraints!"

Everyone laughed.

When it was his turn, this one patient pointed at a sign on the wall. It read.

We are here to awaken from the illusion of our separateness.

"I get that," he said. "My whole life, it's like I was outside the building looking through the windows at the party going on inside."

What a concept. Blew my mind. I'd been in my own separate hell for the past thirty-odd years. Asleep at the wheel. Alcohol and drugs allowed me to function while being disconnected. Nothing was ever sincere. Just rattling bullshit with strangers. Always trying to impress, and the more I tried, the more I grew separate. Now the very truth that had so long terrified me was setting me free. Suddenly, I couldn't get enough of this shit.

Vulnerability, in fact, wasn't a weakness. It made me more human. Everything seemed to be the opposite of what I had thought. I was finding hope and courage and freedom by admitting my flaws. I had been looking for the same such truth in alcohol and drugs for all those years and never finding it. All alcohol and drugs had given me were madness and shame.

CHAPTER SEVENTEEN

At the end of the meeting, the counsellor reminded us that even if they came up with a magic pill someday, allowing us to drink like normal people, we'd still be stuck with ourselves and all this fucked-up shit inside, all the things that made us sick: shame, guilt, fear, resentment.

"You aren't bad people trying to be good, you're sick people trying to get well."

I had heard all this brainwashing before, but now I was beginning to believe it.

Mum walked out of her meeting carrying leaflets and literature. She looked astonished – and relieved.

"Wow! I just learned about the three Cs. I didn't cause it, can't cure it and can't control it. Whoa! And here all this time I thought it was me!"

I was both delighted and mortified by her newfound insights – glad to know Mum was learning about my disease but never having properly considered where this knowledge might lead.

"Look," she added. "They gave me this. It's called *An Open Letter From An Alcoholic*."

I quickly scanned through it. All the ways that alcoholics try to manipulate those who love them was discussed, along with how to keep the active alcoholic in check. My eyes stopped on the last line: "I hate myself, but I love you. To do nothing is the worst choice you can make for us."

"Isn't it great!?" she said and commenced to offload every-thing she had learned. "The man explained that alcoholism affects the whole family and we all become sick. It's a dis-ease of relationships. The symptoms of alcoholism are in the behaviour. You see, I was basically reacting to your behaviour all this time. I tried to show you my love by bailing you out. I never realized how much it's all affected me. And you. They've suggested I go to Al-Anon for friends and family of alcoholics. I've got the number for a lady in the programme. I'm going to ring her straight away and go to my first meeting."

Mum paused to catch her breath and study my reaction. "They've said tonight is family group and they've encouraged us to go, but I understand it might be awkward. I'll leave it up to you."

"Sounds brilliant, Mum. All good information. I'm so glad you're here."

She was a ball of enthusiasm again. I didn't know what else to say. We arranged to meet at 7:45 for the meeting. She went back to her hotel. I went back for a siesta. Sobriety was wearing me out.

At 7:45, Molly appeared at my door with her mum, who had just arrived from the UK. My mum showed up a few moments later and the two were instant friends.

Down in the treatment room we discovered roughly fifty people. Each patient sat with their respective partner, parents or family member. It was like parents' night at the PTA, only Sigmund Freud was running the show.

Molly kicked my shin. "You'd better have some sensible shit to add to this meeting, tosser."

The psychiatrist welcomed everyone to the meeting.

"We'll go around the room, with each family member and patient asking me one question. Feel free to ask whatever you want."

I sat there scanning the crowd. There were some crackin' looking young ladies present and suddenly I felt a bolt of anx-iety. This was one of my most deep-rooted fears – opening my mouth in front of women who attracted me. Mum's presence did nothing to relieve my anxieties. I prepared to pass on the question. No shame there. None that I could see.

One of the birds spoke up. "I haven't really got a question. It's just, my boyfriend didn't come and I don't know what to do. I don't think he wants to support me."

"Recovery is about learning to have a relationship with yourself," Sigmund told her. "To have a healthy relationship with another person, you must be able to have a healthy relationship with yourself. Your recovery has to come first. You'll hear it suggested. Change playmates, playgrounds and playthings. I wouldn't recommend anyone getting into a relationship for at least a year."

A whole year without fucking is what I heard. The anxiety thickened.

Then it was Mum's turn.

"What's the best way I can support my son once he leaves treatment?"

"Attend Al-Anon and keep the focus on you. Learn about healthy boundaries and detachment with love. It's quite a broad subject, so I'll make myself available after the meeting or you can speak to the onsite therapists."

He pointed at me. I noticed Molly holding her stomach and biting her lip. My heart was pounding. I pulled my baseball cap down low and sank further into my chair.

"Er, yeah, my name's Michael. What's the difference between a selective serotonin reu……er, SSRI, you know, my old anti-depressant, and Lamisil?"

The room fell quiet. Even Molly was silent. I heard a couple of sniggers. The shrink was doing his best to maintain decorum, including his own.

"I think you'll find that Lamisil is for athlete's foot."

When everyone else broke out in laughter, he chuckled too. I turned red.

"Oh, I – er – can't remember the name of the medication I take for bipolar. It starts with an L…Lamictal, that's it!"

"I think that's a question best left for a private discussion, so if you want to see me after the meeting, please feel free to do so."

Molly bolted out of the room to laugh. Well, that went mostly as expected.

When the meeting ended and everyone started to file out of the room, I felt people avoiding me like I was a leper. I looked at Mum and shook my head.

"Lamisil, fucking Lamisil."

She laughed and put her arm around me.

"I may be bipolar and manic but my feet look lovely."

We both doubled up with laughter.

"You know, I don't know that you've ever shown me your personality."

"Yeah, I guess it was my way of handling shit. If you thought I was happy, you probably wouldn't give me the money I was scrounging."

The next day, I got the timetable wrong on my twelve-step meeting and walked into Debtors Anonymous. It was the last thing I needed, a reminder of my financial wreckage. Having been acknowledged by the group, though, I felt awkward about leaving and sat down. People were talking about lost businesses and huge debts and spending plans and paying off bills and crap like that. It brought to mind the large sums of money I owed family and friends, ex-girlfriends included, and that wasn't to mention the banks and loan companies who kept a spreadsheet on me.

I left the meeting feeling even lower than when I had gone in and went to sit in the rose garden. A short while later, a black Escalade pulled into the parking lot. The door opened and Natasja spilled out with all her blonde hair. She was wearing a tight-fitting lime-green dress. Her face was partly concealed behind large black Chanel shades.

"Hey, how are ya?" she said as if she'd just gone out to shop and come back.

"One foot in front of the other, ya know."

"I bought you some stuff. It's in the car. Come and help me."

She had luxury duvets, pillows, blankets and warm clothes.

"Is your mum here? I spoke to her on the phone, you know."

"I don't want to know."

I had coordinated the timing so that they would never cross paths.

"We have very different opinions on religion, but it was quite a conversation."

"Yeah, I can well imagine. Where are you staying?"

"The Ritz."

"I need to sign out before we go."

We stood there, the unspoken sins of my past haunting me. I imagined they were haunting Natasja, too. Everything felt awkward and uneasy. You break trust the way I had, it wasn't easy to restore. Maybe never.

"Here, come and meet my friend, Molly," I said, hoping to break the spell.

We walked down the path to Molly's chalet. She was sitting outside in a chair with legs crossed beneath her, smoking a cigarette.

"Molly, meet Natasja," I called up from the path.

Molly nodded. Her nose went up. I saw Natasja's body bristle in response. Her jaw clenched. It was like trying to place the south poles of two magnets together.

"I'm going," Natasja said and stormed off. Molly blew a plume of cigarette smoke in her wake.

Once she had checked into the Ritz, we hired a couple of bicycles and pedalled towards Glendale Gardens. Natasja turned it into a road race and pulled twenty yards in front.

"You know," she shouted over her shoulder. "I've been thinking. I don't really want you as my primary intimate relationship anymore."

Did I just hear that right? I'm to share? And be fucking second in line? She can go fuck herself. I dropped back even further. Our communication ceased for the remainder of the ride, except for hand signals and directions.

When we arrived, Natasja jumped into her photography, ignoring me. You could have cut the tension with a knife.

"Cuppa tea?" I said to her back.

"Sure," she said as if I was the waiter.

We walked to the tea rooms in silence.

"I need a piss," I said as she sat down. "Where are the toilets?"

"How should I know?"

"Right. I'll be back as quick as I can. They'll be round here somewhere."

I wandered around for ten minutes and found the toilets next to the entrance. I tried a cigarette to calm my nerves and returned to the café. From a distance, I saw Natasja in that posture of folded arms and venom.

"What?" I said to the look on her face.

"How long does it take to find the toilet? I knew you'd leave me." She nodded in the direction of the café. "The toilets were there."

"You might have said something. I had no fucking idea."

More silence.

"Fuck it," I said. "Let's go."

I was steaming all the way back to the front entrance. The general area was packed with tourists – pedestrians, buses filled with them – and in the middle of it all, Natasja still oozing poison. I lost it.

"You fucking bitch! That…that fucking back there was a fucking big stitch up. A big fucking abandonment scene. You wouldn't stop till it fucking happened, would you? I'm in fucking rehab. I've just been through fucking hell, and you're here sticking the fucking knife in me, you fucking bitch. I've never been through so much shit in all my life and all you want to do is make things fucking worse. I tell you what if you were a guy I would knock you the fuck out…"

"There's people," she said.

"Fuck every single one of them, and fuck you."

A crowd had formed.

262

"And fuck all of you."

"Michael, please."

Natasja dropped her chin. Her feet turned in, childlike. Finally, she looked back up at me, her eyes glazed. "Calm down, let's not do this here."

"This is what you wanted all along, isn't it? Fucking anger?"

She grabbed my hands. "Let's just go," she said.

I pulled my hands away and went ahead of her, still raging.

Back in her room at the Ritz, we tried solving everything with a fuck. As raw sex went, it was good enough but offered nothing in the way of intimacy. Words, other than four-letter ones, were a threat to our relationship.

Afterwards, she took me back to the treatment centre and left. Half an hour later, my mobile phone rang. It was Natasja.

"I couldn't bear to stay at the hotel. I checked out. I'm going home."

I was glad but didn't say so. Later that evening, she called again.

"I need to know your plans when you leave that place."

"I've got to put my recovery first, that's all I know. I might stay sober better living up here. We can still see each other on the weekends."

"Why don't you come down here? You could stay for a couple of days with me while you find out how to be sober."

"I don't know anyone down there. My whole support group is up here. People who can take me to meetings and help me settle."

"No," she said. "You get to show up for me now."

"I need to show up for me. Just because I'm up here doesn't mean we can't be together."

"I'm not doing this with you anymore," she said and hung up.

I walked to my room and lay on the bed, ready for the free fall of my emotions, the hell that always came when someone left you. I stared at the ceiling, waiting. A knock came at the door while I did.

"Oi, tosser fuck face. Are you in there?"

I opened the door. "Can't I even have a nervous breakdown in peace?"

"What's up? What's wrong?"

"Natasja told me she wants nothing to do with me. I'm waiting to lose my mind. Should happen any minute now."

"You fucking nutcase. Why?"

"Every time I've broken up with a woman, it's the most pain I've ever experienced. I go to pieces."

I sat there like an animal with its soft underbelly exposed.

"Me too," Molly said. "But that's because I was always looking for the wrong things in my relationships. I wanted prestige and power, and got it, and just tried to overdose. Go figure. I'm learning a relationship is nothing to do with any of that. It's what's inside that counts."

"So, it's not just me? Relationships scare the shit out of me, and now I've not got alcohol or drugs to comfort me. Not that they did. Prolonged the agony more than anything else, I suppose. But at least it was temporary relief."

"Do you feel like using or drinking?" Molly asked.

"Not at all. I feel fucking free, to be honest."

We sat there staring at each other. And wasn't that a miracle? I felt no compulsion whatsoever to drink or do drugs.

"I've not felt threatened since I woke up in Santa Monica in those restraints," I told Molly. "Some kind of the truth happened back there. Must have been some sort of spiritual awakening…"

"Then be grateful, Michael. Gratitude is the key to sobriety."

Molly and I attended another twelve-step meeting that evening. She was suddenly my rock, the person I could lean on the most. She was literally leaning on me all through the meeting, her head resting on my shoulder, the occasional nudge in the ribs and squeeze of my hand. Despite all her "in your face" British starch, she was the only person I knew who had been real and straight with me, telling things as they were, her own bullshit included, and I sat there feeling all this love for her.

Up front, the leader was talking about the importance of sponsorship. The first recommendation was to choose somebody of your own sex.

The man knew how to disappoint me. I had Molly down as first choice for the position.

"Find someone who's got something that you want," he concluded. "Someone you feel you can trust with all your secrets."

Now we were talking. I raised my hand at the end of his pitch. "Is Springsteen local?"

That got a good laugh. It took very little for me to feel wanted.

As Molly and I were filing out of the meeting, a younger lady came up to us.

"I have just the sponsor for you," she said to me. "His name's Jim. He's probably coming in to see me soon."

She pulled out her phone and began scrolling through her contacts.

"Who's Jim, by the way?"

"A friend of my husband. He manages The Destructive Divas."

"Is he a nice guy?" I asked as if that really mattered. I was already co-managing the band and sleeping with the lead singer in my head.

The young woman nodded, more distracted with calling this man's number than listening to me. "I'll tell him about you and pass on his number," she whispered, cupping the phone.

I thought to ask if he worked a good programme, but the image of The Destructive Divas came back.

"Voicemail," the young woman whispered again over the phone.

She left a message and jotted down Jim's number for me. I thanked her without much enthusiasm. Sleeping with the lead singer of The Destructive Divas aside, this whole concept of some other bloke running my life was in a head-on collision with my ego.

Two days later, my mum packed her bags for home. "You can come with me," she offered before leaving for the airport.

"I've gotta stay around sober people, Mum. I need to do this for me now."

Then it was time for Molly to leave. She was being released from treatment a couple of days before me.

"Tosser, will you coin me out?" she asked the afternoon of our final group session.

"Of course," I said.

All Molly's fellow patients would share how they felt about her at this final session. As her closest friend, I would be the last one and hand her a graduation coin.

When it was my turn to speak, I cracked a few jokes, then found myself crying.

"I've just never felt so comfortable around someone of the opposite sex."

It was the sort of "pull on the heartstrings" hand I had played to great effect in the past, only now I was completely sincere. Molly, who had welled up herself, reached over and brushed the tears from my cheeks.

"Call me every day," she said after the meeting.

I was handed her baby blue dressing gown.

"You might need this, tosser."

My heart broke as she drove off down the road.

At 4 a.m., I pulled on her baby blue dressing gown and walked across the grounds to Crosby house.

"Where's your sidekick?" the nurse dispensing medication asked me.

"She's gone. I'll be seeing her soon, though."

I walked back down the pathway to the chalet at the end. It was dark and empty now. I took a seat on the patio, pulled the dressing gown tight around me and lit a cigarette. Slowly, the day came to life. My 30 days in treatment were nearly over. How would it be out there? How would I cope? My head filled with thoughts and fears.

On the last day, I was granted access to a computer and checked my bank balance. There was $4,866.79 of Natasja's money in the account. I had one bag of clothes. They were throwing me out onto the streets of LA, where I had to learn how to live sober from scratch. I felt raw and stripped naked.

Not having a car, I rented one and headed down the 134 freeway towards LA. That led to wandering around lost for several hours. Finally, like a moth to light, I followed the tourists and booked two nights at the Universal Sheraton. It was a Saturday night.

I had been told the world would reflect back to me everything I needed to learn in recovery. In the great mirror that was LA, I found vanity, haste and narcissism. I wasn't exactly sure what I was supposed to learn from those things.

Sunday morning turned out an aggressively sunny day in California and, feeling restless, I jumped on the 405 freeway, headed down to Santa Monica, with the not so pleasant memories of Natasja in the back of my head. After wandering around lost for a while, I found a bicycle shop on the beachfront, rented a bike, and started south along the shore.

Nearing Venice and the boardwalk, I found myself increasingly surrounded by people – most immediately cyclists and those rushing by me on roller skates – but beyond them and all along the edges of the boardwalk, a circus of street performers: people break-dancing and singing, standing on stilts and artists with their wares spread out like an obstacle course.

When I arrived at Muscle Beach, I stopped to ogle at the gathering of muscle-bound physiques crowding the shore. There were shaven and tattooed heads, abundant body piercings and blokes in gold thongs working out with their personal trainers.

Sodom and Gomorrah on a Sunday afternoon.

When I caught the scent of marijuana, I did a sharp U-turn and parked at Ye Olde Kings Head, a British-themed pub. That alone flooded my mind with memories of the good old times. Euphoric recall, they had named it in treatment. The compulsion to drink did not start with the first drink, but the memory of the first drink. I downed a Diet Coke and left sharpish.

My deep-seated feelings of unease followed me around for two restless days.

During my stay over at the Universal Sheraton, I lined up a sober living situation in Sun Valley. The joint was out in the country. People roamed the streets on horseback. The manager showed me my room. It was small with a bunk bed on one wall and a single bed on the other.

When I agreed to take it, the manager read me the rules. Regular drug tests, 12 a.m. curfew and proof I had been going to twelve-step meetings. Otherwise, I needed to do something with my day. There was no lounging around the house.

"Wanna help us with putting in the new sewage lines?" he asked.

"Sure," I said. I had served my dues hauling bricks around for Howcroft.

The next day, Molly took me to a meeting.

"I need to call this guy Jim about sponsorship," I told her as we left.

I made a face that suggested fear.

After a few sips of Diet Coke for comfort, I dialled the number. A man answered.

"Is that Jim?" I said.

"That's me."

"My name's Michael. I got your number from a girl in rehab. Hope you don't mind me calling."

I explained the reason. Jim offered me the usual advice about sponsorship and using the phone.

"Call Daniel. He's my sponsor. I'll text you his number. You can call him anytime."

"He's passed me off," I told Molly.

She commiserated. Daniel's number came through and I called him.

"Daniel?"

"Yes?"

"My name's Michael. Jim gave me your number."

"Hey, Michael," he said.

It was a gentle voice.

"I was told to get a sponsor. I'm just out of rehab. Wondered if we could possibly meet whenever you're free."

"How about now?" he said. "Where are you?"

"Coldwater Canyon."

"Which way are you facing?"

"The Hollywood Hills."

"Are you driving?"

"No, I'm just with a friend at a meeting."

"All right. Call me back once you're driving."

I said goodbye to Molly, headed west and got Daniel back on the phone.

"Okay, you want to turn right," he said. "What colour is the traffic light?"

"Red."

"Well, stop."

I stopped.

"When it turns green, start driving and keep in the right-hand lane."

This red light, green light bullshit continued until I had passed under the freeway and was nearing the next major intersection.

"Where are you now?"

"Going through the junction."

"Okay, good. Go down the road and stay in the right-hand lane. Take the second turn and pull up. I'll meet you outside."

I stopped in front of a house under construction. A young Steven Spielberg lookalike came out in a camouflage jacket. He was covered in dust. He exuded peace and kindness. I shook his hand.

"Michael, you made it. And you can take directions. Maybe we can get some work done."

I was a mixture of hope and resentment. Daniel held me in eye contact.

"The thing about being sober is that we start to wake up."

He pointed up to the sky. Three geese circled overhead, nose to tail. "How often do you see that?"

"Never," I said.

"Me neither. You know, they mate for life. They fly together, communicating problems. A goose never leaves one of its own kind behind. If one gets injured, one of the flock stays behind until it gets better or takes its dying breath."

"I know a wild goose chase and that's about it."

Daniel smiled, sort of. "My point is, Michael, you never have to do anything on your own, ever again."

The garbage men pulled up. Daniel went straight over and invited them into the house for a coffee. They thanked him but declined. Daniel waved me into the house.

The interior was filled with stage and screen memorabilia. He was from a long line of Broadway actors. Old posters from his father's films adorned the walls, along with those of Steve McQueen and Judy Garland.

"They used to hang out here with Dad," he said.

Daniel shared his own story. He had been a working actor until alcoholism caught up with him. Now he was training to be a clown at one of those Vegas shows. Right up my street. Just what I needed.

"Come back tomorrow, 6 a.m.," he said as I left.

I worked furiously that night, sketching out what I'd been through at Prospects. At six the following morning, I showed up at Daniel's, all ready to sell him my script.

"Check this out. This would make a funny film."

He gave my handwritten notes a cursory glance. "Let's get you sober first. Are you an alcoholic?"

"Yes."

"Good, then let's start with the steps."

We sat down and began from the beginning.

"We're going to establish a first line of defence against the 'fuck-it's'," he said before I left. "I want you to call me every day at 6 a.m. My phone is on 24/7. Call me ten times a day if need be. It's a thinking problem, so you need to check all your thoughts. Let me do the thinking for you. Call me before you make any decisions, doesn't matter what it is."

Back at sober living, I called him. "I'm about to take a piss, what should I do?"

"What hand do you usually hold it with?"

"Right," I said.

"Contrary action, then. Hold it with your left."

And so it went day by day, sometimes minute by minute.

I walked with Daniel every morning at six. He led the way with a mantra.

"I am willing to be happy. I am willing to be free..."

He taught me to breathe and drew me back to my senses.

"What do you see, what do you hear, what do you smell..."

One day he stopped at a row of flowers. "Can you make one of those?"

"No," I admitted.

"Then you're not God. In the programme we talk of GOD as an acronym for Good Orderly Direction. It's not some physical being sitting up among the clouds."

On another occasion, he placed his hand on his chest and asked me to do likewise.

"In my early sobriety, I went to stay with some Buddhist monks, and one of the monks asked me to do the same thing. 'Can you feel your heart beat?' he asked me. I could and nodded yes. 'Well, do you make that beat? Could you consciously make that stop?' It just blew my mind, realizing how little control I had, how life went on with and without me."

Over time, Daniel listened patiently as I talked through my story.

"You'll write a book one day," he told me.

"I'll need to find the patience to read one first. Apart from porn and simple books when I was a kid, I've probably only read a couple of them cover to cover."

When Natasja e-mailed me, Daniel helped me to respond with love and kindness, and to show through my actions that I was taking responsibility for my life. He helped me access what I came to call my Higher Power.

I watched Daniel be a father to his son: to be firm, fair and friendly. I watched him be a son to his mother; to love unconditionally but also to know when to detach with love and set personal boundaries to maintain his own mental and emotional health. I watched him be a partner to his girlfriend: a healthy, supportive relationship based on trust. He showed me how to do these things in my own relation-ships, with Natasja, with her son, with my own mother and father.

As for Natasja, it was over as a romantic interest. She was like a movie screen upon which the saddest days and memories of my drinking life played out. If there was going to be a new me, there had to be a new her.

One morning, during my usual early walk with Daniel, I thought she had arrived.

Daniel and I were pulling up to the café down at the corner of his block and came upon a woman reading a book out the front. She had a Great Dane lying next to her. Daniel said hello in passing and introduced me.

"Michael, Jessica. Jessica, Michael."

I shook her hand, absolutely spellbound. I had found my new Higher Power.

"She's an actress," Daniel said.

Jessica played it cool. So did I, until I went inside the coffee shop, at which point I rushed to grab a cup and hurried back outside before Jessica had disappeared.

She barely looked up as I took a seat. I kept stealing glances. With beauty like that in my life, absolutely nothing else would matter.

Feeling this inexplicable and utterly irrepressible sense of primal power at being near her, a thought crossed my mind.

"Will you marry me?" I said.

Jessica laughed. "You just want a green card."

She had a point though I elected not to confirm as much.

"Are you British?" she asked over a sip of her mocha.

"Isle of Man."

That led to the obligatory geography lesson. Self-governed. Oldest Parliament in the world. You can still shoot a Scotsman on the beach. The usual pitch of my homeland.

"You should visit," I said.

"I would love to. I just love to travel. Come," she said, tapping the seat next to her. "Sit here and have a look at these photos."

I did, close enough that our legs were touching, but not so close that I appeared to be indiscreet. Jessica continued scrolling through a photo tour of her recent trip to Egypt without missing a beat.

Daniel came out with his coffee, no doubt saw where this movie was headed and started up the block alone. I got back to my tour of the Nile, pangs of jealousy stabbing me as Jessica related how, on the cruise over, one of the masseurs had removed all her clothes and given her a full body massage.

"I recommended it to all the other women on the boat," she said with a laugh.

Given my sudden feelings of jealousy and obsession, I found it hard to smile. As the photo tour continued, I found the image of Jessica naked hard to get out of my head. It had taken precedence over everything else.

I looked up in the direction of Daniel's house. I had promised him to stay away from women until I was done with the steps. Suddenly, I felt a great urgency to finish those bastards.

Eventually, the photo tour of Egypt led to us discussing the world. We were visiting Machu Picchu together, New Zealand. The Isle of Man.

Smelling money, and wondering where it had come from, I inquired about the family background.

"My father's in oil."

"Oh," I said nonchalantly, my head already doing the maths. If Jessica's father is wealthy, by default, so is Jessica.

No use in getting overburdened by the steps. With all that money and Jessica at my side, who needed a programme?

All that night, I obsessed over her beauty and wealth, and I rushed through my usual routine the next morning. Yes, Daniel. Abso*bloody*lutely. Do the steps. Make amends. Morning meditation. Get right with God. All that good shit.

The whole time, my thoughts were completely centred on that corner coffee shop. An Americano would be good. I pictured Jessica down there waiting for me. It was getting towards Christmas – a great time to be striking up a new affair.

Pulling onto the street in my car a short time later, I spotted Jessica sitting in the same seat and my emotions rocketed from the fear of unfulfilled expectations straight to sheer elation.

Then my head kicked in, having its own ideas on how to play this thing. Be cool, it said. Show no emotion. I strolled up with a wave and a nod like I was meeting my mother.

With the morning air crisp and cold, Jessica had her hands wrapped around her mocha. I loved the imagery but could have done without the Great Dane. At least the bastard had stopped growling at my arrival.

"Hey, trouble," I said.

"You're trouble," she said back.

That led to a bit more banter and some playful punches, after which I went in to grab my Americano.

Returning to the bench across from Jessica, I found her staring into my eyes. She stared – and stared. As the seconds dragged excruciatingly on towards a minute, I thought, this is a bit longer than what I'd consider socially acceptable, or comfortable. The realization struck me. It's a fucking challenge. Who's going to look away first? Are you man enough for me?

Fuck this. I had no use for such games, but I wasn't about to let her top me. I held on until I needed eye drops. Jessica finally relented and shuffled across the bench to sit between my legs.

Notch one for the conquering Viking. Apparently I had made the grade. Never underestimate the spirit of a man who had been slow rowing to Valhalla for the past thirty years.

"Rub my shoulders," Jessica said.

I squeezed her shoulders firmly until she let out a moan. Her back arched. I worked on her neck and head and back while she searched for travel adventures on her laptop. That quickly led us back to Machu Picchu.

"I've always wanted to go," I said.

"Let's do it, then," she said.

"Sounds good to me."

We had exchanged contact details before she left. I returned to the scene of the crime first thing the next morning. She wasn't there and my heart sank.

I stretched out a coffee and a few cigarettes over the *Los Angeles Times*. I read through the entire paper without absorbing a thing. My eyes had been distracted up the road every few seconds.

Finally, Jessica came into view and the exchange resumed. A bit of my soul for a bit of affection. I did not need anyone to tell me that I was doomed.

Jessica handed the Great Dane to me and went in for a mocha. Upon her return, she shuffled back right between my legs. There was a tap in the direction of her back. My cue.

She opened up her laptop and resumed her search for far-away and exotic locales. I did my best to keep my erection clear of her perceptions.

We chatted about this and that, with me growing lost in her thick, driftwood-coloured hair. It smelled of fresh citrus shampoo. It also seemed to be a different colour from the previous day. I pulled it back from one ear, thinking to ask Jessica about it, but decided against, no, best to leave that one alone, but then she turned around to look at me, so I went ahead.

"Is your hair lighter this morning, or is it just me?"

With that, she stood, stuffed her laptop in her bag and walked off. The Great Dane looked back – as if sympathizing.

What the fuck just happened?

So maybe I did cock that one up a bit, and yeah, I did have a thing for fiery women, but this was veering way too close to the pathological. Perhaps Daniel was right. Best if I stay away from the opposite sex until I've properly worked through the steps.

Days went by without any sign of Jessica. Meanwhile, my emotions were devouring me from the inside out.

Then, out of the blue, I received an e-mail from her one morning.

Not seen you at the coffee shop recently.

Not seen me? I've been here. Where the hell have you been?

Absolutely baffled, and still wary, I took the bait anyway.

Fancy a coffee?

Sure, she wrote back.

I drove down immediately and waited with my stomach churning.

"I hope I didn't offend you the other day," I said once she had settled in across from me.

She waved off my comment like what had happened was nothing. It was certainly not something we were about to discuss.

"We're still going to Machu Picchu, right?" she said.

"Absolutely," I replied.

And just like that we were back to civility and decorum.

A few days passed without further incident. Then one morning Jessica mentioned that her dog needed medical attention. I made a flippant comment about the high cost of keeping them. "They're sort of like high-maintenance bitches."

Definitely a "foot in your mouth" sort of comment, but meant innocently enough.

Into the bag went the laptop. Off stormed Jessica, the Great Dane looking back once over its shoulder.

With Christmas rapidly approaching, I got word that Jessica had gone off to explore the lost city of Machu Picchu without me. Well, that was that. I wandered around lost and beating the shit out of myself over my big mouth.

Impulsively, I stopped every morning at the same spot for coffee. Then one day Jessica reappeared. As if not a bloody thing had happened, she nestled back in between my legs with her mocha in hand. The photos of Machu Picchu came out. I sat through the travel lecture, filled with envy.

I still had hopes of us being together for Christmas but Jessica had made plans to visit her family and friends in Dallas. My holiday consolation prize was texting with Jessica as she drove to Texas.

You should visit Texas one day.

Love to.

I'm looking forward to seeing Sarah.

I would look forward to seeing both of you.

It was a piss-poor attempt to sexualize the messages.

Go to Bed came back. Like I was a fucking dog being directed to lie in its basket.

And thus ended our text messaging. Jessica had been somewhere near El Paso. The radar went blank for the rest of her entire trip.

My attempt at humour had clearly not translated well in a text.

Tired of giving Daniel lip service, I deleted Jessica's number. The woman was killing me. When it was good, it was good. I was on cloud nine. When Jessica pulled the plug, you may as well have gutted me.

Good God, did I ever need to move on with these steps.

CHAPTER EIGHTEEN

While I spent my first sober Christmas with Molly, her daughter and her mum, visions of Jessica lounging about with the rich and famous back in Dallas were rattling around in my head. Talk about fucked-up emotions. I had such warm companionship, but all my laughter was half-hearted. I was at once grateful that anyone would have me for the holidays and pining for a woman who couldn't be bothered to give me the time of day.

Not having heard a word from her over Christmas, I trudged on wearing my best face but with my heart on my sleeve.

One thing led to another and I ended up moving in with Daniel. It wasn't long before I'd met his mum. She was 15 years sober. She was also old and infirm and in constant need of attention.

Daniel enlisted my help in keeping an eye on her. Among my many duties, I chauffeured his mum around to her doctor's appointments and twelve-step meetings.

One day she had a fall and ended up in the emergency ward. Daniel and I went to see her. A doctor came around and informed us that they had discovered alcohol in her bloodstream. When confronted, his mum denied the whole thing.

"It must have been the Listerine or green tea extract. I've not been drinking."

Nothing Daniel said could put a chink in her newfound armour.

"That's how alcoholism works," he told me as we left.

And so the merry-go-round began. Our trips to the doctor's office and twelve-step meetings were now interspersed with trips to the liquor store – as if I wasn't to notice. The woman began to drive me crazy with her disease.

Then the light went on. So this is the madness I had inflicted on everyone around me. It was humbling. I found my anger at the world transformed into compassion and empathy. I started to forgive myself and others. I was learning what it meant to be a person among persons.

Things were going along quite smoothly in my recovery, except when it came to Jessica. She kept passing through my life like a tornado. There would be the coy text messages, inviting me to coffee. I would agree and find myself listening to all I had missed during Jessica's latest absence and massaging her back as the price of admission.

Then the moment would come when Jessica was suddenly offended, perhaps for good reason, perhaps not, but her response was always disproportionate in my eyes, and utterly baffling. Away went the laptop and off she stormed with the Great Dane in tow. All communication from her end ceased. I deleted her number from my phone. Then we ran into each other at the coffee shop and things started all over again.

I hated myself for giving in to the tease, knowing full well that insult and abandonment were to follow. A typical scene would be Jessica inviting me to a social event then cancelling with no explanation two hours before we were to meet.

I increased the intensity of my weight lifting and training as a way to work off the frustration. In doing so, I began to see the correlation between physical and spiritual well-being. My sights became set on a career as a personal trainer. I had been in communication with Jesse, Natasja's friend, himself a personal trainer, and asked him how to obtain accreditation. He recommended the National Academy of Sports Medicine, where he had gone.

Four months later, I had successfully passed the exams and experienced a slow build up of clientele from Hollywood celebrities to Mexican pool cleaners. I had some of the world's top male supermodels, musicians, TV personalities and people who had never seen a treadmill.

At one point, Jesse was called off on location and asked if I would train his clients while he was away. When he returned, I was invited to a birthday party for one of his mates. It turned out to be a small gathering of the A-list crowd.

I had to laugh at the birthday boy scenario. He had been the leading character in a prime-time stateside drama some years back and I'd wasted away more than a few Sunday mornings back on the Isle of Man, smoking heroin and watching him on the telly from my bed.

In the following weeks, I was introduced to the cream of the British entertainment industry. Jesse invited me out to the theatre and Dean, a British actor, showed up. He had starred in a recent blockbuster that had been nominated for multiple Oscars. Dean followed up with an invitation to an afternoon BBQ up in the Hollywood Hills. I found myself strutting up to the door of a luxury mansion. A glamorous blonde named Mandy welcomed me in and steered me outside to the pool. The barbecue was in full swing. The view of Los Angeles stretched from one end of the horizon to the other.

Camped on the opposite hillside, a pack of paparazzi were zooming in on the pool area with photo lenses the length of your arm. The pool area was buzzing with some of the top British entertainers. A handful of the hottest American TV actors rounded out the team. Paul McKenna was sculling backward across the pool on an inflatable raft.

Amazing, I thought. Of the few books I had read in my life, his *Change Your Life in 7 Days* was one of them. I had passed the hours with it on that long flight to New Zealand.

Later in the day, Paul and I got chatting.

"Why don't you come over here for a workout this week?"

He pointed to the side of the house. "We've got the gym in there."

We met a few days later and that led to the two of us training together on a regular basis. When he was called out of the country on business, I was asked to look after the house.

"Range Rover and the Bentley are in the garage," Paul told me upon my arrival. "Keys are on the side."

Off he went. I sat down inside and took in the view, hardly believing that anyone would trust me with that much stuff.

On the second or third afternoon, I noticed a Starline bus head up to the top of the road and turn around. The tourists were all hanging out of the windows for a better view of the celebrity houses as the bus came back down the hill. The names along the street read like a *Who's Who* of Hollywood: Brittany Murphy, Ryan Phillippe, Val Kilmer, Jason Statham. The list went on and on.

The following day, I kept a keen eye out for the Starline bus going up the road and was all prepared by the time it had turned around – the garage door open and me seated in the Bentley, a pair of aviator shades on and casually looking over my shoulder.

No place like Hollywood for the craic!

Conveniently, Jessica had texted me that day with ideas of luring me back into her lair. I texted back.

Come up to the house, the view's incredible. I'll feed you grapes by the pool.

I thought I had nothing to lose by trying to seduce her. Her response came like a sucker punch.

I'd be much more impressed if it was your house.

Aloof bitch. Always looking for a fight. Why did I even try?

I responded with a cutting note of my own and that quickly escalated into several heated exchanges. Then silence. The Cold War was back on.

One rainy morning, after Paul had returned, I drove over Laurel Canyon on my way to his place for a workout. On the other side of the valley, a car braked in front of me and I went into a skid on the wet asphalt. Having slammed into the back of a black Cadillac, both the other driver and I got out. He looked over his bumper.

"I'm so sorry," I said, walking up.

"We'd better get this sorted. Here's my card. I'm Steven. Hey, listen, do you act?"

"Not really but it feels like I've been doing it my whole life."

He was all business, sizing me up.

"Look, forget about the scratch. I'm putting together a film noir and you've got the right height and rugged good looks. Are you interested?"

Why not? A few months earlier in my sobriety, I might have choked, but I had nothing to lose by now.

Arriving at Paul's place, Mandy answered the door. I explained the story.

"LA's the only place where you can crash into a car and get a part in a film out of it."

"Be careful," Mandy said. "Did you get his name? What company was he with?"

I retrieved the card and read the name out loud.

"Hustler. Who are they?"

Mandy burst out laughing. "Michael, I hate to break this to you, but it's porn."

"For fuck's sake," I said and skulked off to my workout with Paul. "Just my calling."

Mandy came in and had a good laugh with Paul over my new career path. Bastards. It was hard to believe how still in the fucking dark I was at times. Naïve, and in my early thirties.

Paul had a radio show to attend after our workout and jumped in the shower. I heard a mantra emanating from the bathroom.

"I can, I can, I can."

It was positive reinforcement. The same thing I had been learning in recovery. Everything starts with your inner attitude.

That following week, I designed some business cards. MICHAEL up top, CANNAN below it. Black background with white letters. The I and CAN were highlighted in red. I CAN. Over the top, perhaps, but it served as a reminder of my sobriety. I had no idea what a liability this card would become for me in the days to come.

The summer rushed by, littered with barbecues and the British elite. One afternoon I recognized the Scottish model James Brooks across the pool. He was renowned for having a healthy portfolio of celebrity girlfriends, an A-list actress being the last. He was certainly surrounded by quite a few women on that day, the Duchess of Cornwall's niece, Emma Parker Bowles, amongst them.

I wandered over to see what one-liners I could pick up from him. The discussion had turned to the pressing question of whether bleaching your arsehole was a requirement for successful integration into LA culture. Emma kindly offered us a two-for-one discount on bleaching ours. Out of deference to the Queen Mother, we declined.

By the time the sun had gone down and the barbecue was growing cold, Mr Brooks and I had become good mates.

"I'm out of the country on a couple of assignments," James said on his way towards the door. "But I'll give you a shout when I'm back and we'll have a workout."

On his return, we met and drove over to LA Fitness on Hollywood Boulevard. His phone beeped as we pulled in. He picked it up and started to laugh.

"What?" I said.

He held up the phone to show me the text.

I WANNA EAT YOUR FACE OFF!!!!!!

"Who the hell's that?" I asked.

"Just between you and me. Alissa...Alissa Klein."

"Are you fucking serious? Let's see if I can staple you beneath the bench press and break the bad news to Alissa. She'll need a shoulder to cry on."

He had a good laugh.

After the workout, while we were sitting down for a steak sandwich, a group of hysterical Japanese birds came around begging for his picture. Getting out of there was like a Kodak commercial or a scene from *A Hard Day's Night*.

A paparazzi chase through the Hollywood Hills ensued. The scramble was all about getting a photo of James with Alissa. As a means of escaping them, James pulled in to visit a friend of his in the neighbourhood. We left a short while later for a jog in Runyon Canyon. I decided to change clothes at the boot of his Range Rover. With my arse hanging out of a ripped pair of Calvin Klein boxers, I noticed James pissing himself laughing.

"What?" I asked.

"There's a paparazzi behind you taking photos."

Christ. There was no privacy when you knocked about with that crowd.

Back at his house, we found more paparazzi hiding in the trees across the road. It was everything I had imagined about LA – glamour and privilege – but sprinkled with a pinch of madness and anxiety I'd not anticipated.

Inside, James was fielding calls from his agent and deciding which designer threads to sport for an event with the missus. Major contrast that. I was worrying about the wreckage from my past and my tourist visa. The visa permitted me to remain in the USA for six months at a time, which meant very soon I would be obligated to head back to the Isle of Man. A nice trip, aside from having to face all the people I'd fucked over before getting sober.

CHAPTER NINETEEN

The months flew by against a backdrop of Hollywood stars and their opulent lives, played out on and off the silver screen. My life was altogether another thing. Ever cognisant of the amends before me, I found the idea of going back through my life, person by person, and owning up to my part of the wreckage a matter of dread. I knew it had to be done if I wanted to be free, but major progress had yet to materialise.

Before I knew it, an entire year had flown by since my stay at Forest Hills rehab. It was October and a warm Santa Ana wind was blowing in from the desert. I was alone and feeling lost and wanted someone to know it was my sobriety birthday.

Unannounced, I stopped by Jim's house, the manager of the Destructive Divas and the man who had introduced me to Daniel. Jim was still in bed when I knocked. He came to the door looking groggy.

"Michael. What are you doing?"

"Hey, brother, one whole year sober. Would you believe it? Thanks so much for everything."

"Unbelievable," he said. "Well done, man. That's amazing."

"Greatest achievement of my life. And the bravest."

"Me too. Come in, come in," he said, coming out of his fog. "Get yourself in that cupboard. Something in there for you."

I lifted out a black Hugo Boss suit, with black shirt, black Armani belt and black Armani shoes.

"This?" I said, holding it up.

"It's all yours."

"Thanks, man!"

"Every alcoholic needs a black suit. If nobody dies before you, we've got something nice to bury you in."

"Lovely thought, mate."

That evening I wore the clothes to an event at LA Fashion Week. During the break I walked outside to smoke and check my phone. There was a text from one of Molly's friends.

Oh Michael. I'm so sorry. It's Molly. She's dead. So so sorry.

I slumped against the wall and wept. When I was able to gather myself, I called her friend and learned that Molly had relapsed a few weeks earlier. That day, she left a note and threw herself off a building in Playa Del Rey.

I had not seen Molly for a few weeks. The last time was when we were out shopping around together for her new house. I had kept an eye on her daughter while she viewed each property with the agent.

"I heard my mum tell a friend that she loves you on the phone," her daughter had told me.

Unsure if that was meant to be as a friend or a romantic interest, I did not know how to handle the situation and backed off. Then we'd lost touch for several weeks.

On the day of the funeral, Molly's friend gave me Molly's one-year sober chip.

"She would have wanted you to have it."

I watched Molly's daughter throw a red rose on her mum's coffin, a mess of tears.

"My mummy loved you," the little girl told me.

Christ, what a sad day. I thought of her dad killing himself. Maybe it was something genetic. The stress of divorce too. Or just the simple fact that alcoholism is a killer. I had a sense that Molly would not be the last. I recalled her telling me that whatever I put before my recovery, I would lose. Her death was just a grim reminder of that. Recovery always had to come first in my life. Without it, I had nothing.

I went to visit the psychiatrist at Forest Hills, determined to move on and get off all the meds if I could. I was still taking Seroquel and Lamictal for my bipolar disorder. The psychiatrist agreed that I could get off the Seroquel, but not the Lamictal. I asked him about a long-term strategy.

"It's something you will have to take for the rest of your life. Think of it as using a condom."

It was not what I wanted to hear. I was more determined than ever to get at the truth of my problems and find a way to free myself from prescription drugs.

My mum and sister came to visit soon after Molly's death, and Sal and I talked for hours about our past experiences. She had always been the strong one, always protecting, and in some way I would always be her little brother, but the dynamic had changed. We were more like equals now. My recovery had given me a sense of my own place in the family. In any case, for the two of us to talk about how we had dealt with the same shame and guilt growing up was very healing.

I had this urge to revisit the Prospects treatment centre and took my sister along for the ride. I had not been back since the day they carted me out on a gurney.

As we came up the driveway, Jaz appeared. I got out of the car and called to her. She looked astonished to see me.

"Are you okay or are you coming back for more?"

"Over a year sober," I said.

"How wonderful, Michael. You know, when you were here, your mum called and said we should get a priest to perform an exorcism on you."

I smiled but was heartbroken inside. To think my Mum had believed that shit. She must have been terrified. I suddenly felt such compassion for the poor woman.

"It was worth a try, I guess, but I've done it without one."

Soon after my mum and sister left, my tourist visa issues resurfaced to confront me. My stay was up, a fact that had been hanging over my head for the past six months.

On the Saturday before I was due to leave, James Brooks and I booked a table at the Chateau Marmont. The maître d' escorted us to our table and pulled James' seat out for him. James eyed me and nodded over his shoulder. Alissa and one of her A-list actress friends were at the table behind us. James had split up with Alissa but out of common courtesy walked over to greet her.

Shortly after his return to our table, Noah Mills and another fella in the modelling business joined us for dinner. Alissa Klein stopped by later while we were still eating and engaged in some lively banter before sauntering out of the restaurant.

I couldn't keep my eyes off her arse as she left.

"Would you look at the fuckin' legs on that," I said.

"Mate, let me tell ya," James said. "It doesn't matter whether you're in a crack house in Glasgow or on the beach with Alissa, you're still left with your own thoughts."

Of all things, his comment had me thinking about the amends I needed to make to my old man. It seemed like an opportune time to address them, what with my visa requirement to leave the country every six months. The hour of reckoning had arrived, and I booked a flight back to the Isle of Man.

Before leaving, I sat down with Daniel to read the ninth step. Making amends to all the people I had screwed over and all that.

Halfway through, I received a text from Jessica.

Why don't you come over and give me a massage?

Game on. I could conveniently add her to my amends list.

Daniel's phone rang about the same time. It was another recovering alcoholic. The two of them went on and on. I used the opportunity to slip out of the door.

Daniel had told me that the devil comes in many forms, but particularly in the shape of high heels and a short skirt.

Soon, I had Jessica between my legs, doing my penance at her back and shoulders. The whole time I could hear Daniel saying, "Leave her the fuck alone." Well, off came her top but I left her alone. Anything this good was worth the wait. I only wished this twelfth step would be over sooner.

I drove home with my cock hard. I went to sleep that night in no way signed up for this priesthood business. I awakened the next morning in the same state of mind.

While making tea and feeling regret over not fucking Jessica, I went to make a call and realized I'd lost my phone. I e-mailed Jessica to see if she had seen it. She hadn't.

I had a sudden urge to see her again and used the opportunity to open up the dialogue with a few goading comments. That was the only way I knew how to express my emotions at the time, which once again did not translate well through the use of modern technology.

Before I knew it, Jessica and I were in another royal battle via email.

It came down to:

Fuck you!

Fuck you!

I had been trying to get in the last word, but of course Jessica beat me to it:

You're an asshole.

And she was gone.

I messaged her back several times, but all my subsequent attempts were met with silence.

On the day of my flight, Daniel gave me a ride to the airport.

"Any last words of spiritual advice?" I asked him as we pulled to a stop in front of the terminal.

"Don't forget who's at the top of your amends list."

"Who?"

"You. The twelve steps are an amends to yourself more than anything else. Don't forget that."

We hugged.

"I love you," he said.

"Same here, mate."

I boarded the long flight to London, then caught a connecting flight to the Isle of Man. Dad picked me up. I was staying with him.

The following morning, I sat down while he was making breakfast.

"Dad, do you have a moment to talk?"

He looked surprised. "What, then?"

"Can we sit down?"

His dining table overlooked a garden.

"You know how I've been going through this recovery?"

"Yeah."

"Well, part of the process is to make amends for my past behaviour."

He quickly stopped me and jumped on his feet. "Oh you don't need to do that with me."

"No, Dad, I do. Please. I need to so I can move forward. Will you listen for a moment?"

He reluctantly sat back down. Perhaps he thought I was going to point the finger at him. I had no intention of doing so, but no doubt there were skeletons in his own closet and he'd just as soon avoid them. Ever since the divorce, the whole family had been haunted. An unspoken background noise had troubled all of our interactions. Until this moment, I had never known how to broach the subject.

"I realize how difficult I made your life, so I want to apologize. Ya know, for being dishonest about my drinking and drug use. I lied for years."

"You really don't need to do this. I'm just glad you're okay. That's all I ever wanted to know."

"Please, can I finish, Dad? I know I hurt you when I dishonoured the family and I'm sorry. I'm sorry that I shut you out of my life and ignored you when you were trying to help me, and I'm sorry that I stole money from you. I broke into the house when I was younger and I used it to fuel my addiction to gambling machines."

"I knew you nicked the money."

"I wasted the deposit you gave me for a house. Spent it all on drugs and gifts for my girlfriends. Didn't even realize that you'd paid half for my treatment in rehab. Im so grateful for all of it and it's my intention to pay everything back."

"You don't need to do that. It doesn't matter. Just as long as you're okay."

I watched him fidget. Clearly he wanted the conversation to end but I forged ahead.

"I appreciate your generosity, but it matters to me. Even if it's a small amount each month until I can afford to pay you back the whole lot. Dad, I held on to all these resentments towards you and never let you be my dad."

Seeing his discomfort, I reached to touch his forearm.

"I never took the time to understand the breakup of the marriage or the difficulties you faced in your life. I was in no position to judge you. I was pissed off because you were having an affair. I understand from my own experience that you were doing the best you could with the information you had. I forgive you for the affair. For all of it."

The tension fell away from his body and he sat back in his seat.

"I've been waiting thirty odd years to have this conversation. It broke my heart to leave you kids. I've not been able to live with myself. Until you have kids, you'll never quite understand. If I'd have been there I might have been able to prevent everything that you've gone through."

"Don't ever feel guilty, dad. Everythings exactly as it's meant to be today. If you'd stayed it might have been worse. I might never have hit the bottom I needed for me to get well. I might have never found recovery. It's not just about stopping drink and drugs; it's a whole new way of life. A new freedom."

He smiled a bit.

"Alcohol's definitely been in the family," he said. "My mum's brother and her nephew were both alcoholics. Both died of alcohol poisoning."

I had never heard this side of the story before. Directly or indirectly, we had all been hit by the effects of alcoholism. I felt a new level of compassion for everyone involved, me included.

Dad continued, "Aye, mum said her brother was the biggest liar in town, only behind me. She reckoned I was a bigger liar than him. Tom Pepper she used to call me."

"Tom Pepper?" I said.

"Yeah, she reckoned Tom Pepper was thrown out of hell for lying."

"Must be in the blood. Hell of a legacy I picked up there. I reckon I've got you both beaten."

It felt good to laugh together.

He started to explain his reasons for going to Australia when he was younger.

"I had to leave. I had to get out of the house. Mum became seriously depressed after my little brother died. She'd already lost two of her brothers to Scarlet Fever. Had a mental breakdown. I had to go and live with my grandparents. She was medicated for years. It affected her so much she was angry and frustrated all the time. I couldn't bear it. I wished my dad had left for the woman at work. She'd treated him well."

Sensing this was an attempt to justify his own divorce, my heart sank. He still could not take responsibility for his choices. I did not judge him but wished he had something like the twelve steps to deal with his problems. I wanted him to be free. If not for alcohol and drugs, I would never have found the answers to my own life.

After we had talked for hours, I came back to my own amends.

"Is there anything you can remember where I shamed or angered or humiliated you, Dad? If you can remind me it would help because I fucking never want to go back to where I was. I want to be a good son."

"I'm just so proud of you," he said and gave me a hug.

"I love you, Dad,"

"I love you, Mikey."

Suddenly he was a human being and friend and not the father figure I had feared. It was the most healing thing I had done in sobriety.

Now I had another small amends to make to my old friend, Gavin. He had asked me to be his best man, and in the run-up to the wedding, my drug-induced behaviour had crossed unheard-of new boundaries of debauchery.

"Gav, how are ya, mate?" I said when he answered my call.

We had not spoken for four years.

"Fuckin' hell," he said. "Is that who I think it is? How the hell are you doing?"

"Is there any chance I can come and see you?"

He gave me his address and I drove right over. He opened the door and we hugged. He was living with his wife, Lucy, and their children.

"I knew the day would come," he said.

"Can we talk, then?"

"Yeah, take a seat. I'll be with you in a second."

I walked into the conservatory. Gavin came in with two glasses and a bottle of cheap champagne.

"Let's get started," he said.

"Not for me. Thanks, mate."

"Why's that then?"

"Had to stop, mate. I'm sober twenty months now."

"What, you don't drink?"

He poured a glass each for him and his wife.

"I'll leave you two to it," she said. "I'm sure you've got plenty to catch up on."

"No, Lucy, do you mind staying? You need to hear this too."

She stood at the conservatory door.

"I had to get sober and I've seen how my actions affected the people I loved in my life. And I really need to speak to you both."

"Oh, you don't have to do that," she said. "I'm going."

"Can you please stay?"

"I know what happened," Gavin said, "and you don't need to do this."

"Gav, I do. I betrayed your trust. I realize that before I left the island my actions were inappropriate and I want to apologize for making advances towards your wife. For ringing and trying to, ya know? You, Lucy."

I gestured to her. Tears filled my eyes.

"I consider you one of my best friends. You didn't deserve to be treated that way, and I'm sorry."

"I'm leaving you two to it," Lucy said and left.

"Mate, I knew it wasn't you. You became someone else with the drugs and all. I didn't know you."

"I was making phone calls to Lucy, and it was wrong and I just want to apologize. I'm sincerely sorry."

"Mate, listen. I've got some natural wine here. Get a scoop of this."

I laughed. "Mate, I can't have anything. When I drink, things die. Honestly, it's not for me today."

"You're seriously never gonna drink again for the rest of your life?"

"Well, if I thought like that, I'd be in trouble. I just take it a day at a time."

We sat up until 4 a.m., just talking. I gave him an unedited account of the last few years: New Zealand, America, the hedonism, the addiction, the sickness, the nut houses.

He looked angry and frustrated.

"You bastard. The only thing I'm mad about is that I wasn't right by your side the whole time."

He shared his story. His family ripped apart by alcoholism and addiction.

In the following days, I also spoke with my uncle and auntie, my mum's sister. I apologized for my past actions and shared many of the same stories. My auntie in turn shared some of her own background. Information that helped me to understand everything my mum had gone through. Mental illness had run through the family. And yet there I was pointing the finger at mum.

294

At the end, I once again asked if there was anything from my past that I might have forgotten.

"Well, there was that incident at the golf club," my uncle said.

Only then did that particular episode come back to me. On drugs, I had pulled a small knife on a friend in an argument, terrorizing and embarrassing everyone at the country club in the process.

Add it to my amends list. Jesus, some of this stuff was enough to make your skin crawl.

I didn't stop until I had seen almost everyone on my list: family members, friends who had become estranged through my behaviour; old girlfriends I had hurt and to whom I owed money; dead friends in the graveyard; old places of work and old work colleagues.

Some people I came across in the street and made spontaneous amends to them. Some people I called would not agree to see me. They only knew the old me and did not feel comfortable having me past the doorstep, but I was willing and tried to do whatever I could to heal those old relationships. Years of shame and guilt dropped away with each amends.

The whole time I was on the Isle of Man, I obsessed over Jessica. I started pumping iron with a fury. I'd be ripped to shreds. Then wait until she saw me. She would not be able to resist.

I had to get back to America.

A month after arriving on the Isle of Man, my mum invited me to visit Cyprus, where she was still living and working. It was one of my last amends. The two of us had communicated regularly, and through her participation in Al-Anon, I knew she understood the disease of alcoholism, but I was still nervous about the impending confession.

At the airport on the Isle of Man, off to London and my connecting flight to Cyprus, I spotted a familiar face from across the terminal. Hilary Kaighen. I hadn't seen her since our school days. She had suffered from clinical depression back then and I'd often mocked her. Jesus, you never knew when these amends would come creeping round a corner. She was near the top of the list, and I had often thought of her while sitting in that nut house but hadn't thought I'd meet her like this. Karma was catching up with me.

Clearly she didn't recognize me and I was struggling with the courage to face her. I found a cubicle in the bathroom, pulled out the notebook with all my amends and flicked through to the part where I had taunted Hilary at school. It was painful. Flight departures to various destinations were called out over the intercom; mine included. I prayed for the right words and headed back out to find her gone.

Deflated, I boarded the plane, only to find she was seated directly in front of me.

Poking my head between the seats, I asked if Hilary remembered me. She did a double take.

"Michael Cannan, is that you?"

The recognition came to her as something less than pleasant. I stumbled through the start of my amends. My sincerity finally got through and we talked at length the entire flight. Addiction, depression, the lot. I felt like I had known her all my life.

In London, we disembarked and walked to the train station together. I finally got on to a proper amends.

"Hilary, I'm genuinely so sorry for the way I treated you at school. Can you ever forgive me?"

"Oh sure, Michael. Forgiven."

We were both choked up and shared a heartfelt hug and agreed to stay in touch.

Mum picked me up from the airport in Cyprus.

"Mum, you know about the amends, don't you?" I said once we had settled.

"I do, but there's nothing left to say. I think I pretty much know everything. Don't I?"

"Well...can you take a seat?"

She picked up a box of Kleenex. "Will I be needing these?"

I was so relieved to sit with her and be specific about my behaviour, to take responsibility for the past: for lying, cheating

296

and stealing; for letting the house fall into disrepair; bringing women into the house out of disrespect; for my wallowing in self-pity and depression; driving drunk in her car; stealing her time; putting her in a position where she was covering my arse again and again.

"And all the money, Mum, where do I start?"

"Forget about it. I realize you need to pay me back for you, but you can do that in fifty years' time for all I care. You do it when you can afford to do it."

"Thanks, Mum. And thanks for being there. Without you, I wouldn't be here today. You were the one who stood by me through all this. I'm so touched that you were willing to go to Al-Anon."

"Al-Anon helped me. It helped me to see the issues that I've had in my life. I wish I'd had the chance to know my own mum. She became ill when I was born."

Mum opened up further about her experience and family background.

"Al-Anon gave me the tools to help me be more objective about all my relationships. I was born seven years after my sister, and I'd been told that my mum had become ill during my birth. Because of this illness, mum had needed help looking after me. When I found out about all this I felt guilty – I felt that I was to blame. Mum became a semi-invalid for many years and died when I was twenty. Al-Anon helped me to understand that this was not my fault."

With all my amends done, as best as I could do them, I caught a flight from Cyprus to London, and one from there to Los Angeles via Chicago. I was stopped at customs in Chicago and detained for questioning by Homeland Security.

Before being questioned, I was allowed to use the bathroom. I had no bloody idea if any cameras were watching me, but I got on my knees. A phrase from a spiritual guidebook came to mind, something a man I knew had used when times got tough. "Holy Spirit, guide me now." It seemed a bit dramatic, but it was the only thing left in my bag of tricks.

Back out with security, they searched my suitcase and found a blue notebook. It had my amends list and the dollar amounts next to everyone's name. To them it looked suspiciously like a drug dealer's list. They rifled through my wallet and found that business card I had so proudly designed with my I CAN logo on it.

Now I was suspected of having worked illegally in the States. They gave me an opportunity to withdraw my visa. I would need a new one to re-enter the country now. I wavered. After several hours two officers arrived and showed me some handcuffs.

"Are you going to do this the easy way?"

I relented and they walked me to a nearby jetway. I was made to face the wall while the jet crew reopened the door. Then I was escorted onto a full plane. I felt like the only thing missing was an orange boiler suit.

I arrived back at Heathrow with no idea what to do next. Wandering around the airport, I noticed a counter for Cyprus Airlines in the far corner and enquired about the flights. They had one seat left on a plane departing in a few hours. I was able to get hold of Mum and explain the situation. She met me at the boarding gate as I disembarked.

Still the prodigal son. She gave me a much needed hug.

To obtain an H-1b visa and return to America, I needed to show skills in a specialty occupation. My degree gave me an opportunity to apply for a job in graphic design. A friend of mine in Los Angeles owned a graphic design agency and offered me sponsorship. Thus began the visa application process. The first stage involved getting my hands on the actual paperwork. The second stage would take place some three or four months later and involve an interview at the American Embassy. If the interview went well, I was on my way.

That was a big if. I would be questioned on my previous attempt to enter the USA in Chicago and why I had been refused. My attorneys in the USA levelled with me. The prognosis for success was not good and suggested I hire another attorney in the UK to help me gather supporting evidence for the application and walk me through the process.

Still obsessing daily over Jessica, and feeling all the more vulnerable as the result of my legal status, I decided to e-mail her and explain the situation. My visa had been withdrawn and I was now living in the Mediterranean with Mum. The facts dealt with, I decided to place my heart on my sleeve.

I truly regret our misunderstanding and the breakdown in communication. I value our relationship. I've been thinking about you endlessly for the last 83 days. I miss you greatly and hope to hear back.

Reading back through my note, I thought surely she still cared. Visions of us living happily ever after had lodged themselves in my head.

Then again, maybe not. As an afterthought, I added a PS.

I just reread this e-mail and it's quite heavy! This should give you an idea of what it's like to be holed-up in 112 degree heat in an isolated Christian monastery in Cyprus with nothing to do but think!!

Nonetheless, if you are still reading this, I really do miss you.

Having hit the send button, my feelings of vulnerability soared exponentially. I walked a tightrope between my fears and romantic dreams the next few days.

Jessica's reply finally came. In part, it read.

…I think you're a great guy and any woman would be lucky to have you as her husband and protector. However, I've been seeing a man for almost a year now that I can see myself with in 50 years, hopefully more, God willing.

ALMOST A FUCKING YEAR!!!

And there I was, hanging around your fucking house, giving you a fucking rub down! At your fucking invitation! You fucking bitch!

Apparently on a fast track through the five stages of grief, I found myself on the floor, bawling my eyes out and laughing all at once, a mixture of devastation, relief, sadness and elation. Just wait until I get back to America and you see me, you bitch. Fuck six-pack abs. I'll have eight. Five percent body fat. I'll reinvent myself and write a *New York Times* bestseller. Pulitzer Prize. I began writing the book immediately. Twelve hours a day. Day after day. Wait until I'm an internationally renowned inspirational speaker, recognized for his endless humanitarianism.

That'll get her attention.

Disillusioned about my immigration status and still moping around the island of Cyprus over Jessica, I was at least afforded an opportunity to know my mum in a way I had never known her before. I washed a lot of dishes. I put a lot of trust in a power greater than me. My daily actions became my most sincere form of amends.

With lots of time on my hands, I located a copy of the *Diagnostic and Statistical Manual of Mental Disorders* and began looking into the spiritual emergencies of other people. Kenneth Ring, in his study of near-death experiences, had concluded that these psychotic episodes were symbolic renderings of inner psychic changes, not a prediction of future events. Prophecies did not point to the end of the outer world, at such and such a date. They were representative of inner transformation. In effect, a person was working out their shit. I read the case of a Christian woman in her early thirties who had experienced a ten-day period of euphoria and union with the universe. As a result she turned her life over to God.

That sounded a lot like my mum and turned my thoughts back to the spiritual experience she had shared with me when I was a boy.

"I need to apologize for judging you on your religious beliefs," I told her. "I get it now. Can I ask you what happened with the experience you had?"

"I should never have shared that experience with you," she said. "It was a God experience – a rebirth. I went into a state of complete bliss for about two weeks. I felt such love for everyone, most of all for Dad and you kids. I shared my experience, expecting to be embraced, but instead people ridiculed me. I couldn't deny it, so I turned my life to God. That's when I experienced the breakdown of my relationship with your dad."

I stared at her with the most profound sense of love and forgiveness. I had judged my mum for her religious beliefs. Now things had come full circle. Religion or no religion, we both had a God according to our own understanding.

As an amends to myself, I began to study the Bible and came to a startling realization. Jesus had been a 33-year-old single man, living in the Middle East with his mum. I felt like we had a lot in common. We had even shared the miracle of resurrection.

While I waited for the visa to process, I put my skills in graphic design to proper use. I had mostly been a hack at it with my addictions, but once back to work, I discovered my skills weren't as shameful as I thought.

My first job was for the bishop at St Paul's Church, Nicosia, building a website for the Diocese of Cyprus and the Gulf. I would help to carry the Christian message throughout the Middle East.

As part of my continuing amends, I designed posters and leaflets about addiction and distributed them to hospitals and institutions. I also set up a local twelve-step meeting. In my efforts to raise awareness about drug and alcohol abuse and recovery throughout the island, I discovered the police had not even heard of twelve-step programmes.

To receive my bipolar medication, I had to register with a local psychiatrist. He was a German expatriate and, during our first meeting, we talked at length about my experiences.

"I thought I was Jesus! Well, with a slight variation on the theme, mind you…"

"I zink you have a borderline personality disorder," he said in response to my story.

"Lovely," I said.

"Vel, it could be worse. I don't zink it's bipolar disorder. In my experience, you seem too balanced for dat. It sounds like you have been deeply affected by religion, divorce, shame and guilt. What are your feelings on religion now?"

"All the stories throughout the ages seem to be part of the same spiritual journey. Enlightenment, resurrection, whatever. Western religion, Eastern philosophy, Greek mythology. They all tell the same story to me. One of love and unity within the universe. All rivers running into the same ocean?"

"And how is ze depression?" he asked.

"The twelve steps have really given me a chance to find my way out of depression. My sponsor tells me depression is just me not getting my own way."

"Vat do you vant to do about ze medication?" he asked.

"I want off."

"Okay, it vill be an experiment. Ve vill do it gradually."

I introduced Mum to the shrink and provided her with the names of local psychiatric wards and emergency hospital numbers.

"In case they find me dancing naked in the street or something."

She laughed.

After eight months of waiting, I received a seven-page request for evidence to support my visa application. One of the requests was for photographs of the office where I would be working. The registered address for the office was Wilshire Boulevard. The physical office address was Downtown Los Angeles. On the application, the attorney had given the registered office address. The attorney stated that the photographs did not match the address on the visa application. The only thing she could do was withdraw the entire application and reapply for the following year. In May 2010, I started the visa application process all over again.

While I waited for my second visa application to move forward, James Brooks came to visit me. Mum was gutted. She had to be away that week but insisted that James sleep in her bed. She called one day. "I've been telling all the girls I've got a supermodel in my bed! I didn't say I wasn't there, though."

"Mum, your secret is safe with me!"

Over the many months in Cyprus, I continually reduced my medication until I was completely clean. For the first time in sixteen years I was not medicated. Feelings slowly began to emerge from the depths of my soul in response, feelings I had never known, at least not since I was a boy, and even those I could hardly remember. I felt a simple joy from attending church with Mum on Christmas Day, then going to a joint twelve-step meeting for alcoholics and their families. I felt a renewed sense of responsibility and reached out to Natasja in a letter. It had always been my intention to make amends to her face-to-face, but suddenly things could not wait. In my letter, I omitted nothing and Natasja responded with appreciation and gratitude. It meant everything to her that I had validated her feelings.

A month later, I received another Request for Evidence to support my new visa application. My gut feeling was, the chances of me returning to America were slim, but three months later, I received approval for the first stage of my H-1B visa. The interview at the American Embassy was next. In keeping with the tenets of my sobriety, I decided to be completely honest and declared my treatment for addiction on the interview form. I met a man at St Paul's Church, Nicosia, who worked at the American Embassy, and he gave me a character reference. I also had a character reference from my psychiatrist and well-respected figures in the community.

On the day of the interview, the woman in charge of my case questioned me thoroughly on my previous failed entrance to Chicago. At the conclusion of the interview, she said it appeared that I had been banned from re-entry for three years but requested transcripts of my statements. I returned with them the next day, to receive her final judgment. Miraculously, she overturned the ban and approved my visa.

Three days later, I received an e-mail from Jessica.

Just curious to see how you're doing. Have a girlfriend? How's life? What are you up to?

Unbelievable. I had been obsessing over that woman for two years. What the hell had I done wrong? Why didn't she want me? Now here she was, out of the blue, ready to fuck with my head again.

I wrote back:

Would you believe it? I've been away two years tomorrow. Currently married, two kids, third on the way...

I thought better of taking the piss and added to the end of my note.

No, not really. No girlfriend!!

Jessica wrote back.

Good to hear you're still free. Do you ever allow people to come and visit you in Cyprus?

Incredible. After all this heartache, asking to visit.

I wrote back:

Just got my visa. I'll be heading back to America shortly.

CHAPTER TWENTY

After two and a half years away and a long, exhausting international flight, I landed back in LA and headed for the Best Western Motel in Sherman Oaks. It was relatively cheap and close to my support group.

Wasting no time, I e-mailed Jessica first thing the next morning.

Are you in town?

Jessica e-mailed back.

Yes

My stomach churned as I wrote back.

Coffee? The place on the corner?

There was no response. A wiser man would have cut his losses, but not me. Faced with feelings of rejection, I only grew more determined.

Twenty-four hours went by before I heard from Jessica again. The note came as if there had been no delay.

Meet me at the coffee shop. Noon?

As instructed, I drove over to the place where we first met. Jessica hardly looked as I parked. She had on a pair of form-fitting jeans, boots and a white t-shirt. Her shades were a pair of those slick designer numbers.

I had dressed to make sure she could appreciate my new form.

"You look skinny," she said.

I could not bloody win.

305

We hugged and exchanged a few coy glances and fumbled about with some banter. Jessica already had her usual mocha. I excused myself and went off to grab my own. As I stood in line, my head was trying to construct one sane thought out of all my fears, anxieties and expectations.

I sat back down with Jessica, still trembling inside. Without alcohol as a social equalizer, I felt like a drunk trying to get the first shot of morning muscatel up to his mouth.

After skirting around the unspoken issue for a few minutes, I queried her.

"So, what the hell happened to this other man you had in your life?"

"What other man?"

"The man you told me about in your e-mail. The man you saw yourself being with for the rest of your life."

She stared, confused for a moment. Then the light went on.

"Oh, that. I just said it to put you off. I wasn't with anyone."

Games. Constant games! I just wanted to fuck the life out of her and be done with the whole thing.

Small talk ensued, during which time I seethed inside over her comment. Then Jessica appeared ready to leave. Her book went into her bag.

"I'm going hot air ballooning for my mom's birthday tomorrow."

"Well, take care and keep inside the basket," I said, standing up.

We hugged and went our separate ways. I drove off with visions of being the one to shove her arse out from five thousand feet.

A few days on a recovery meeting binge and I felt reasonably sane. No woman was going to fuck with my head, least of all a beautiful one.

So much for the plans of mice and men. The following week, I landed the position of graphic designer for actress and supermodel, Alexis Newton. There was no getting away from them.

First day on the job, the CEO gives me a shout.

"Meet me in the boardroom. I've got Alexis on a conference call."

The three of us exchanged the usual formalities and started knocking things around a bit. Alexis was asking this and suggesting that.

Steadily, as the conversation continued, the intensity of her breathing mounted. I was half expecting Alexis to throw in a few moans and go all x-rated on us. You'd think I had dialed one of those 900 numbers.

The CEO gave me a look, his eyebrows up, a shrug and a grin. Apparently he couldn't believe his ears, either.

On and on it went, with the three of us talking business and all sorts of visuals going off in my head.

After about twenty minutes, Alexis said, "Well, I guess that's about it for now, guys."

She let out one last great sigh, like she'd climaxed.

Then we heard a thump and several more heavy exhales.

"Oh god! Enough of this treadmill for one day!"

The CEO and I had another look at each other. You had to laugh. Man and his imagination. We were working on a porn film. Alexis was getting a workout.

If nothing else came of the thing, the CEO and I had just forged a special kind of bond.

Out of the blue, a few days later, I received a Facebook friend request from Dylan Freeman, Natasja's son. Women. I smelled trickery. An inner voice told me, they'll use any means to get you by the balls.

Half of me wanted to say, bollocks to that, but I accepted. An e-mail from Dylan followed soon after.

I saw you on Facebook and that you were back in Los Angeles. We're living in Beverly Hills. Mom wanted to know if you'd like to come by for tea.

Trojan horse, but I accepted and drove over that same night. They were living barely twenty minutes away from my Best Western up the 405.

Dylan answered the door when I knocked. Natasja appeared with a shocked look on her face.

"I had no idea you were coming," she said, tapping Dylan on the legs. "When did you get back? What are you doing?"

"Should I give you the answers out here or come in for a chat?"

"Oh, sorry," Natasja said, opening the door all the way.

We were eventually seated in her living room with cold drinks and catching up on things. Dylan mostly listened. Then he butted in.

"You can join the local rugby team and I can watch you play."

He still thought I was a pro rugby player. More amends. I had already confessed to Natasja in a letter. She and I exchanged glances. I pretended to cringe, and she laughed. What the hell. Some things were better left unsaid. I patted Dylan on the leg and we forged ahead as if nothing had happened.

"Thanks for continuing to pay back the money," Natasja told me when Dylan ran off. "You know, you can come and stay here with us if you want."

Feet up in Beverly Hills. Very tempting.

"Actually, I've just arranged to share a house in Sherman Oaks. My recovery's really about standing on my own two feet now. I even have my own bank account."

Natasja laughed.

"A two-figure bank account and a rented car, with quarter of a tank of petrol. But I just got my first ever bill in my own name."

"Now you're showboating," Natasja said.

"Some things never change."

This time we laughed together.

"Yeah, the truth is, Natasja, I still share a credit card with Mum, but I'm working on it."

"God, I'm so proud of you for staying sober, Michael. It'll be four years in a few weeks, right?"

"One day at a time an' all that. You should come and give me a cake at a meeting."

She agreed. After a bit more banter, I got up to leave. We talked a bit more at the door. I drove off and watched the easy life disappear in my rearview mirror.

Back home, my heart rate escalated when I found an e-mail waiting for me from Jessica. She had just returned from the ballooning holiday and wanted to know if I'd join her for a film screening at the Directors Guild of America. I did, and that led to regular dates.

At Daniel's instruction, I had vowed to stay away from sex for as long as possible. The idea was to build trust. We went for hikes in the wilderness. We had dinners out. Two weeks passed. Then three and I'd still not laid a finger on her. This was all new territory for me.

After a month, I finally kissed Jessica and that quickly led us to bed. It rained hard that night. It was as if the universe was expressing my relief.

By then I had taken over the job of art director for Alexis Newton. Dealing daily with celebrity-endorsed brands. Surrounded by fame and fortune.

The reality of it was far different from the image I had conjured up in my head. Having it all seemed to be a soulless enterprise. No matter what their position, I saw individuals at war with their own demons.

Jessica and I had become an item, but I was still somewhat surprised when she invited me to join her for Christmas at her parents' home in Dallas. You could smell the crude oil driving up to their property and taste the money. Concrete lions topped the gateposts. The mansion was big enough to get lost in.

"I love the stone lions," she said.

Alcohol dominated everything Jessica's family did. Some of it was festive, in keeping with the season. Mostly it was rampant. It became very clear to me in that moment what a huge impact alcohol had had on Jessica's life.

Her mum pulled me to one side at one point and said that Jessica had never brought a man home for Christmas. In fact, she hadn't had a boyfriend for several years. For the first time in a long time, I felt like I was enough for the woman in my life.

On Christmas Day, four generations of the family gathered around the Christmas tree to exchange presents.

Out of nowhere, Jessica squinted and gritted her teeth at me. "Avert your eyes."

"Avert them from fucking what?" I whispered.

"I saw you giving her the eye."

"Who? Your grandma?"

"You know who," she said and nodded in the direction of her brother's girlfriend.

She was seething. I sat there baffled and dejected. It was beyond crazy. I had purposely ignored the woman, fearing I might ignite Jessica's jealousy.

Her venom bled into the festive moment. I turned to find some of the family members staring, and I flashed a nonchalant smile. Jessica smiled as well and bided her time, but as soon as we were alone, all hell broke loose. I went off in search of somewhere to hide in that giant mansion.

By that same time the next day, I was on the phone trying to organize a flight to get out of there. It was the same insanity I had always known, except without the drugs and alcohol. I didn't know how to live with Jessica. I didn't know how to live without her. As in my past life, I just went along with the drama and chaos as if there were no alternatives.

We would survive our holiday excursion and settle into a relative period of calm back in LA, but things soon spun out of control again. Like a Zen master whacking me over the head with his bamboo stick, a light went on. She's absolutely nuts, and I'm with her, so what does that make me? Nothing I could do was going to change or fix this situation. The disease was in her, and the only person who could deal with that was her.

We broke for three months until I ran into her at a frozen yogurt shop in the plaza. We went back and forth again, in bed and then another round of screaming.

Finally, I went to the yogurt shop one evening, almost against my will. Its windows looked out onto Laurel Canyon and I was staring in that direction, watching cars pass, when a black Porsche pulled up at the traffic lights. One glance at the number plate and I knew it was Jessica. As the car came by, I saw a man sitting in the passenger seat.

I was suddenly cured of frozen yogurt.

CHAPTER TWENTY-ONE

Months went by with me moping around in a daze again. I attended my meetings. I worked with others. I did everything that was expected of me in recovery and still felt as if the colour had been taken out of my existence.

Then Alexis Newton decided to sell her operation, and the new owners wanted to put me on commission. Without my salary, I'd be the equivalent of a glorified telemarketer.

Seeing no other choice, I went back to work for multiple clients. One of them was a guy named Zakhar, a Russian of Chechen origin I had met through random friends. He was a tall, menacing-looking fella jacked up on steroids, and frankly scared the crap out of me.

Ever since we first crossed paths, there had been vague references to the Russian Mafia. He had interests in the diamond trade. He always paid in cash, which further added to the mystique.

A couple of grand for an evening meal was nothing to him. I barely had enough to cover the rent and pay my bills. I couldn't help but look in the mirror and wonder: What am I doing wrong?

Amidst all the indulgences, Zakhar related his ongoing battle with drugs and alcohol. Apparently, no amount of money could buy you freedom from that shit.

Not yet done with the celebrity scene in my life, I accepted an invitation to a rooftop party one evening – 360-degree view of Hollywood – tigers, llamas and a crocodile paraded around for entertainment. Members from Cirque du Soleil were there to perform. The paparazzi were circling overhead in helicopters.

By the fireside, naked women painted as cats licked at bowls of milk. More naked women posed as statues on podiums surrounding the pool. Midgets dressed as pirates displayed their sword skills. A sumo wrestler in a pink tutu played chess with the queen from Alice in Wonderland. I had just fallen down the rabbit hole. The bright lights of Hollywood served as a backdrop.

The party grew ever more debauched around me. Empty cocaine wrappers littered the bathroom. People came out of the door with their noses dripping blood, but grinning from ear to ear. All that fame and fortune and they reduced themselves to this?

At one point, I felt my phone vibrating and pulled it out to look. The call was Zakhar, my mobster friend. The two of us had been out on the town and checkin' out the odd strip joint here and there.

I answered the call. "What's up, mate?"

"Oh, man, work. Pressure. You know, all this shit. I'm drinking heavy and I can't stop. I need to get sober."

"Start with the basics. Keep it simple. Go to meetings and don't use between meetings. Call me tomorrow when you're straight. That's it."

"Yeah, yeah. So, are you cool?"

"Yeah, I'm good. Still sober. One day at a time."

"What's all that noise?"

I explained about the party, then wondered if it had been the wisest thing to do, under the circumstances.

"Okay, well, I've got to go," Zakhar said.

He was always in a rush that way. Hellhounds on his trail. His situation desperate. Zakhar went about life as if standing still were painful.

I hung up and looked around at the party. What the fuck am I doing here? I wasn't sure, but it was going on four in the morning by the time I crawled into bed.

The phone rang around ten. It was Zakhar. He wanted to go to a meeting.

The two of us hung around together that day, and somehow Zakhar got through it without using. I still wasn't sure if he was sober. With him, it was hard to separate neurosis from potential substance abuse.

Zakhar disappeared again and I didn't hear from him until the end of the week. Seeing his name on the caller ID, I picked up the phone but the line was dead.

I dialled the number back. Someone answered without saying anything.

"Zakhar, what's happening?"

Silence.

"I haven't heard from you for a week. Are you sober or what?"

"No, Michael. I'm fucked up. Are you still sober?"

"I am, mate."

"Fuck, I can't seem to get it, man. You gotta help me. My life is so fucked up."

He kept going. I finally interrupted.

"Look, mate. Do you want to get clean?"

"Yeah, man. I want to get clean."

"Then let's get you into a treatment centre."

"Yeah, let's do that. Come get me right now."

"Where are you?"

"The Peninsula Hotel in Beverly Hills."

I set off down the 405 freeway, trying to arrange a bed for Zakhar at my old rehab, Forest Hills, as I drove. Zakhar kept calling me the entire way, but every time I answered the phone, I heard only silence.

Upon my arrival, Zakhar came storming through the reception area wearing only a dress shirt and a pair of swimming shorts. The shirt was covered with blood. His face was dripping with sweat.

"They fucking robbed me," he said. "In broad daylight. Took my trousers and wallet to get my address."

"Who?"

"The Mexican Mafia. This is fucking serious. We gotta get outta here."

We were soon driving through Beverly Hills. I kept glancing at him.

"How did you get that blood all over your shirt?"

"The stitches burst."

"What stitches?"

"The stitches in my chest. I did too many steroids and grew bitch tits. I had to have them removed. The blood's from the surgery."

Amidst all this madness, God was working in my life, holding up a mirror to remind me of where I had been. I felt an enormous wave of gratitude, even as I had to pity this poor fella.

"Come on, man, drive faster," Zakhar said with glances over the seat. "They're coming after me. And don't stop, whatever you do."

I looked over at him. With the blood and shorts and wild eyes, he was a sight. "You're not supposed to drink, no matter what," I offered up as wisdom.

"I know. Fuck, I know but I'm in deep shit. My past has caught up with me. I couldn't take the pressure and drank. Fuck, I've been doing crack and heroin."

"What pressure? What's happened?"

"They got my father. Tortured him and broke his ribs. They threatened my mother to find out where I was. Everyone's deserted me. My cousins had to leave the country. I've fucked up, man. I've put everyone in danger. I've been so fucking stupid."

Zakhar was looking at himself in the side mirror. I was stealing glances at him.

Over the time I had known Zakhar, he had confessed to all this dark shit in his past and suddenly he was confessing to more of it. And given his history of drugs and mafia involvement, I had to assume these latest stories weren't bullshit.

So now the gangs were seeking retribution on him. If they were out to kill him, I had to assume they would take out the chauffeur too.

Every time a vehicle came up alongside us, I feared the worst. At every traffic light, Zakhar looked like he was ready to shove open the door and bolt.

"So what? Is there a contract on you?" I asked him.

He nodded. "If they don't kill me, I might as well kill myself." He glanced at me nervously.

"They've been following me for the last six years. The last deals I did are on camera. They've got me fucking confessing on camera."

"Who's got you on camera? Who's following you?"

"The Feds. The CIA. Now the Mexican Mafia."

"Let's get you safe. I've got you a bed lined up in treatment, but you're gonna need five grand for the first week – we'll figure something out from there."

"I've got a kilo of heroin and a kilo of crack at the house, along with a hundred grand."

I diverted our journey through Beverly Hills in that direction. At the next stop, a blacked-out SUV pulled up alongside us. I noticed one in front of us and another one behind. I was waiting for the windows to come down and hit men in ski masks to appear. My life flashed before me.

If I die right now, am I all right with God? I'm clean. I've done everything in my power to clear away the wreckage of my past and heal all the old fucked-up relationships. I have experienced what it is like to be a free man. Whatever waits on the other side, I'm okay with it. I don't really fear death, but I don't really want to die, either.

Amazingly, the phalanx of blacked-out SUVs turned out to be pure coincidence. The light changed and everybody raced forward.

Soon, we left Beverly Hills behind for West Hollywood. From there I pulled onto the 101 and headed north towards Zakhar's apartment in the San Fernando Valley. A normal day in LA involves police roadblocks and helicopters. This day was no different.

Zakhar continued to confess his sins. "I've been so fucking stupid."

He repeated more or less the same thing, over and over again, the entire trip. Every time we stopped at a traffic light, he looked ready to bolt. The energy in the car was toxic.

Finally, half an hour later, we pulled up outside his apartment complex.

"I can't go in there. They're waiting for me. The last thing they told me was that they wouldn't stop until they killed me."

"Give me the keys," I told him.

It was not one of my better ideas, but I was driven by adrenaline to put an end to this madness.

Zakhar and I argued back and forth. He didn't want me to go in on my own. We finally settled on the two of us going in together.

We rode the lift up to his penthouse in silence. In the hallway outside his place, we stood there listening. It was completely quiet. I put the keys in the lock and opened the door.

More silence. We went in, still expecting guns and ski masks. Instead, we stumbled upon crack, cocaine, and heroin spread all over the coffee table. Zakhar ran into his bedroom and rushed back out holding an empty Wells Fargo pouch.

"All the money's gone. They've been and taken it."

I was sceptical. Why wouldn't they have taken all the drugs, too? But I was in no mood to argue.

"Look, Zakhar. I already checked with a few of the free treatment centres, but there aren't any beds available."

Zakhar was running his hands through his hair.

"Have you got a debit card? We need money to get you into treatment."

"No, I only deal in cash. I'll call and have some delivered."

He got on the phone with someone. In all the madness, I felt a pang of envy. All he had to do was pick up the phone and someone would deliver a bag of cash.

"Have a beer," I told Zakhar when he hung up.

He grabbed one from the fridge and had a long slug of it. That led to him taking a seat. Anything to help ease him down. His nervousness was agitating the hell out of me.

"I need to call my mother and father," he said, bolting upright again.

"I'll call them."

"The phone's tapped, so be careful what you say."

I called and spoke to his mother.

Without asking, she confirmed the story about the father's broken ribs.

Zakhar shouted at the phone. "Where are my cousins, Mom?"

"They've left the country."

She was crying now and pleading for Zakhar's safety. I told her that I was getting her son into treatment. He'd be safe from himself and others.

Getting off the phone with her, I called around and finally arranged a treatment bed for Zakhar the following day. In the interim, he'd gone through all the beers in the fridge. He had no cash. I had $60 in my bank account. Knowing the drink would lessen the effects of his withdrawal, I purchased him some beer and cigarettes.

He downed a few more beers upon my return and quickly fell asleep. I was left staring at a table covered with drugs. When your bank account looked like mine, drugs quickly acquired a dollar value. It took a fair bit of willpower for me to clean them into a bag and drop them into the rubbish chute.

The following morning, I went out on an errand. When I returned, Zakhar was gone. I drove home and didn't hear from him until the following day.

My first question was: What happened?

"They came to my house," he told me. "I need to see you."

"We're taking you to treatment. Have you got the money?"

"No, but I'm picking it up now. I'm on my way to your house."

318

He arrived looking wild-eyed and worse than ever. He was twitching and darting looks around the room. I didn't need to be told that he'd been smoking crack and couldn't stop, but he told me anyway – and he needed a lift to get the money. Thinking it was for treatment, I agreed.

I followed Zakhar's instructions to North Hollywood, where he suddenly told me to pull to the side of the road. A man jumped into the car and handed him two baggies – one with white powder, the other with white crystals. They did an exchange and the man jumped out.

"Okay, let's go," Zakhar said.

"Enough!" I said. "Fuck this. This stops right here. Get rid of the fucking drugs."

"This is the last, I promise."

Livid, I drove back to my house. Inside, I watched from the living room as Zakhar headed for the kitchen. I turned on the television, then realized it was probably the worst thing I could do for someone in his condition. He came out of the kitchen looking even more wild-eyed.

"Turn that fucking thing off."

"Yeah, you probably think the TV's trying to communicate with you."

"Oh, I see," he said, gritting his teeth, his eyes filled with terror. "So you're in on it."

I hung my head. My heart was trembling. This was me, five years earlier. From my own experiences, I knew he'd crossed the line into full-blown psychosis. I had to get him out of my house. My housemate was upstairs and we were all in danger now.

"You've been recording all this, haven't you?" Zakhar said. He looked from me to the phone and back again. "When are they coming, Mike?"

"Look, let's get out of here," I said and reached for his arm.

In response, he ran into the bathroom. In his mind, it was all a setup for torture. When he reappeared, I urged him again to leave, but every time I moved towards him, he retreated to

319

the kitchen or bathroom. Soon, he was scurrying back and forth between them. Whenever he stopped, his eyes were darting around the room in a wild state of paranoia.

"You're fucking scaring me," I told him.

"Get me to my uncle," he said.

Thinking his uncle's would be a safe and familiar place, I agreed to take him. Anything to get him out of my house.

Before we left, I texted my housemate and told her to leave the house immediately and stay away until I contacted her.

On the way across town, Zakhar devised a mafia scenario from my every move. When my phone bleeped from a text, he nodded.

"Is it time now?"

"Time for what?"

"Time for me to do it?"

"Do what?"

He made a gun shape with his hand and put the fingers in his mouth. "End it. End it myself before they do?"

"NO!" I screamed at him. "It's all in your fucking head! Fucking drugs! This is what they do to you, you fucking idiot! They fuck you up! You're paranoid! You're deluded and you're scaring the shit out of me!"

That shut him up until we arrived at his uncle's office in Woodland Hills.

"Give me your drugs," I told him.

I wanted the option to call the police if he got out of hand, but I didn't want him busted for drugs. He thought it was all another scenario.

I was delighted when his uncle took over. He promised to sort out the money and take him straight to rehab. I left, torn between my compassion for what he was going through and the need for my own sanity.

As I drove down the 101, my conscience got the better of me and I turned around. I knew it wasn't safe for his uncle to be with him alone. On my way back up the 101, Zakhar called.

"I have to meet you at your house," he said.

I tried to dissuade him without luck. I had a notion to disappear somewhere for the day, but I had to think of my roommate.

Arriving at my house, I found Zakhar waiting outside with his ex-girlfriend.

"I left my keys inside," he said. "I've got to go in and get them."

"You're not going in my house."

"Why?" he said, getting into my face.

"It's too dangerous. My roommate's upstairs and she's scared half to death."

"Let me in," he shouted.

"You're not going in."

We were standing toe to toe, eyeball to eyeball.

"You're not going anywhere near that house."

The shouting match continued, but eventually Zakhar gave up.

"Tell me where the keys are, and I'll get them."

Inside the house, I locked the door and went in search of the keys. Before long, Zakhar was banging on the door and trying the handle. Unable to find the keys, I stepped out of the front door.

"He stashed his drugs in there," his girlfriend told me outside.

"I just want my drugs," Zakhar said. "I'll flush them, I promise."

"Tell me where they are and I'll get them."

He began to plead with me. He was so scared that I was going to flush them.

Finally, he confessed that the drugs were hidden inside my toilet. I made him promise to sit still and went off to retrieve them. The minute he had his hands on the bag, he buried his face in it. He came back up covered with white powder.

"That's all I wanted," he says.

Yeah, I knew the feeling, until the drugs wore off and the insanity returned. I gave him 30 minutes if he was lucky.

Still committed to helping my fellow alcoholic, I guided Zakhar back to Woodland Hills. Along the way, I called the emergency psychiatric response unit.

"I've got a friend of mine here having an acute psychotic episode. He's been smoking heroin and crack and has severe paranoia and delusions an' all that. He really needs help. It's been going on for at least three days and he's now talking about suicide. I reckon he needs to be hospitalized."

"How can you be so sure?"

"Because I've been there."

They informed me that all their units were dispatched. I tried his uncle's place again, but he was gone. Thinking a beer would help Zakhar come down, I stopped at the liquor store. When I came back out, he had disappeared.

There was a lesson for me. I'm powerless to save another alcoholic. I had given it my best shot. Now it was time to say thanks for my own sobriety and let it go.

As if I needed another reminder that I had no control over anything in this world, including whatever the hell kind of demons were haunting Jessica, she fired a shot across my bow by way of a text message the next day, wondering if we could be friends now. Had enough time passed? She had a work project and wondered if I could help.

I had no stomach for going down that road again and decided not to respond. I might as well have been dating Zakhar. I had come to like who I was and the peace I had found. Who needed that kind of insanity?

Several weeks later, another text arrived from Jessica, this time while I was driving home on a Saturday night. She was down in Bali, living it up with all the money in the world.

This is it. If you don't respond, it's the last time. I'm never going to try and contact you again.

I had come to expect nothing less from her.

I pulled to the side of the road and punched the stereo off, needing to have a dialogue with my Higher Power. I was too drawn by the illusion of an easy life that woman represented, ready to sell my soul at the drop of a hat. Sobriety seemed like such a bitch right then in comparison – a modicum of peace gnawed away at by a never ending parade of uncertainties. Yeah, my worst day sober was better than my best day drunk, but I had yet to experience much security – financial or otherwise – and Jessica could offer me that in spades.

I started to talk to God out loud.

Listen, big fella, I need your help. I need you to help me get out of my own way. I need to have a relationship with you, not just me puking up some set prayers whenever I feel desperate. All that thee and thou and I'm willing to surrender bullshit. I need a real relationship where I can talk to you about anything and actually turn my life over. You've never let me down before, but things never turn out the way I plan. I'm guessing you can hear me, but I have no clue how this is supposed to work. Whatever it is – that universal power or energy or spirit of the universe – whatever the fuck it is, please show yourself to me so I can see it. Be bigger than every little problem I have. Come on, let's have it.

My phone rang that very instant, another alcoholic I knew on the other end of the line, struggling to stay sober.

"Mike, I need help," he said when I answered. "I'm trying to get into a treatment centre."

And there it was. An answer to my plea. Just one drunk talking to another. At least in moments like that, my destiny was perfectly clear to me.

EPILOGUE

Two years later, I was on the beach at Del Mar, just north of San Diego, kicking back on a clear, blue sunny day when my phone rang. I glanced at the screen.

Dear God. Zakhar again. What now?

At least he was alive. The last time I saw him, we were engaged in that fiasco up in LA, trying to find him a bed in a treatment centre. A lot of water had gone under the bridge since then, like my old childhood friend and partner in crime, Finnegan going down for the count. They had found him dead from a heroin and alcohol overdose, and at the very same Viking Hotel where the old man had been hanging out with his new bird. Images of Finnegan and me throwing rocks down by the shore passed through my days. That seemed like ages ago now, and it was all gone forever.

I was devastated. Finnegan had been a catalyst for my own recovery. Why couldn't he have found the freedom that I had come to know? How tragic can something be…?

During that same time frame a chance conversation at a party in LA led to a job opportunity down in North County San Diego, a situation that quickly went balls up due to my ongoing visa troubles. In need of having my visa stamped at a foreign embassy, I flew to Amsterdam and did the honest thing there by declaring my addiction issues, along with that excursion through a treatment centre. Now the Yanks wanted blood tests, x-rays and a full physical exam to prove I was clean and sober before they'd let me back into the country. With my passport confiscated, a five-week saga ensued. By the time I made my way back to San Diego, my new boss had given me the boot.

On a right old downer, and fearing my only option was a one-way ticket back to the Isle of Man, I did what I had learned to do a long time ago in recovery – ask for help. That was never easy for me to do, but I set aside the old pride and approached a good friend. It did not hurt that he also happened to be a very successful businessman. He'd been through the wringer himself a few months back, and I'd given him a hand getting up off the floor.

"So, just wondering, mate," I said after explaining my situation. "Think you could use someone with my skill set?"

Being the man he was, always ready to reciprocate a kindness, Kavanagh immediately put a hand on my shoulder.

"Are you kidding me? We spend hundreds of thousands of dollars a year on what you do. Start as soon as you can. I've always wanted to have you on board."

He made me an offer on the spot, at double my previous salary, and threw in sponsoring my visa with the bargain.

In a series of events that can only be described as uncanny, I had soon rented a property half a mile from where I originally lived in Rancho del Cielo with Natasja. Then my new boss, wanting to extend his business into North County San Diego, secured an office a few hundred yards from the cheap motel where I had embarked on my last alcohol-fuelled drug binge, eight years earlier.

So there I was, with all that water under the bridge and Zakhar ringing me on the phone.

My first thought was: Don't answer it. The man was nothing but trouble. But what if he was looking for help?

I hit the accept button.

"Zakhar, what's going on?"

He started to laugh. "Michael! I just wanted to call and thank you, man. I'm so grateful for everything you did for me."

His voice sounded clear and steady. No drugs or mafia hit men appeared to be in the movie.

"How's everything going?" I asked.

"I'm clean and sober. Two years now. My life is incredible."

"That's so good to hear, mate."

"Listen, I'm on my way out of the country right now, but I'd really like to see you when I get back. I owe you an amends."

"You can come and see me anytime, but ya know, the best amends you could ever make is just this. Stay clean and sober and help another alcoholic."

"That's exactly what I'm doing. I already have two young guys I'm sponsoring."

Incredible. What a feeling of satisfaction and fulfilment that was, to think I might have helped one man. So many people had helped me and I could never repay all the love and kindness and generosity that had been so freely given.

"That's excellent," I said. "Just pay it forward, Zakhar."

"I am, man, but if there's anything I can ever do for you, anything at all, it's yours. Just name it."

That grabbed my attention for sure. A laundry list of all the shit I thought I needed flashed through my head. A fast car. A big house. A big chunk of cash.

I caught myself before opening my mouth. That was another thing I had learned in my eight years of sobriety. None of those things could give me the peace of mind I had always been seeking.

Sobriety was an inside job.

Concrete Lion season was now over for this Viking.